JEMMA KENNEDY

Jemma Kennedy is a playwright and screenwriter who began writing after a career in the music business in London and New York. She was awarded a Jerwood Arvon Young Playwright's Apprenticeship in 2006 and was Pearson Playwright in Residence at the National Theatre in 2010.

Plays include *Genesis Inc.* for Hampstead Theatre; *Maggot Moon*, *The Prince and the Pauper* (also National Theatre of Greece) and *The Summer Book* for the Unicorn Theatre; *Don't Feed the Animals* for National Theatre Connections; *The Grand Irrationality* for Lost Theatre Studios; *The Gift* for New Vic Theatre Hoard Festival, and *Second Person Narrative* for Tonic Theatre's inaugural Platform series. Film credits include *Captain Webb* (Marathon Films). Jemma is working across a variety of projects for stage and screen. Read more at: www.unitedagents.co.uk/jemma-kennedy

Jemma has worked as a dramaturg and playwriting tutor for twenty years, and led the National Theatre's first adult playwriting course, where she also created New Views, their online playwriting course for young people. She lives in London.

Instagram: @kennedythescrivener

**Other Books on Writing
from Nick Hern Books**

Being a Playwright
A Career Guide for Writers
Chris Foxon and George Turvey

How Musicals Work
And How to Write Your Own
Julian Woolford

How Plays Work
David Edgar

Playwriting
Structure, Character, How and What to Write
Stephen Jeffreys

The Secret Life of Plays
Steve Waters

So You Want To Be A Playwright?
Tim Fountain

So You Want To Write Radio Drama?
Claire Grove and Stephen Wyatt

The Writer's Toolkit
Exercises, Techniques and Ideas for Playwrights and Screenwriters
Paul Kalburgi

Jemma Kennedy

THE PLAYWRIGHT'S JOURNEY

From First Spark to First Night

Foreword by Joe Penhall

NICK HERN BOOKS
London
www.nickhernbooks.co.uk

A Nick Hern Book

The Playwright's Journey
first published in Great Britain in 2022
by Nick Hern Books Limited,
The Glasshouse, 49a Goldhawk Road, London W12 8QP

Copyright © 2022 Jemma Kennedy
Foreword copyright © 2022 Joe Penhall

Jemma Kennedy has asserted her moral right
to be identified as the author of this work

Designed and typeset by Nick Hern Books
Printed and bound in Great Britain by
TJ Books Limited

A CIP catalogue record for this book is available
from the British Library

ISBN 978 1 84842 580 4

MIX
Paper from
responsible sources
FSC® C013056
FSC
www.fsc.org

For Paul Kennedy (1941–2020)
who loved a good night at the theatre

CONTENTS

FOREWORD
Joe Penhall

This is a very, very smart book which left me nodding in sage agreement with every chapter. As a writer I'm used to studiously avoiding books on how to write, because they're so often written by people who either don't know what they're talking about or don't know how to convey it. Jemma Kennedy is that rare exception, a writer with the gift of laying bare the most complex, convoluted ideas with exquisite lucidity, wit and empathy.

Far from trying to simplify things, Jemma respects her readers and takes for granted their sophistication, intelligence and ambition. She obviously has a wealth of significant achievement to draw on and writes with hard-earned authority. Nothing escapes her attention. She anatomises all the big complexities with the skill and attention to detail of a keyhole surgeon. There is no issue too minute, subtle or complex for her.

I spend a lot of time talking to other playwrights and this is how the best ones talk. Playwriting can seem like a foreign language, but Jemma speaks it fluently. A substantial and rare aesthetic achievement which every aspiring playwright, producer and director should read and respect.

INTRODUCTION

Think for a moment about the last play you saw. It might have been a piece of new writing in a black-box studio above a pub. A Shakespeare at the RSC. An amateur production of a twentieth-century classic in a local community centre. Or an epic new play on the National Theatre's Olivier stage.

In each case the show will have been the result of the work of many people, including a director, actors, set and costume and lighting designers, perhaps a musical director, a dramaturg, a voice or movement coach, alongside the stage managers and technicians and casting directors and assistants and as many members of the company and the theatre itself that you can find credited in the show programme. In other words, the team of people who turn a written text into a performed play. They are generally highly skilled craftspeople, who have been through some sort of rigorous educational and/or professional training. In fact the only people in the theatre who are rarely trained to the same degree in any technical sense, who are usually self-taught, and who have blundered into this exhilarating, challenging creative world without any kind of formal learning or apprenticeship are the authors of those texts. Playwrights.

Of course, opportunities to study and learn playwriting already exist and continue to expand. There are bachelor and master's degrees in writing for performance, short playwriting courses, residential writing retreats, and a growing library of books on the subject. But the double bind of being a playwright is that once you've perfected your play on paper, its work is only just begun. A dramatist's real apprenticeship only truly begins the moment their texts start to be performed, if not to a paying audience, then at least to a roomful of students or peers or theatre folk. Like a bungee-jumper, you leap off a platform into thin air and hope your cord holds. And, while it's important not to underestimate the unique technical challenges in telling stories for the stage, craft alone cannot make a good play.

Anyone can pick up Aristotle's *Poetics* (the book every playwright is told to read) and teach themselves how three-act structure works, or take a course on the mechanics of theatrical dialogue, narrative and stagecraft. Not everybody can become a working playwright. Plays are constructs, but they are also made of organic matter. Thoughts and feelings, experiences, intuition, emotional intelligence. These are the things that make a play come alive, first on the page and then on the stage. You might call it spark, or voice, originality, energy – the unique DNA that is found in any individual playwright's work, and which starts with their creative instincts. These instincts are, in a way, the direct opposite of craft, and they cannot be learned by rote. If you're currently writing a play yourself, I'll bet that you're not staying up all night hunched over your keyboard or working through your lunch-break simply because you want to practise crafting a dramatic form. It's because you have a burning desire to tell a story and communicate something about human behaviour.

I never studied theatre formally myself. I learned to write, as most of us do, by trial and error. Watching plays. Reading plays. Studying their structure. Discussing productions with friends and colleagues. And slowly, tentatively, starting to write myself. It was hard. I had readings, I got commissions, I was invited to theatre-writing groups. More often than not, the plays didn't make it on to the stage, beyond a rehearsed reading. It took ten years from writing that first play to having my first main stage production, and along the way I have learned some pretty good lessons. This book is intended to help you on this journey. I hope it will encourage you to interrogate your creativity and explore your connection to your material, while finding ways to harness them to writing craft. In other words, to explore the process of playwriting via the heart as well as the head. Incidentally, I never made it through the first chapter of Aristotle's *Poetics*. But I have sat in the ruins of the Theatre of Dionysus at the foot of the Acropolis in Athens, and looked at the stage where Aeschylus, Sophocles and Euripides, among others, debuted their plays. Thousands of bottoms have worn the marble seats smooth. Human beings, not textbooks, make theatre.

Over the last decade I've also taught many hours of playwriting. To BA and MA students; to adult learners; to young writers; for new-writing theatres, on residential courses, universities, up mountains and by the ocean. Part One of this book is loosely based on the format of my long-running class for developing writers, which I went on to teach at the National Theatre in London. It's pretty simple: I meet with a small group of playwrights once a week for three hours. We start with a quick theatre catch-up, so we can talk about plays we've seen and enjoy some heated debate about who liked what and why. I'll lead a short workshop or exercise on a particular aspect of playwriting craft, often using a published playtext. Then I give the floor to one student, who will share a number of scenes from the play they're working on. We read the play aloud as actors (to the best of our abilities), and then we discuss the writing.

I always encourage students to be brave enough to bring in their problem scenes, rather than their best work, so that they can get the most out of their feedback sessions. And it's interesting how many people have told me that although the dedicated analysis of their own writing is helpful, what's even more useful is the time spent evaluating other people's work. Not only is it far easier to be objective about writing that isn't your own, it's even more instructive when it's imperfect – as is any work-in-progress. In learning to understand where someone else's play isn't working to its full potential, we begin to understand how to correct and improve our own.

This is rather different from seeing brilliant plays brilliantly directed on professional stages – although that's equally instructive, and, hopefully, inspiring. So, although I'll refer to contemporary and classical texts in this book, I'll also use examples from plays – some produced, but mostly not – written by former students of mine who have generously given me permission to describe the genesis and development of their work, and how they dealt with problems and challenges. These are the case studies given towards the end of most chapters. The interrogation of text that is detailed in these case studies is probably the closest the developing writer can get to being in an actual rehearsal room. They should give you a taste of the sort of rigorous questioning process that you might encounter in rehearsal yourself one day.

Most of the plays referenced in this book are published, and most are examples of what we'd call the traditional 'well-made play'. This is simply because they are more open to analysis on the page, whereas more experimental forms of writing, including much devised work, are either a) unpublished and/or b) often make more sense in production. The texts include two of my favourite classic twentieth-century plays; Lorraine Hansberry's *A Raisin in the Sun*, and *A Streetcar Named Desire* by Tennessee Williams. It might be worth reading them before or while you're reading this book. But the exercises and guidelines offered can be applied to many forms and styles of theatre.

I've also rounded off each chapter with a practical exercise on a relevant aspect of writing craft, which you can complete in your own time. Some I invented myself to address a question or issue that arose in a class. Others were originated by other teachers and/or playwrights – where that's the case I've hopefully identified them correctly. Either way, I can truthfully say that I've road-tested them all myself, and so have many of my students who have gone on to have their plays produced.

Developing playwrights also naturally want to know about the practicalities of having their script turned into a show. Part Two lays out some of the steps on the journey towards production and offers some practical advice about how to navigate this exciting but sometimes baffling process.

You might have a burning desire to write for the theatre but no prior experience. You might have written your first play or, perhaps more likely, started several plays that you haven't been able to finish. But if you've only been to the theatre a couple of times in your life, and/or never read a playtext, I'd advise you to put the book in a drawer for a few months, read some contemporary and classic plays and plan some theatre trips (if that's not possible, then *imagine* them on stage as you read them – it'll be good training). It will help you to have a degree of familiarity with the theatre as an audience member before you begin writing, and before you dive into this book.

Finally, it goes without saying that I offer no hard and fast rules for what a good play is, or should be, or how it should be written. Creativity is a fluid, mysterious thing, bubbling up from our unconscious minds. It can't and shouldn't be forced into formulaic shapes. You must allow yourself time to daydream, to *feel* your way through your writing process, as well as applying craft to those base materials. Then you can find and harness the patterns, rhythms and devices of theatrical narrative – and of language – in order to tell your story. Your play may be a 'well-made play' in the traditional sense; it may be a one-woman show or a devised piece of performance or an adaptation of a literary work or anything in between. Whatever it is, I hope to share some knowledge and experience that will help you to keep going and finish the draft that might one day make it on to the stage.

To set the scene, here is James Baldwin, writing in 1976 about seeing Orson Welles' 1936 production of *Macbeth* with an all-black cast, as a thirteen-year-old boy:

In the darkened Lafayette Theatre – I watched the narrow, horizontal ribbon of light which connects the stage curtain to the floor of the stage, and which also separates them. That narrow ribbon of light then contains a mystery. That mystery may contain the future – you are, yourself, suspended, as mortal as that ribbon. No one can possibly know what is about to happen: it is happening, each time, for the first time, for the only time... everyone seemed to be waiting, as I was waiting. The curtain rose.[1]

– PART 1 –

1
THEATRICAL STORYTELLING

THEATRICAL STORYTELLING

Plenty of people who have an urge to write drama will aim for the stage first. It stands to reason. Practically speaking it is generally far easier to get a play staged than it is to have a TV series commissioned or a screenplay optioned – not least because the latter both cost so much to produce. This is one of the reasons there is no 'fringe' television, no 'black-box' cinema and far less of the admirable energy and innovation that we see from 'let's put on a show' theatremakers (although of course digital technology is making this more possible in film and TV). Plays can and do flourish in pubs, hired rooms, public buildings and, increasingly, in site-specific locations. I once saw a memorable series of short Tennessee Williams plays staged in a hotel room for an audience of twenty. The theatre is also a great training ground for new writers because it allows them access to actors, performance spaces, rehearsed readings, and a strong writing community.

This is all good – theatre *should* feel accessible, egalitarian and doable. But sadly it doesn't mean that writing a play is easy – or that all plays *should* in fact be plays. There are plenty of films that have begun their lives as plays, and novels that have been adapted into plays, and more and more films that end up on the stage, too. But don't let that lull you into a false sense of security. I read lots of new plays that should probably be novels, and some that should be poems, and even more that are really television shows. And most of them share a key characteristic, which is a distinct lack of theatricality.

WHAT IS THEATRICALITY?

This concept often baffles writers new to playwriting. Doesn't the fact that their story is performed on stage in the presence of an audience make it inherently theatrical? The answer is an emphatic no. Theatricality is a term that covers the broad set of tools available to theatremakers, present in physical stagecraft *and* in writing craft. These tools will always be utilised in a good play. Even an apparently realistic play will employ deliberate theatrical techniques which are present in the writing as much as the performance. In the theatre, the gap between 'actual' reality and the reality represented on stage can be very small or very large.

As an example of the latter, the play that Simon Stephens crafted from Mark Haddon's novel *The Curious Incident of the Dog in the Night-Time* uses movement, music, graphics and lighting (performative theatrical devices) to allow the audience to experience life through the eyes of its hero Christopher, an autistic teenage boy (although the condition is never explicitly named in the book or the play). There are also theatrical devices written into the text by the playwright, including the fragmented non-linear timescale, and the scenes between Christopher and his teacher, where we experience his life as written in a book for a school project. This particular play and its staging has a high level of thrilling and sophisticated theatricality. It's easy to see why the novel became a play, with some clever theatrical thinking by playwright and director.

At the other end of the spectrum is realism – 'life imitates art' theatre – which is still the dominant form of modern Western theatre. These sorts of plays aim to depict a real situation, with linear shifts forward in time and place, in order to mimic reality as closely as possible. (Linear storytelling is a presentation of events in their chronological order as they happen.) It is often also known as 'fourth-wall' theatre: the action on stage is surrounded by three walls, with the audience positioned where the fourth wall would be, as a privileged but unseen witness. An actor would never 'speak out' and address the audience (which is known as 'breaking' the fourth wall) – because it disrupts the convention that the audience actually isn't there.

An example of this is Joe Penhall's play *Blue/Orange*, which creates a realistic depiction of a couple of days in a psychiatric ward. We meet two doctors, one junior, one senior, and their patient (who also happens to be called Christopher). During the play we witness the two doctors clash over the right treatment for Christopher – is he ready to be released from the hospital or not? One doctor thinks yes, the other no. The play, which has three acts, leads us through a day and a night in the hospital; as each doctor interviews the patient and fights their corner, we learn that each has their own personal agenda with regards to Christopher's diagnosis.

So where is the theatricality in this play? It is everywhere. It is present in the heightened dialogue, which may sound completely realistic to the audience, but on close inspection of the text turns out to be far more poetic, structured and deliberately rhythmic than 'real-life' dialogue ever is. It is present in imagery and symbols embedded in the text – not least the blue orange of the title, which creates metaphorical meaning for the audience. It is present in the three-act structure which gradually allows the audience to change their alignment from one doctor's argument to the other's and, finally, perhaps, to Christopher's. It's a far less *formally* theatrical play than *Curious*, but it is just as theatrical in its essence, its *play-ness*.

Blue/Orange is a theatrical exploration of a political subject played out by personally conflicted characters, set within realistic constraints; *Curious* is a theatrical exploration of the interior state of one particular character, whose experience of life is externalised in action, both realistic and profoundly expressionistic. Both are plays; both are theatre; both succeed on their own terms.

THEATRICAL STORYTELLING VS CINEMATIC STORYTELLING

After its successful run in London, *Blue/Orange* was turned into a film for BBC Four, which was a very faithful adaptation of the play. But it's worth noting the key differences in both forms. The play has one setting: the treatment room. All the action takes place within it. In contrast, the film has many locations, as well as a slightly different time scale. The breadth of visual storytelling is far greater in film – audiences generally get bored with one setting and a lack of spectacle, and there are very few films that successfully use such contained and constrained time and place. Because, as a rule, we are far more familiar with film and television narratives than theatrical ones, it can take a while to train yourself as a playwright to imagine onstage action in your plays without the lens of cinematic reality. To the untrained eye, a play's basic action and spectacle can seem very simple, and very achievable.

Let's take the iconic shower scene from Hitchcock's *Psycho* as an illustration – it's easy to find online if you don't know the film. The character Marion is enjoying a hot shower. We see her, framed from the shoulders up, under the jet of water. We (the camera) look up into the showerhead. Back at her. Then we pull back to show a menacing female figure appear in silhouette behind the opaque shower curtain holding a knife. She yanks back the curtain. Now Bernard Herrmann's famous chilling music starts – and we see Marion scream. The camera zooms in in extreme close-up on her terrified face and open mouth. The mystery killer begins to slash at Marion with the knife. Hitchcock uses a fast sequence of different camera angles here to portray the chaos and violence as the killer attacks Marion – including the 'point of view' (POV) of the knife slashing downwards – and then blood darkens the running water in the bath. The killer disappears. We zoom in on Marion's hand sliding down the tiled wall, before ending on her dead face, eyes open. It's widely regarded as a masterpiece of visual storytelling. (Of course, although we consider film to be a far more 'realistic' medium than theatre, it is still a carefully constructed montage of visual fragments that creates an illusion of reality. I've been told that Hitchcock shot the forty-five-second scene over seven days using eighty different camera positions.)

As an experiment, try watching a film or TV show some time with the sound turned down, and see if you can still understand what's going on. In a good film there is a mass of information that is conveyed purely visually; for example, a close-up on an actor's face to convey emotion; a shift in location, time or place to show us that time has moved on (e.g. from day to night). Now imagine sitting in the theatre and watching an entire play with your ears plugged. How much could you understand? You should be able to detect action, however subtle, through the arrangement of the space and the movement of bodies through it, and find meaning created in the physical setting. You'll probably also be able to guess at certain relationships by how people physically interact – but the subtle intricacies of the play's meaning will be lost. The action or spectacle may appear static, visually simplistic, even dull.

But open your ears and everything comes alive. Dialogue – and the use of language in general – is the playwright's great tool, and one that is pushed to its furthest capacities in theatre, far more so than in film or television. We'll look at this in more detail in a forthcoming chapter.

Back to our *Psycho* sequence, which creates crystal-clear meaning and narrative without a single word of dialogue spoken. Could we replicate Marion's murder on stage? Yes. That is to say, we could easily show a woman on stage taking a shower, who is disturbed by a killer and violently stabbed to death. But our experience of watching the same action would be entirely different – and, perhaps, far less disturbing. Why? Because the tension and fear created by the film version comes almost entirely from what is *not* shown. The camera shots, editing and music create a cinematic subtext that a stage production cannot replicate. The eye of the camera is intimate, privileged and detailed, and it moves wherever it wants.

A theatre audience has a very different communal eye. Although we are skilfully manipulated by some of the same elements – lighting, blocking, physical action and dialogue – the panorama of the stage is generally static, and action ebbs and flows into it. We can't zoom in and out like a camera can, or privilege the audience perspective in the same intimate way. There's a good reason why certain filmic staples are very rarely shown – and rarely work – on stage. Sex is one. Dying is another – by which I mean actual physical death. I can think of a few great death scenes: Shakespeare was, of course, pretty good at them (though there's a bit too much talking), and the Greeks knew how to throw a gory punch. Seán O'Casey's *The Plough and the Stars* has a devastating one. Chekhov was fond of the offstage gunshot. But we rarely see as many bodies drop and blood spurt as we do in the cinema, certainly not often in contemporary drama. These things are hard to stage, hard to act, and often seem melodramatic.

Somebody clever, whose name I cannot recall (feel free to write and tell me if you know the original quote) said, 'Classical drama tends to ask, "What's going to happen next?" (i.e. it is plot-driven.) Modern drama tends to ask, "What's going on right now?" (i.e. its drive is psychological/emotional/behavioural.)' Modern stories for the stage thrive in the realm of the psychological. Death is present in much great drama, but more often at a symbolic level or as an offstage presence. If *Psycho* is ever adapted for the stage, I'd imagine a clever director could create some sort of visual spectacle to mimic the iconic moment, but the play would live or die according to the onstage tension between the key characters. And that would make use of playwright's craft. Subtext. Complex behaviour. Symbolism.

THEATRE IS ACTIVE

Of course, it takes time to learn these sorts of elements of playwriting craft. And it's hard not to be influenced by filmic storytelling. This can sometimes lead the developing writer to unconsciously borrow from film and television as a kind of shortcut to creating theatricality. I'll often hear new playwrights describing their play like this: 'It's set in an airport and it uses video projection to show planes taking off and landing to create an airport atmosphere.' Or, 'My play is set in a remote forest in America in 1950, and a bus depot in England in 2011, and I'll have a filmed backdrop to represent the forest and a bus on stage to represent the depot.'

There's nothing wrong with the desire to shift between theatrical realities. And in principle there's nothing wrong with video projection to help create a world or setting – many productions do this successfully using highly stylised staging. (Theatre companies Frantic Assembly, who worked on the *Curious* adaptation, and Complicité are masters of this.) But these sorts of devices, which use the camera to help create an onstage reality, can often function more as a safety net for the inexperienced writer: *I'll show moving images to the audience which will allow them to fully understand my context and give the work a visual veracity.* And this can be dangerous.

Why? Principally because audiences are far cleverer *and* far more active than we might imagine. A good writer, director and creative company will easily convince an audience that they're watching both 1950s natural woodland and modern Britain, using only a bare stage and a few lighting and/or music cues. In the theatre the audience is already primed to accept a heightened theatrical version of reality with the most subtle sleight of hand. The language, flavour and tone of the play, plus costume, staging and so on, all help create this theatrical reality. Try to remember this when you're writing so that you don't end up spoon-feeding information to your audience, leaving no room for their collective imagination.

Also remember that no two performances of a play are ever the same. From the moment the curtain goes up, the audience enters into a creative contract with it. We collectively agree that this chair is a tree. This woman is a child. This is sixteenth-century England. We are asked to participate in the reality, and we do. (Or don't, and will probably leave at the interval.) Actors will often talk about a sense of creative transaction that takes place between audience and performers in the theatre.

This is because we shape the performance in our live reactions. When we laugh, gasp, or react emotionally to a single moment in a play, that moment becomes part of the organic fabric of the collective experience. Actors will react, and hinge off a reaction. They will alter their timing – pause, suspend, stretch, or quicken – like an orchestra responding to the baton of a conductor. This creates a wonderful sense of active participation by the audience and provides a creative, almost spiritual transaction between the preacher (i.e. the live storyteller) and the worshippers in the pews (i.e. the live audience).

Here is our first case study, in which a writer allows us to share in his process and give an overview of the genesis, development and execution of his play.

CASE STUDY: *Coma Girl* by Hinrich von Haaren

Hinrich brought his play *Coma Girl* to workshop in my class at the National Theatre. I'm going to let him describe how he went about turning his original impetus into a play in his own words – starting with his own synopsis.

SYNOPSIS
A girl owes money to a doctor.
The doctor and his sister want their money back.
A young man is hired to threaten the girl but things go badly wrong.
The girl is beaten into a coma.
The young man's girlfriend thinks he should be paid for the job anyway.

Who is culpable? Who can shift the blame? Who will be punished?

The initial idea for the play came from a story a friend told me. She had bought a flat, and the tenants were refusing to pay the rent. On the way home, my partner and I were joking that our friend could hire someone to 'rough up' the tenants a bit. This was of course ludicrous as our friend is the sweetest person. But something about the incident stuck in my head and I carried it around with me for months. Firstly, this was because my own reaction surprised me. As someone with a left-wing moral conscience I would have usually sided with the tenants. Only suddenly, in this case, I found myself on the side of the person who was making the money. Secondly, it was because I couldn't stop wondering just how far certain people might be willing to go to get what they want.

The initial draft was only about twenty minutes long, but it gave me the basic outline for the play. It really helped to have a concrete event that everything revolved around (a girl is injured accidentally in a fight and goes into a coma). From this event I spun out three different story strands. They were their own individual stories involving individual characters, but they were all linked in some way to the girl in the coma.

The play became a series of two-hander scenes and the central event (the violent act that puts the girl in the coma) takes place offstage. It's only ever talked about. Keeping that big action offstage gave me the opportunity to show it from a different character's perspective in each scene, through their retelling of the story. So you get partial information about how or why it happened in each scene and then the next scene might contradict that narrative. I wrote the first draft very quickly, then left it sitting in a drawer for ages, and finally took it to Jemma's playwriting class at the National Theatre.

After we workshopped the play, I started revising. But first I had some actors over, and we did a read-through at my house. All the things I thought were terribly clever and funny sank like lead balloons. The scenes that I thought were mundane because the dialogue was seemingly about nothing worked the best. So I went back and cut, cut, cut.

Another important thing happened when we did the reading, which was that the actors (there were six of them initially) asked how I saw the play being performed. I had an image of all six actors being on stage together, and realised that this was far too large a cast for a new play to have a reasonable chance of production. I looked through the play and saw that I could double the actors quite easily as the scenes were all two-handers. So I decided to make the play for three actors only. I also realised that this would make the play more theatrical.

Hinrich is a published novelist (in German, his first language, along with other European translations) and I asked him how, when a new idea for a story landed, he went about deciding if it had greater potential for a novel or for a play.

With *Coma Girl*, I knew from the start it would be a play, because I saw all the characters existing in one space together, although in different locations, for the whole duration of the story. Whether it would ultimately be staged like that or not, I don't know, but the sense of single contained space and time was very strong. I also knew that the absent coma girl was a sort of physical void that would bring all the characters together. That would never happen in a novel, because I'd want to describe her, take the reader there and get inside her head.

Also, when I have an idea for a novel it usually starts as a much bigger sprawl involving more characters and situations, and I have to slowly evolve a plot from those elements. I see the characters in 'real' situations and I also hear them thinking – I sort of tap into their inner thoughts. But with a play, I immediately hear characters speaking out loud. I sort of feel my way through the story using their verbal interactions – and silences – it's a kind of dialogue that you don't find in prose or on screen. There's more freedom for me in writing a play than a novel – it's a very 'playful' process. I can write short scenes and move them around; cut things up and puzzle them back together.

In a way, for me, knowing a particular story *has* to be a play comes from understanding the story's limitations. That it isn't necessarily epic, that it should happen in one room and be contained by its setting as well as by its central idea. There's some sort of tension that I feel when I imagine the characters speaking that can only be experienced live, not described in prose or by a close-up of a character's face. That tangible sense of a story's theatrical potential is quite elusive really, but I'm getting better at spotting it early on!

Hinrich's play went on to win the Nick Darke Award in 2016.

As you can see, Hinrich found the opportunity to create theatricality at various stages of the writing process. Early on, he hit on the idea of using three actors to play six characters (one that is generally unique to the stage). This turned out to have several functions. Firstly, the doubling of actors added to the comedy of the play and its absurdist, darkly comic tone, as well as its entertainment value; audiences take great pleasure in watching versatile actors inhabit contrasting roles. Secondly, it helped underpin the play's themes about mistaken identity and moral weakness in the characters' entwined fates. This device does have its challenges. A literary manager who read the play astutely commented that the doubling of actors with such a small group of players might end up seeming glib. Could the audience invest properly in the characters with such an overt game of theatrical 'pass the parcel'? Time will tell, but it was a good starting point for marrying story, theme and form.

Another key choice was Hinrich's decision to make the central event of the violent attack on the girl an offstage event that we never see. Although this might fly in the face of conventional wisdom and invoke the usual set of worries about basing a play around something that involves a lot of telling but no showing, it was actually a smart move. The bungled accident that led to the coma girl's hospitalisation is far stronger left to the audience's imagination. Presenting the same central event from three different points of view also allows the audience to make an active choice about which character's version of events is the true one. The *retelling* of the accident, in this case, becomes not only a plot device but a central theme in a play that is both an existential whodunnit and an exploration of personal and social responsibility.

If you steadily interrogate your material as you write it, like Hinrich did, you will find the spaces that will allow for theatricality in performance. But be true to your vision for your play, however simple or small or plain that might seem in comparison to the work of others. Don't embellish your script with unnecessary theatrical flourishes just to try and give it a stagey pizzazz – these may have the opposite effect of weakening your script if they're not germane to its essential story.

Finally, remember that theatre audiences demonstrate a persistent hunger to suspend their disbelief and to participate in a play's sleight of hand – even when it goes wrong. I once read an interview with a young actor who told a wonderful story about his first professional performance. I can't remember the exact play but it was a classic – it might have been *Romeo and Juliet*. The climax of the action required him to fall on his sword and die. This moment had been carefully choreographed in rehearsal so that the actor would fall, in his death throes, on a precise mark where a fountain of fake blood was concealed. This would release on impact and bloody his shirt, creating the effect of the fatal wound.

One night the actor, to his horror, missed his mark, and fell to the floor some way from the fountain. He had no choice but to die on the spot *without* the prop blood, judging that to drag himself several feet to his mark would ruin the verisimilitude of the moment. As he died, the fountain triggered several feet away, sending a spout of blood up into empty space.

The actor, as we can imagine, died a second death of professional mortification and slunk offstage when the curtain fell. And then later, in the bar, he overheard two members of the audience discussing the moment. 'Wasn't it incredible,' one of them remarked, 'when the man died and blood symbolically jetted into the air. What a brilliant piece of theatre.'

EXERCISES: FINDING THEATRICALITY

1. *Instinct questions (feeling your way through)*

This set of questions should help you to start exploring some of your conscious *and* unconscious connections to your material. You don't have to have a finished draft yet. If it helps to imagine your play here as a physical performance, go ahead. But if you're not ready to do that, just write down any feelings or impressions you have when you think about your play, even if it's as yet unwritten. Either way, try to answer the questions spontaneously, without overthinking your answers. And don't beat yourself up if you can't answer them easily. This is meant to be a playful exercise, not a test.

→ What are the colours, smells or tastes of your play? Describe any sensory impressions that come to mind when you summon your story in your mind.

→ Is there any music (featured in the play, or not) that encapsulates the essence of your play?

→ Describe your play as if it were a building; what is the architecture like? Baroque, Rococo, Gothic, Modernist? Is it dark or light, big or small? Cluttered or minimalist? Be as literal as you like, or as abstract.

→ Picture your play in your head as a mass of feelings that you want to dramatise: write down a list of key emotions that come to mind.

→ Which human emotion does your story lead with? Is there one word that sums up the key feeling that is communicated by the play?

→ What are the opposing poles of the play – its north and its south? (e.g. love and hate; peace and war; forgiveness and revenge; intellect and emotion.) Is there change from one or more elemental force (emotional, behavioural, active, visual, thematic, etc.) to another in the play?

2. *Craft questions (thinking your way through)*

When you feel ready, this next set of questions might help you

---

interrogate the inherent theatrical potential of your story. If you don't know all the answers, or even if your answer is 'no' to most of the questions, that's fine. You don't need to know everything in advance. You can always come back to this exercise when you're further on in the writing process.

→ What are the 'theatrical spaces' of your play? Can you visualise the physical settings, locations and world of the play on stage easily?

→ Are there any more abstract theatrical spaces in your play – for example, a dream space, a memory or flashback sequence – something that isn't tied to a concrete 'real' location?

→ Are there any theatrical devices you can use to convey meaning? These might include storytelling forms like monologue or direct address, and use of props or symbols (physical and abstract.) How do they carry meaning or subtext that is not 'told' in dialogue?

→ Is your play linear in form and narrative (if so, that's fine!) or does it lend itself to other non-realistic narrative shapes or forms? i.e. does it move back and forth across time and space or juxtapose more than one theatrical reality?

→ Is there a sense of spectacle to your play, however small? What are you inviting your audience to witness when they watch your play?

→ If you're writing for a particular space, how close can the audience physically get to the action? Will this affect the text? Might any physical limitations of the space be used to advantage in your storytelling?

2

GETTING STARTED:
THE STATUE IN THE
STONE

GETTING STARTED:
THE STATUE IN THE STONE

Stories spring from many different places, both conscious and unconscious, concrete and abstract. A play can start from a single scribble. It might be a line of dialogue, a character note, a place and time, or a strong feeling about a particular topic. Some playwrights begin from an intellectual place of enquiry via theme, idea, proposition or theatrical concept. Others start from an emotional impetus to dramatise a character journey, relationship or some aspect of lived human experience. But turning these initial inspirations into a fully fledged play is a whole different story.

The novelist Ursula K. Le Guin describes the writer's process of discovery as looking for 'the statue in the stone', inspired perhaps by a famous quote from Michelangelo: 'The sculpture is already complete within the marble block, before I start my work. It is already there, I just have to chisel away the superfluous material.'

This is easier said than done, especially if our play is still half-submerged in our unconscious mind. The statue, Le Guin adds, 'is what the craft works on, and shows, and sets free... How does the artist find that, see it, before it's visible? That is a real question.'[2]

For any writer, the blank canvas – or the smooth block of stone as yet untouched by the chisel – can seem terrifying – it's both too empty and too full of possibilities. The worst thing that can happen, and often does, is that an inexperienced playwright plunges in randomly after their initial spark of creativity, and then proceeds to write and rewrite the same scene over and over for any number of weeks, months or years, before giving up in frustration.

If you are one of the rare and lucky writers who has a great story to tell for the stage, with a clear beginning, middle and end, and a strong sense of character journey before you've put anything down – congratulations! In my experience, most playwrights usually start in an enthused but creative muddle, and must painstakingly chip away at their block until their statue begins to emerge, line by line. Some of you reading this book may already have an entire draft of a play written, but others only a few scenes, a sketchy outline or just a lingering idea that feels full of dramatic potential. Whatever stage you're at, this chapter is intended to help you chip away at your block of stone. Some plays require careful mapping before you start writing. Others will tumble out in a stream of consciousness and then need shaping afterwards. Whatever our starting point, we have to find a writing methodology that works for us.

TRUST YOUR PROCESS

Developing playwrights often worry that they're missing some vital universal skill that will enable them magically to complete a draft. They also invariably want to know how successful playwrights go about their business. Over the last few years I've spent many fruitful weeks working on various projects as a writer on attachment at the National Theatre Studio. On the top floor of the building there are five small writer's rooms, equipped with desk, chair and computer; each containing a playwright or director or small creative team beavering away on a new project. There's usually a certain amount of friendly visiting between writers in their respective rooms to borrow paper, gossip, or offer a tea break.

An observer might notice that when we enter the inner sanctums of each other's writing rooms, we're all covertly looking for *signs of process*. Who has a series of filing cards taped to the wall with each scene outlined on it? Who listens to music while they write and who doesn't? Who works from a diagram, a flow chart, a sketch of the stage? Who records freeform dialogue on their phone and then types it up afterwards? Who has a daily page limit, a word count, a map of their play drawn on Post-it notes?

Deep down we all secretly believe that someone else might have cracked the ultimate writing system. For some reason we never consider our own process in any way useful or creative – but we should – at the beginning it is often all we have. You must learn to trust your process from the get-go, even if you don't think it's very professional. There is no vital universal methodology that is a fail-safe route to success.

You will also need to practise patience. Give your initial thoughts, feelings and ideas adequate time and space. Write as many notes as you need; spout monologues, create character sketches or emotional maps – whatever feels fruitful. And don't be afraid to change your course at any point.

FINDING A FOOTHOLD

I usually spend quite a bit of time doing research before I start writing a new play. It's not only useful for those writing a drama that requires biographical fact-checking or extensive historical knowledge of an event or world or person. Any kind of research – whether that's talking to someone who has personally experienced some element of your story, reading around your subject matter, or visiting a place or location you want to write about – can help you ground your ideas and provide concrete details to inspire your storytelling. The human imagination feeds on detail. It's no accident that many directors encourage their actors, once a play is in rehearsal, to visit places, people and locations similar to those in the play, so they might immerse themselves in a concrete reality to add veracity to their performance.

Harold Pinter has talked about how he often started his plays with a couple of characters in a particular context, and then set them speaking, and then wrote down what they said. Many playwrights find this infuriating, as it suggests an effortlessness and confidence which few of us experience when writing. But his advice here, given in a speech made at the National Student Drama Festival in 1962, is invaluable: *'The context has always been for me, concrete and particular, and the characters concrete also. I've never started a play from any kind of abstract idea or theory.'*

If you were asked to go away and write a scene 'about love', where would you start? Who is in love? What kind of love it is? Where is the inherent drama in the scene? As a starting instruction, it's far too abstract and vague to be useful. But if you were asked to go away and write a scene about romantic love between two teenage girls who cannot reveal their relationship to their school friends, it would suddenly get a lot easier.

Concrete particulars. Two characters, A desires B. There is an external obstacle to that desire. A series of potential settings: classroom, bedroom, playground. And a set of dramatic stakes – e.g. the potential for consequences that might create drama for the two characters and others. This would likely give us enough to easily invent a time, a place, a 'now' –

a concrete context. These choices may not stick – those two teenage girls may morph into two boys; or a man and a woman working for the same company; or any number of variations, as you discover what holds your interest – but they will have anchored you enough to start exploring.

To chip away at this a bit more, I'm going to give some examples of plays both published and performed, as well as those workshopped in my classes, detailing the genesis of the play from a particular concrete element.

STARTING WITH A CHARACTER

You might have a character in mind that you can't stop thinking about. Why? What interests you about them? What do you want to know about them? What drives them? What do they want? What is their conflict – with themselves, with others, with their world? Do they change or learn something during the story? Or is the character in fact a group of people going through a unifying experience?

→ Anne Doherty's play *I Vow to Thee* began with a desire to explore her own parents' experiences as Scottish workers transplanted to England in the hostile 1950s. Note the inherent conflict between their native background and their new world, which contained the seeds for her story. (More play details in Chapter Three.)

→ Lucy Flannery's play *Hippolyta's Handmaiden* was born out of her interest in a minor character from Shakespeare's *A Midsummer Night's Dream* – a woman forced to marry against her will. The story grew from Lucy's desire to dramatically explore what this action might have cost her character emotionally, and what choices she may be forced to make in accepting or challenging her fate. (More play details in Chapter Five.)

→ Sylvia Paskin's play *A True Friend of England* was also based on two characters from her own family's history – a Christian German and a Jewish German in Berlin during the Second World War who were forbidden by law to fall in love. Again, inherent conflict (and danger) within their political and social worlds meant the potential for drama. (More play details in Chapter Ten.)

STARTING WITH AN EVENT

Many plays are led by a key event that has either happened in the recent past (and before the curtain comes up), or takes place early on in the play.

It's no accident that births, marriages and deaths feature prominently in dramatic narratives – they are both unifying and divisive communal events, which usually invoke strong emotion. The same goes for a war of any kind – political, cultural or personal.

The most classic and common event to kickstart a play is, as Christopher Booker calls it in his book *The Seven Basic Plots: Why We Tell Stories*, 'A stranger comes to town.' This could encompass literally hundreds of plays, and is at the heart of many of those referenced in this book: *A Streetcar Named Desire* by Tennessee Williams; *Love and Understanding* by Joe Penhall; *The Weir* by Conor McPherson; *The Children* by Lucy Kirkwood. In other words, *change*.

The 'stranger' doesn't have to be a person arriving; it can be anything that changes the status quo for the play's characters. But *something must happen* around which you can build your story. Is it a promise, a betrayal, a declaration, a fight? An inheritance, a visit, a trauma? How might it unify or divide your characters, create tension, or set them on a new path of action?

Chimerica – another play by Lucy Kirkwood – starts with an American journalist witnessing the Tiananmen Square Massacre of 1989 from a hotel window. He goes on a quest to find out what happened to the man who famously stood in front of a line of military tanks with his shopping bags. The play uses a real historical event as the central plot device, but cleverly embroiders a personal journey of discovery around it for the three main characters.

My former student Catherine Willmore's play *Property* had its genesis after the London riots of 2011 that started in Tottenham, London, and spread out across the country. She was fascinated by the social, racial and class conflicts that fuelled the riots, and wanted to explore what they might have meant to a variety of people living in the same area of London in very different circumstances. She invented a constellation of characters to carry her story, but this real-life event was the creative hub of the play. (More play details in Chapter Nine.)

Writers starting with an event, real or imagined, must think carefully about how to bring that event on stage, or decide if it's necessary to show it at all. If the event *does* take place on stage and in the action of the play, is it physically stageable and does it have theatrical life? More importantly, how does it create action for your characters? If the event takes place *offstage* at any point in the play, how will you bring it on stage thematically? Plays can be hampered by long exchanges in which characters have to explain to each other (and so to the audience) exactly what happened and when. Some exposition is always needed to set up a story, but too much of this sort of 'storytelling in the past tense' can weigh down a scene, and rob it of energy. It is often far harder for an audience to invest emotionally in an incidence of anecdote-telling, than it is in witnessing the actual event now, on stage.

Of course, there are exceptions. Remember that Hinrich chose *not* to show the central event/act of his play *Coma Girl* (see Chapter One), but to leave it to the audience's imagination. The retelling of his story's central event offstage by various characters, and their contrasting versions of events, was part of the fabric of the play, so his decision earned its place. In Conor McPherson's play *The Weir*, 'a stranger comes to town' and reveals a key offstage event from her past to four strangers. The basic synopsis for the play might be: *four men from the same village and a woman who is new to the village, spend a single evening in the local pub, telling each other stories.* Put like this, it sounds pretty simple and without very high dramatic stakes. Is is it dramatic? Yes. Is there some sort of change or transfiguration? Yes. The men come to view the woman in an entirely new light after she has told her story, and it subtly changes their own relationships. It may be a simple story, but it is one with great emotional power. More on story in Chapter Four.

STARTING WITH A WORLD OR PLACE

Is there a geographical location or a particular social/political/cultural/ historical world that grips your imagination and is a creative cauldron for your story? If so, what are its key elements? Is it a natural landscape or a man-made urban sprawl? A public environment such as a workplace, or a single room containing a private domestic world? How might it provide, in Pinter's words, a concrete and particular context for action? Is there also a level of metaphorical meaning in the physical and sensory geography that you put on stage?

→ Viv Edwards's play *The Bevin Boys* arose from both event and world. He was interested in the Welsh mining villages that hosted Bevin Boys during the Second World War – young men without any prior training who were conscripted to mine coal for the war effort. His imagination was fired by thinking about the collision of a small closed community infiltrated by strangers (another 'stranger comes to town' set-up). He was also intrigued by the theatrical possibility of setting scenes in the mine itself, which might play out in near total darkness. (More play details in Chapter Four.)

→ Inua Ellams's big-hearted hit play *Barber Shop Chronicles* is set in a variety of different barber shops in different African capital cities (as well as London), where customers and staff watch the same championship football match on television. The match thematically connects and unifies the various locations and personal stories that emerge from this jigsaw-puzzle portrait of the African diaspora.

STARTING FROM A PROP

Most plays use props – physical items brought on stage – to create a world and theatrical physical setting. But some can be used more strategically to carry metaphor and subtext. Is there a key concrete prop in your play around which action might revolve? Props are often overlooked by new playwrights, but used well, they can help create meaning and focus the audience's attention.

→ Tanya Ronder's play *Table* uses a large dining table as its central prop, around which six generations of the same family play out their domestic dramas through different historical eras and locations. The table shifts from Victorian farmhouse to African mission to 1960s commune and more, taking in a century of change and social evolution.

→ Lydia Marchant, a former student, wrote a funny and touching play called *After Party* about a group of teenage girls who go on a boozy package holiday in Magaluf after graduating from high school. Lydia knew she wanted things to start well, with the girls in high spirits, but then to slowly disintegrate as tensions between the friends escalated, and new alliances and hostilities were formed. Along the way the girls' carefree hedonism is replaced by concern about their futures. The single setting and continuous action created a lovely pressure-cooker environment, but not enough was happening – in the draft we workshopped, the scenes tended to descend into talky stagnation. There was a moment of tension in the play when a new and expensive dress belonging to one of the girls was borrowed by another character. The dress symbolised its owner's dreams for her new life, and functioned as an idealised projection of her status, beauty and desirability. That felt potent – and dangerous. What if everyone in the play had a relationship with the valuable dress? Once pristine and an emblem of adult hope, it might end up soiled and imperfect by the play's end – but perhaps allowing the characters to find a new equilibrium. The evolution of a minor prop gave Lydia a strategy to approach her new draft, building the action of the play around this central, valued and fought-over object.

STARTING WITH A THEATRICAL DEVICE

By 'theatrical device' I just mean any kind of storytelling convention that is used on stage in a play to create meaning outside of the dialogue – and which generally takes the play beyond straightforward realism. For example, a narrator who tells parts of the story directly to the audience, or a character who speaks 'out', breaking the fourth wall. Use of a chorus, monologue, flashbacks or dream sequences and non-linear narrative form are all theatrical devices, as was Hinrich's use of three actors to play six different characters in his play *Coma Girl*.

If you have an idea for a key theatrical device that you might build a story around, make sure that it is woven into the play's DNA, rather than simply sitting on top as a purely decorative element. Are your devices organically linked to your material? Do they mirror your themes or create dramatic subtext? For example:

→ A man slowly descends into dementia and loses his grip on reality. His growing confusion is dramatised on stage by a) the use of different actors to play the same characters in his personal life, and b) the changing theatre set, in which the furniture in an initially cluttered living room slowly vanishes piece by piece, scene by scene, eventually becoming an empty, sterile hospital room. (*The Father* by Florian Zeller.) The play's theatrical form and physical world not only mirror its theme but are part of the story itself – it becomes a compelling visual suspense puzzle for the audience. debbie tucker green's play *generations* also uses a 'vanishing' device, but in this case with characters and dialogue. The gradual truncation of the same scene, enacted five times by dwindling family members, dramatises the decimation of the family by AIDS, without ever metioning the disease.

→ A doomed love affair is presented to the audience backwards, in a reversal of linear time. The play begins with the unhappy parting of a couple having had an extramarital affair, and works backwards in time as the play progresses, ending with their first optimistic romantic encounter. (*Betrayal* by Harold Pinter. This narrative device is also used to great effect in Stephen Sondheim and George Furth's musical *Merrily We Roll Along*, based on the play by George S. Kaufman and Moss Hart, and the play *Skåne* by Pamela Carter.)

→ Joyce Lee, a member of my NT playwriting group, wrote a play called *State of Mind* about a character, Sasha, who is suffering a form of mental psychosis. The play begins with a group-therapy session, in which various characters who've experienced similar issues talk to (and often over) each other. Slowly we get to know each of these characters in more detail... only to realise eventually that they are all personifications of the various 'voices' in Sasha's mind. Joyce used this expressionistic theatrical device as a way of showing the schism that Sasha's psychosis creates in her identity. The audience is intended to believe that the characters are entirely different people existing in empirical reality. Using this device as the starting point for her play threw up some challenging questions. At what point should the audience learn what's going on? At what point should the *character* learn it, or does she already know? Is her realisation a liberation or an entrapment? The play's form enabled Joyce to create a theatrical and sensory experience that mirrored the experience of psychosis and took her audience directly into the mind of her protagonist.

DIGGING THE GARDEN

It requires a lot of energy to keep chipping away at your stone, and it's all too easy to craft yourself into a dead end, losing the vital creative spark that you need to keep going. Alan Ayckbourn has a succinct piece of advice for when writers are stuck: go and dig the garden. (If you're lucky enough to have one.) Mine would be: go for a walk. Or a run, or a swim. Something interesting seems to happen when the body is fully involved in routine and rhythmic activity, particularly if it's based in nature – the brain starts to float, dissociate and spark.

Overly analytical thinking, then, while essential to the problem-solving aspects of playwriting and the logical decisions that must be made, is only one side of the coin. So know that the seeds of your story might be buried somewhere deep, and pay attention to your creative instincts. I'm now going to move on to some more intellectual or abstract starting points that might also grow into a play.

STARTING WITH AN IMAGE

Although plays are wordy things, they can also spring from visual sources, both real and imagined. The aforementioned play *Chimerica* was inspired not only by the historical events of the Tiananmen Square Massacre, but by the iconic photograph of 'Tank Man' – the unknown Chinese protester who stood before the approaching tanks.

At the opposite end of the visual spectrum, Arthur Miller famously took his starting point for *Death of a Salesman* from a single imaginary image. If asked to guess what that image was, we might think, an empty briefcase. Or any of the images or props contained in the play, e.g. a packet of seeds. An expensive fountain pen pilfered from a director's office. Actually, it was this:

> The first image that occurred to me... was of an enormous face the height of the proscenium arch, which would appear and then open up, and we would see the inside of a man's head. In fact, *The Inside of His Head* was the first title. It was conceived half in laughter, for the inside of his head was a mass of contradictions.[3]

Is there an image that captures the essence of the play you want to write, concrete or abstract? If so can you study it, draw it, or even make it? The playwright David Greig is known to ask students to draw a single image to encapsulate their play, and I've found it a really useful exercise in intellectual disassociation. I once attended a workshop where he asked us to create a tableau of our play, or that of a famous one, using a bowl of fruit. A memorable *King Lear* was crafted from a melon with three clementines arranged in a semi circle around it. A funny but also utterly precise depiction of the energetic essence of the play...

STARTING WITH A PROPOSITION

What is a proposition?

> *A statement or assertion that expresses a judgement or opinion – e.g. a theory, hypothesis, thesis, argument, premise, idea, statement.*

As a starting place for a play, this might sound a bit dogmatic. Much contemporary theatre tends to present the grey areas of human life; half-truths, maybes, contrasting perspectives. But a *story* proposition is very different to an overt political ideology or manifesto. (As examples of the latter, communism is a political ideology; the American Declaration of Independence is a manifesto.)

By and large, audiences don't want to be force-fed the writer's value system masquerading as drama. The playwright Anthony Neilson had this to say on the subject:

> Many critics still believe theatre has a quasi-educational/political role; that a play posits an argument that the playwright then proves or disproves. It is in a critic's interest to propagate this idea because it makes criticism easier; one can agree or disagree with what they perceive to be the author's conclusion. It is not that a play cannot be quasi-educational, or even overtly political – *just that debate should organically arise out of narrative*. (My italics.)

In other words, let your play be the carrier of your argument by all means, but not at the expense of your story. If your starting point is an intellectual proposition – something that angers, inspires or moves you, politically or otherwise – ask yourself if you can articulate the idea in *dramatic action* for your characters. If you can't yet, go back to the drawing board and think about how you might organically coax a story from it.

Another way of coming at this is to ask yourself if you want the ideas in your play to provoke a particular response in your *audience*. (Provocation: *an action or speech that makes someone angry, especially deliberately*.) Again, you should use your characters to do this work for you. Whether they love or loathe them, audiences will invest far more deeply in interesting onstage characters doing interesting things, than in abstract ideas.

→ Proposition: By oppressing the old pagan values of ancient Britain and suppressing freedom and creativity, something precious will be lost in modern-day Britain. (*Jerusalem* by Jez Butterworth.) Provocation: the price for it might be anarchy, which can also be destructive.

→ Proposition: The public-school system allows young men total liberty and no punishment for their transgressions based on their economic and class background. (*Posh* by Laura Wade.) Provocation: this is not only morally wrong but can lead to the normalisation of criminal behaviour such as physical violence and sexual exploitation.

I can't tell you if either writer went into their process with such a well-defined intellectual concept, but both plays pose fascinating questions about our wider society. We could say they also both make specific political judgements on our society, but never at the expense of character or story. Right now you may not know what, if any, propositions or provocations your play makes. It's more a question of making sure that if you are writing from a strong place of opinion that it isn't better off in an essay than a play.

Anthony Neilson goes on to say:

> I can't tell you how often I've asked an aspiring writer what they're working on, and they reply with something like: 'I'm writing a play about racism.' On further investigation, you find that this play has no story and they've been stuck on page 10 for the past year; yet they're still hell-bent on writing it. You can be fairly sure the play, should it ever be finished, will conclude that racism is a bad thing. Newspapers, or news programmes, are the places for debates, not the theatre. (*The Guardian*, 21 March 2007)

As a counterpoint to this, here's a short extract from Lynn Nottage's play *Ruined*, which won the Pulitzer Prize for Drama in 2009. The play is about the systematic rape of women in the Democratic Republic of Congo and how they find the strength to endure their experiences. Here, Salima, a farmer's wife, describes her rape to a friend.

> SALIMA.   One of the soldiers held me down with his foot. He was so heavy, thick like an ox and his boot was cracked and weathered like it had been left out in the rain for weeks. His boot was pressing my chest and the cracks in the leather had the look of drying sorghum.

The horror of the experience is packaged in poetic and powerful language that pins us, the audience, to our seats, just as the soldier's boot pins Salima's body to the ground. In this way, the dramatist confronts a subject that many of us might turn away from in the news or a documentary. 'Rape is bad.' We all know this going into the theatre. But our theatrical experience of this play gives us so much more than a moral lesson. More on dialogue and theatrical language in Chapter Seven.

STARTING WITH THE NOTION OF 'AN EXPERIENCE WITNESSED'

As in *Ruined*, we are always bearing witness to a series of events and experiences when we watch a play. These can be big or small, minor or major on the world stage. But we are invited to watch, judge and feel. If you've not yet evolved your story and you're still at the dreaming stage, another way into thinking about the piece of theatre you want to create is to consider the audience experience beyond their intellectual engagement. What are you asking them to bear witness to? How about:

→ Witnessing the experience of depression and its opposite, euphoric love (*The Effect* by Lucy Prebble). Provocation: is it 'real love' or love artificially stimulated via drugs? Does this matter?

→ Witnessing the experience of addiction (*People, Places and Things* by Duncan Macmillan). Provocation: can an addict ever truly change if those closest to them cannot?

→ Witnessing the healing power of storytelling (*The Weir* by Conor McPherson). No overt provocation here – the power is not questioned, but uniquely dramatised.*

Coming at your play this way might release you from snarly plot mechanics and get you thinking about its energy, atmosphere and spectacle.

To round up the chapter, the following case study leads us through the genesis of a play by a former writing student, and describes the different story seeds, or starting points, that eventually grew into her finished play.

CASE STUDY: *The Lighthouse* by Rachael Claye

Rachael's play came to life on the back of a group workshop I held on using play settings as dramatic metaphors. It was based on a similar workshop I'd once attended by playwright David Harrower. Everyone had to choose one element from three different lists (physical place, character, theme), and try to bring them together in an opening moment. The idea was to use the composite elements to create meaning on stage before any dialogue was spoken, thinking particularly about the symbolism of the physical location in which the action was set.

---

* McPherson's play is harder to analyse according to the general 'rules' of most good playwriting, particularly in regard to the absence of traditional plot and dramatic stakes, but I'd argue that his exceptional use of language allows him to set his own rules here as a theatrical storyteller. The American playwright Annie Baker might also fit into this category.

From her three elements, Rachael evolved a story about St Nicholas of Patara – the 'original' Santa Claus – and a young girl named Rose, who meet on Christmas Eve. Over the course of one day and night, this odd couple develop a deep friendship that allows them to heal each other. Rose is able to become a child again, and St Nicholas to become a saviour of children. It was an emotional but resolutely unsentimental story, which turned St Nicholas into a real person and dispensed with all the clichés we have come to expect from the commercial myth of Father Christmas. The genesis of Rachael's play came from this random mental exercise, not a deep-seated desire to tell a particular story or convey an idea. She had some abstracts: an emotion and a theme. And some concretes: a place and a character. They were all she needed to build her story organically.

Here's Rachael on the development of her play.

> My list of three things was: an iceberg (setting), a child with a secret (character), and the theme I've forgotten – perhaps isolation, perhaps salvation. Anyway, the opening moment then became Father Christmas (or rather, his original incarnation, St Nicholas) crashing in fog on an iceberg and being unable to fix his sleigh. He hears the sound of oars pulling through the water towards him, and this turns out to be a little girl, offering to rescue him and take him back to the lighthouse that she lives in with her father. The idea of St Nick crashing on an iceberg just made me chuckle – it was an absurd situation, as was being rescued by a capable child.

> The lighthouse on the iceberg, to me, symbolised loneliness and loss, but also communication and hope. It reflected each character's underlying need to shine a light on their strengths and believe in their powers again. Once the opening moment of the play was there, from the collision of place, people and theme, it was just a question of following it along. The world of the play was very vivid right from the start, and the dynamic between the two characters very clear. But I had no idea what to do once I got them into the lighthouse – two people talking at each other for an hour? What helped was that Rose, the child, had a secret she didn't want to admit to herself, let

alone to St Nicholas, so dropping clues and evading answering them provided some fuel. (The secret was that her father, the lighthouse keeper, had gone missing, and she was alone.) Plus, St Nicholas wanted to keep his identity secret, but had somewhere to be rather urgently. Having the two opposing problems and goals of him trying to get off the iceberg to deliver his toys, and her wanting to keep him there also helped. Also – and this was really important – I fell in love with the lighthouse as a physical place, so it was fun to make that intricate.

What also helped was keeping a sense of two crises coming along the line for both of them – St Nicholas had to fix his sleigh and get away, but had lost his magical powers; Rose had to keep the lamp lit in the lighthouse to give her absent father a beacon to return to, but was running out of oil and believed her only hope was in having St Nicholas stay and help her. Again I think that remembering the symbolism of the lighthouse on the iceberg helped keep me going. It was the starting point for my entire plot but also each character's underlying emotional state, being cut off from the world and, for very different reasons, in need of help. The other really useful thing was setting the play over a few hours with high-stakes deadlines for both characters, so there was a sense of urgency built in, and I could keep ramping that up and pushing the story forwards.

Rachael's initial burst of creative instinct within a simple writing exercise was crafted into a theatrical narrative over a period of five years. Her play was eventually produced at London's Space Theatre in 2016, as their Christmas family show – and it was magical.

EXERCISES: FINDING A WAY IN

If you can't easily answer any of the following questions in relation to your play, don't panic. Do as many that feel relevant or useful and ignore the rest. Try to retain a sense of playfulness when you go through them. It's just a chance to step outside your comfort zone and look at your play from different angles.

1. *Concrete elements*

Make a list of all the concrete elements that you already know about your play. Are they organically linked? Do any feel anachronistic or out of place? Which element do you feel the most interested and invested in, and confident about? Conversely, which parts of your statue do you feel ambiguous or doubtful about? If you chiselled them off, would this free up more space for your play?

→ Who is the main character or who are the main characters? Write a character sketch of one or all of your key characters, describing their personality, beliefs, values, desires, needs. What is at stake for the protagonist, or for the group if it's an ensemble piece?

→ Is there a key event (there may be more than one) that shapes the play, either before the action begins or during it? How does this event drive the story? What chain reaction does it force for the characters of the play? What are its dramatic consequences?

→ What is the world of the play – social, cultural, political, physical? Does the world and its settings allow for your themes to be expressed? Would the play benefit from a single setting, to create a pressure-cooker environment? Or a more panoramic set of locations to help anchor story and theme?

→ What is the time scale of your story? Do you give your audience the luxury of real time spent with your characters, or do you want to cover the sweep of an era? How will you move between your different time locations? Might they overlap, clash or progress in a non-linear way?

→ What theatrical devices does your play currently use, if any? How do they convey meaning on stage and create tone, texture, shape, narrative complexity or thematic relevance? If your play is a piece of straightforward theatrical realism, try, just as an exercise, to take one of the devices mentioned in this chapter and reimagine your story using it to shape the action. Does this crystallise or focus any key elements of your play's story, theme or idea?

→ Are there one or more key props in your play that might express theme, idea or story? Make a list of any props in your play that feel significant. Might any of them be used more strategically to carry meaning?

2. Abstract elements

Now think about the more intellectual or emotional attachments to, or intentions you have for your play.

→ Try to distil your play into a single image – it can be as concrete or abstract as you like, but it should encapsulate some element of the meaning of your play, to you. Describe or draw the image – or make it in 3D; with Lego, plasticine, or even pieces of fruit if the desire takes you!

→ What are you asking the audience to bear witness to when they watch your play? (For example, an experience of addiction; a romantic betrayal; a battle; a descent into madness.)

→ Is there symbolic and non-literal meaning encapsulated in your setting, world, a key prop, a key action, or your structure? If there isn't, try articulating the core meaning of your play into a sentence or paragraph, and then write a list of visual metaphors that might help carry that meaning, just to stretch your imagination. Referring to Rachael's description may help: *'The lighthouse, to me, symbolised loneliness and loss, but also communication and hope. It reflected each character's underlying need to shine a light on their strengths and believe in their powers again.'*

3. Questions to help you dramatise

Some of these questions may seem impossible to answer when you start a play – or even when you finish it. They're just another tool to help you gently interrogate your material.

I'll use *Romeo and Juliet* as an example here to illustrate what I mean, as it's a universally known love story.

→ Is there a *dramatic question* at the heart of the play – one that your characters (and audience) will answer and resolve over the course of the play? If so, put it into a sentence, e.g. *Will Romeo and Juliet's love survive the opposition of their warring families and can they be together?*

→ Is there a *thematic question* at the heart of the play – relating to a notion, idea, proposition or provocation that you want your story to test? e.g. *Is it better to experience romantic passion than familial duty, even if that passion results in death and violence? Or should an individual sacrifice happiness in love to benefit their family or society?*

→ Finally, what do you want to discover as you write this play – about your characters, your story or yourself? What draws you to it/ them? Why do they feel important to you? What is it about them that won't let you rest?

3
CHARACTER:
YOU CAN'T ALWAYS GET
WHAT YOU WANT

CHARACTER:
YOU CAN'T ALWAYS GET WHAT YOU WANT

Sometime in 1968, Mick Jagger wrote the famous line 'You can't always get what you want' in a song of the same name, which ended up on the Rolling Stones' 1969 album *Let It Bleed*. Aside from writing a classic rock anthem, Mick unwittingly created a maxim that I believe sums up all great drama. It's an idea that begins with a universal truth – that human beings are constantly searching for things to make us happy.

We can see this in the great heroes and heroines of classic drama who pursue their desires to tragic or comic effect, showing us the dangers inherent in acting on impulse, falling in love, having ambitions, and generally indulging in the seven deadly sins of pride, envy, wrath, gluttony, lust, sloth and greed. And conversely, they show us the sacrifices required to create acts of humility, generosity, kindness, temperance, diligence, unconditional love and selflessness.

WHAT YOU WANT VERSUS WHAT YOU NEED

One of the most familiar tenets of dramatic writing is: give your characters something to want, then put an obstacle in their way. This is a useful starting point, as drama will inevitably come about through the conflict of the competing goals of different characters. But to really explore your characters' motivations and actions, you need to go deeper, and think about the second half of the Rolling Stones' lyric: 'But if you try sometimes you might find you get what you need.' The tension of much great drama walks a line between *desire* and *need*, which are, of course, quite different things. This line separates our deepest, darkest secrets and our idealised selves; our individual wants from our communal requirements; our spiritual pursuits and our physical urges.

Although a particular character may well have a definable, conscious goal that drives the story, often this want is actually not what they *need* at all. They may think it's the right thing for them, they may think they'll die without it, but they're often mistaken. To be clear, the 'need' I'm talking about here is usually not something the character is aware of, in contrast to the conscious 'want'. But it's a need – generally psychological and emotional – that the *audience* will be aware of.

Let's say that in real life, our best friend has decided to chase blindly after an inappropriate romantic interest, despite the fact that it's clear the person they're fixated on is never going to make them happy. At a certain point we realise that all we can do is sit back, watch it play out and be on hand with the tissues/chocolate/whiskey when disaster strikes. And we'd be lying if we said we didn't derive a tiny bit of pleasure from witnessing the whole debacle. We get to feel, comparatively, sane and happy. We get to think 'I told you so' even if we don't say it out loud. So it is for audiences watching characters spin out of control on stage, when we are one step ahead of them.

This is otherwise known as dramatic irony. When we are really invested in a character it is thrilling to watch them struggle to achieve something that we know isn't good for them, whether because of a failing in their own personality or because of the obstacles and limitations placed on them by others. Where desire (which is generally conscious) and need (which is more often unconscious – until the point in the story when the character realises something about themselves) meet and clash, you'll usually find powerful drama.

To explore this further I'm going to use Tennessee Williams's play *A Streetcar Named Desire* as our model. It's a classic protagonist/antagonist set-up with Blanche DuBois and Stanley Kowalski wending their irrevocable way towards violence and brutality based on their great clash of desires. If you don't know the play, you might want to read it before or after you finish this chapter. (I can guarantee you a pleasurable couple of hours.) Alternatively, perhaps search online for a synopsis of the play or watch Elia Kazan's film adaptation, which is a very faithful transposition of play to screen.

BLANCHE AND STANLEY

Blanche DuBois wants a home and security; to be admired by men; a husband. She is aware of these goals as much as she is able to be. She knows she is flawed, weak and vulnerable, but she uses what powers she has left – her beauty, her charm, her seductive powers – to try and get what she wants, which includes her sister Stella's affections, and those of her husband Stanley's friend Mitch. But we could say that what she truly *needs* is to accept the reality of her situation; that she is poor, ageing, unmarried and an unwanted guest in the marital home of her sister and her brother-in-law. She also needs to exorcise the ghost of her dead lover, who shot himself years before, and who haunts her still. Perhaps above all, she needs to forgive herself for her past transgressions. Only then might she extricate herself from the mess she is in.

Does she get what she needs at the end of the play? Arguably, no. In the final scene she is betrayed by her own sister and taken away to an asylum. And also arguably *yes*, as seen in the wonderful moment when the doctor offers Blanche his arm, like a gentleman, and her resistance subsides. She allows herself to be escorted away on his arm to the mental institution, because she has always depended on 'the kindness of strangers'.

I've held raging debates among playwrights about this ending. Some feel that Blanche is better off living in her twilight world of fantasy than in the harsh reality of her rape by her brother-in-law Stanley and her abandonment by her sister and Mitch. Others feel that her final descent into madness has robbed her of any agency. But whichever way we interpret the ending, the power of her character comes in the main from this endless clash between the conscious desires she pursues, and the unconscious needs that propel her forwards.

Blanche's antagonist Stanley, in contrast, wants simple things: a home; a good meal; a card game with his pals; his wife, Stella; a child; and to rule his small empire without rivals. Blanche's arrival changes all that. What does Stanley *need*? An audience might have a hundred different answers to this, ranging from 'a sharp kick in the pants' to 'a lifetime's therapy' or 'a prison sentence'. But psychologically, emotionally and morally, within the world of the play, he needs to see that his power has limits. And ultimately, although he 'wins' the battle for Stella, home and hearth over Blanche in the most horrible way, he also sows the seeds of his own destruction, because Stella will never trust him again. His marriage is now doomed. At least that's how I read the play; but like many great plays, there's room for a variety of responses. Although we may imagine different lives panning out in different ways, we can have no doubt over how the status and power of each character has shifted.

There is a similar bittersweetness in the resolution of Lorraine Hansberry's *Les Blancs*. What her hero Tshembe *wants* is to leave his troubled country, his two estranged brothers, and his white colonial antagonists, and return to England to be with his wife and baby son, to watch television by the fire. And we want that for him too, in as much as we want him to be safe. But his *needs* – both personal and political – slowly work their way up through his consciousness as the action of the play ramps up. Ultimately he rejects an easy retreat in order to murder his brother, fight for his country, and take a stand against colonial martial law. We can see the value of that too, but we are torn between our desire that he lives, and our desire that he fulfils his moral imperatives.

So, although your key characters might acknowledge a concrete goal or desire, actually achieving it will probably be a) difficult and/or b) misjudged. Whether or not your characters achieve their goals in your play is up to you, but it's important to think about how much they are aware of what they want at the beginning of the play, and how making it less straightforward for them to achieve them might make your story more interesting.

BLANCHE AND STANLEY ON THE COUCH

Freud's famous psychoanalytic model – which separates the human psyche into three distinct drives: id, ego and superego – explores how our behaviour is influenced by conflicting desires. His model can be usefully applied to fictional characters to look at the power play between their wants and needs, and isolate significant actions that arise from it.

ID

The id is the aspect of our psychology that demands instant satisfaction (another rather famous Jagger/Richards musical investigation). It's the primal impulses in all human beings: for food, warmth, connection, sex, pleasure. The id is not about rational decisions but about primitive instincts. Stanley Kowalski is a great example of an id-driven character. Stanley lives for his wife, for sex, poker, beer, steak, with a good fistfight to clear the air. He is also easily reduced to tears, bellowing for Stella when he messes up, like a toddler who's lost his mum. Id-driven characters can be great fun for an audience to watch, because they often lack social filters and impulsively say, think and do exactly what they want. For this reason they are often vehicles for comedy. Examples include Shakespeare's Falstaff, Francis Henshall in Richard Bean's *One Man, Two Guvnors* and Rooster Byron in Jez Butterworth's *Jerusalem* – albeit a man with a burst of superego at the end, but more on that later. *Who's Afraid of Virginia Woolf?* by Edward Albee pits a husband and wife of equally appalling id-driven behaviour against each other, before lust, competition, marital punishment and one-upmanship eventually descend into tragedy. And, of course, Stanley's rape of Blanche at the climax of *Streetcar* arguably is the ultimate id-driven moment.

EGO

The ego is the part of us that consciously attempts to devise a realistic plan to get what we want, but in a logical, rational way. This will change according to the social values, conventions and expectations of our times. If the id operates through the Pleasure Principle (the driving force behind instant gratification), the ego operates through the Reality Principle. It is still goal-oriented, but it accepts there are necessary boundaries in human behaviour and modifies its behaviour accordingly. It accepts the need for deferred gratification for the greater good. Freud described the ego as: '*like a man on horseback, who has to hold in check the superior strength of the horse*'.[4] Stella is a good example of an ego-driven character. She has primal needs, as expressed through her love for Stanley, but she also tries to accommodate Blanche, to moderate Stanley's behaviour, to keep the peace, and to act as a reasonable diplomat in the raging emotional war between her sister and her husband. An ego-led moment might be when Stella rationalises to herself that Blanche must be lying about the rape, and says as much to her neighbour. If Stella's goal is a happy marriage, she must sacrifice something, and in this case she chooses to believe that Blanche has made up the rape accusation. Stella accepts the reality of the situation and makes a rational, if cold-hearted, choice to preserve her marriage.

SUPEREGO

The superego is all about the moral conscience. It inherits dominant values from parents, teachers and social institutions, and understands that society demands certain modes of behaviour; for example, that it's not right to kill, steal or lie to get what we want. There are limits to human behaviour that must be accepted if human beings are to evolve and live among others. If the ego gives in to the demands of the id, then the superego will punish us. Our conscience will prick; we will moderate our behaviour because we understand it's wrong. Conversely, the superego can reward us for good behaviour by making us feel proud and self-validated. Mitch from *Streetcar* typifies a superego-driven human being. He still lives with his ailing mother and is very worried about what she will think of Blanche; he cannot accept that Blanche is a woman of loose morals, and breaks off their engagement when he learns she slept with many men before him. Superego-driven characters are often tragic: think of John Proctor in Arthur Miller's play *The Crucible* and Bernard Shaw's Saint Joan. Lorraine Hansberry's Tshembe, arguably, sacrifices his own personal happiness to his need for political and social justice.

In Freudian terms, all human beings possess and exhibit all three drives, and they are in constant conflict. But it's interesting how many memorable characters lead with one particular drive, and how that particular drive will define the action of the play. They might also begin the play with certain wants, needs and psyche-driven actions, and end up consciously adopting very different ones at the end. In Ibsen's *A Doll's House*, repressed but id-driven Nora ends up taking a huge superego-driven action; she leaves her family for the sake of living an honest life. (Or, is this an even bigger id-driven action? Discuss.)

We might say that the id is the drive towards pleasure, the ego towards reality, and the superego towards morality. If we combine our Rolling Stones and Freudian models, we might get the following: *the id can't always get what it wants, but if the superego tries sometimes, the ego might find it gets what it needs*. Not quite as catchy, I know, but possibly a useful model for helping think about how character psychology creates drama.

SHORT-, MID-, LONG-TERM GOALS

Human beings have many different goals (and needs) at any given moment or hour, on any different day, week or year. Each conscious or unconscious desire will contain a certain potential for dramatic action (i.e. action with consequences for ourselves and the people around us). Single protagonist plays will often contain a single overarching goal that drives the action in the whole play and is present in every scene. This is usually very clear in classical drama. (Hamlet's goal to avenge his father; Macbeth's goal to become king; Antigone's goal to bury her brother.) Considering the urgency or immediacy of any one particular desire – and how easily it might be fulfilled – can be a useful way to shape a unit of action in your play.

A *short-term* goal – I want to make up with my mum for the row we had this morning at breakfast – will naturally create a different set of potential actions and story drives than a *mid-term* goal – I want to learn to speak fluent Arabic within three months – than a *long-term* goal – I want to have three children one day.

A short-term goal will usually help shape a short unit of action – a scene or story beat. Mid-term goals might shape an act or sequence of scenes, of course depending on the time frame of the story. A long-term goal may help shape an entire play.

For example, in *Streetcar*, Stanley is playing the long game. He wants to a) get his hands on any money that might have come from the sale of the DuBois family home (mid-term goal), after which he can b) get rid of the interloper Blanche forever (his long-term goal and super-objective, to use a Stanislavskian term).

Blanche's mid-term goal, which becomes conscious once she's met Stanley's friend Mitch, is to find a husband, which means she might realise her overarching long-term goal and super-objective of finding a stable home. About halfway through the play, Blanche secures a proposal (or as good as) from her suitor, Mitch. But, this being a gothic Southern drama, there is more to come that will complicate matters. The second half of the play gives Stanley the opportunity to expose some less than savoury truths about Blanche, and so bring about her downfall.

However, each scene in the play is also clearly driven by a short-term goal for either Stanley and/or his nemesis, Blanche, which pits them against each other. For example, Stanley wants to play poker in peace with his friends; to make up with Stella after a fight; to use information he's discovered about Blanche's past to discredit her. Blanche wants to take a hot bath; to impress Mitch; to get Stella to take her side over Stanley's. These clashing short-term goals create narrative momentum and escalate the drama, moment by moment.

As always, this sort of analysis is not meant to offer a prescription for writing your own play, but to get you thinking about what drives your characters. Will they ultimately get what they want or what they need at the end of the play? (Or both?) And how will your audience feel about that? These are big questions, and ones that you probably won't be able to answer when you begin. Many playwrights would argue that it's actually problematic to know everything in advance, and that having your characters' journeys schematically mapped out before you write your play deprives you of any space for discovery. However, in my experience, playwrights who ignore all of these questions entirely and plunge straight into the writing process without at least a couple of firm footholds often end up writing in circles for years.

Personally, I've learned to stop worrying about the ending of my story if it's not clear when I begin. If you start your play with a strong sense of your characters' wants, needs, conflicts and drives, then you will usually find situations to put them in and events to challenge them with. When you do get to the end of your play, however, you may also find that you're not sure any more where your character stands, emotionally, psychologically or morally speaking.

TREASURE/OBJECTS OF VALUE

Another useful concept here is the notion of theatrical treasure, which is a term the American theatre academic and director Kathleen E. George uses to describe something of value that is fought or negotiated over by various characters in a drama. Treasure is really another way of coming at character goals, but it allows the playwright to think about their characters' relationship with the physical and symbolic dimensions of their story. There is usually an overall treasure or two buried in each play as a whole – something valuable that is desired, competed for, lost or sacrificed. A treasure can be concrete or abstract, real or imagined, but the more specific it is, and the more people know about it in the play, the better. In *Death of a Salesman* we could say that Willy Loman's reputation as a terrific salesman is a key treasure of the play, as is his two sons' beliefs that he is a good father, as is (a more concrete treasure) the family home and its material contents. These three 'things of value' slip further and further from Willy's grasp as the play progresses, until he can't stand their loss any more and takes his own life.

In *A Raisin in the Sun*, the two concrete, financial treasures that drive the action are Lena Younger's insurance-policy payout for her dead husband, and the new family house she plans to buy with the money. The house is also a symbolic treasure, representing social progression and greater autonomy for the family. As in *Salesman*, these two 'thing of values' are threatened, firstly by the racist Neighbourhood Committee who want to prevent the Younger family from moving into their neighbourhood, Clybourne Park;

and secondly by Walter Younger's rash investments in and subsequent loss of the remaining inheritance. However, unlike Willy Loman, the Youngers ultimately manage to find a new and different collective, *emotional* treasure through their adversity, as we'll see below.

COSMIC JUSTICE

Depending on your philosophical position, you might already subscribe to the notion of fate or karma. You may believe that the universe metes out justice and punishment on the basis of eternal moral and spiritual laws, and that people will be rewarded or punished accordingly. What about within the universe of drama? Despite our modern thirst for more ambiguity and psychological complexity than the Greeks or Shakespeare gave us (you can blame Freud for spearheading that sea change), I believe that we still hunger for narrative cosmic justice (or injustice) on stage. This doesn't mean we want reductive stories about two-dimensional characters, but that we yearn for a sense of inexorability. Or cause and effect. Or spiritual logic, if you like, according to the emotional and psychological struggles of the characters, and the social and political laws of the world in which they operate. We want to get to the end and feel, whether uplifted or despairing, angry or joyous, devastated or optimistic, that the play could only have ended that way, because the forces of the drama were unstoppable, based on the characters' growth and change – or lack of.

In a great play we often have a sense of the 'rightness' of its endings – not in a moral sense, but rather in a sense of its inevitability. In *Streetcar*, we certainly can't say Blanche deserved to be raped. There is no cosmic justice there, not by any value system. But there is a terrible inexorability to what happens. Stanley famously comments, before he brutalises her, that this is a 'date' they've had from the very beginning. We didn't see this moment coming, but now it's upon us, it feels horribly, tragically inevitable. David Mamet puts it another way when he says that, in the great plays, the seeds of the ending are buried in the beginning. We can trace the climactic moment back to the first meeting between Blanche and Stanley. They flirt, lie and dance around each other; the fluttering genteel moth and the violent ape. We can also anchor the terrible climax of the play in the competing drives of Blanche and Stanley, their clash of wills, their collision of strong wants and needs. And ultimately, perhaps, we are allowed to feel a fleeting sense of cosmic justice right at the very end, when it becomes clear that Stanley's terrible act has forfeited him the thing he values the most – Stella (more on this at the end of the chapter).

As already mentioned, Willy Loman from *Death of a Salesman* takes his own life at the play's climax. It hurts us that he does, but it makes sense on some deep emotional level. By lying to his family, and to himself, and by idealising his sons, he destroyed them. Taking his own life is a way of freeing his family financially – and perhaps giving both his sons a chance to live out a different fate. In classical tragic terms, a catharsis has taken place. In the universe of this play, the perpetrator has been punished and has redeemed himself through self-sacrifice. He has gained self-knowledge.

Miller's *The Crucible* plays out a different way, when at the climax of the play, John Proctor is sentenced to death. His wife, who has never told a lie in her life, lies to save her husband. But John Proctor's morality is too sophisticated for his society. He is ahead of them in his humanity; they are still blinkered by their total bondage to Puritan ideals. We watch a good man go to his death. Again, it hurts. There's a powerful sense of cosmic injustice playing out. The laws of this world seek to oppress a truth-sayer, because he is dangerous. And that is exactly the message that Miller sought to convey with this allegorical play, at a time when McCarthyism was raging through America and destroying many left-thinking liberals.

PUNISHMENT OR REWARD?

It's crucial, then, to think about the dreams, ambitions and desires of your characters in the context of the political, social and cultural laws of their world. These may be personal laws that operate in a particular family, organisation, gang or tribe. If so, where do your main characters sit? Are they inside or outside the laws? How do they transgress, if so? And what is their punishment – or their reward? Remember that if your play has an ensemble cast, rather than a traditional antagonist/protagonist set-up, the questions I've explored in this chapter can also be applied to groups with a collective set of values, wants and needs. What does the group of people you're dramatising want to achieve and who or what will hinder their joint efforts?

Of course, there will be variation within that group. Each member of the Younger family in *A Raisin in the Sun* has their own beliefs, dreams, strengths and flaws, and their conflict with each other forms much of the drama. But they are also forced to pull together in their opposition to the oppressive racism of their society. This institutional bigotry and prejudice is personified in Karl Linder, the white representative of a neighbourhood 'Improvement Association' who attempts to pay off the Youngers in order to prevent them from buying a house in his own predominately white neighbourhood of Clybourne Park. We could say that while the family is collectively punished by the daily cosmic injustices of racist American society (and will continue to do so after the play ends), the Youngers are also rewarded by their strengthened personal bonds and renewed commitment to fight that injustice. This is dramatised at the climax of the play, when Walter, the most id-driven character in the family, has a change of heart and refuses Linder's offer. It's a moment of personal cosmic justice for him, his family, *and* the audience – despite the new battle that will no doubt begin when the family move into their new house.

As a more contemporary example, Rooster Byron in Jez Butterworth's *Jerusalem* is a drug-peddling, booze-guzzling, anarchic vagabond (a pure 'id' character) who may or may not have seduced an underage teenager. But his strongest desire is to protect his home, a rickety caravan in the ancient woods that he loves, and defy the council who want to evict him. (Clear goal, clear obstacle.) At the end of the play, he torches the caravan before the council can raze it, and instructs his young son to fight on in the name of their ancestors, and of pagan Britain. It's an act of violence but it's also simultaneously an act of sacrifice, because he wants to try and preserve something precious about English culture that he believes is being fatally eroded. The 'id' character is transformed by a final act of superego – and transcends his own weaknesses in a glorious celebratory moment. He may or not have redeemed his earlier actions – the audience must decide – but either way, there is change, movement and growth.

THE GREY AREAS: CHARACTER VERSUS STORY

Contemporary drama is often more about the grey areas of psychology and emotion than it is about binary human extremes. Villains and heroes are found in franchise Hollywood movies, but rarely on stage in modern writing, outside of pantomime. But even if our modern hearts and minds lean towards the subtle and complex ambiguities of human behaviour in our dramas, that doesn't mean that audiences don't long for clear resolutions to the narratives they see on stage. Here's where it's important to distinguish character from story. The two are inextricably linked, of course, which is all the more reason to think about them separately for just a moment.

Certain writers are naturally more predisposed to create small, delicate plays on a miniature canvas, and they can make for beautiful theatrical experiences. But unless the writers have immense skill, these kinds of plays can ultimately feel rather slight and underwritten. I see plenty of shows (particularly in theatre studios) that abound with gorgeous character detail and skilled observation, but which don't quite deliver enough narrative to satisfy their audience. I think this is often no accident – the writer has consciously set out to do this. Why?

In class, when I've tried to encourage a writer to push the elements of their story further and create a clearer narrative arc, I have often heard the plaintive response: 'But I *want* the story to be ambiguous.' The playwright's intentions will always be sound – they wish to avoid offering easy solutions to their characters' human dilemmas and/or avoid serving up heavy-handed or melodramatic moral lessons. My answer to this is usually the same: 'Subtlety is great, but your audience still wants to be told a story.' A lack of story is actually nearly always rooted in underdeveloped character goals, and the narrative ambiguity that the playwright seeks is really just papering over the cracks. However, it is possible to leave space for audience interpretation while also providing narrative satisfaction – if you do the right exploratory work.

Back to *Streetcar*, which manages to achieve both these things. The climax of the play (in its penultimate scene) is Stanley's rape of Blanche. In this act of violent degradation, the fundamental battle of the play is won. Stanley 'conquers' Blanche, and this tips her into madness. In the final scene, some weeks later, the status quo of Stanley and Stella's life has, on the surface, been resolved. Stanley and his pals play poker in the kitchen, while Stella and her neighbour Eunice prepare Blanche for a 'trip'. Unbeknownst to Blanche, they are waiting for a doctor who will take Blanche away to a mental hospital. Stanley's main goal throughout the play has been to get Blanche out of his apartment and away from his wife for good. So the ending is a definitive win for Stanley – or is it?

Because in this final scene, we see that Stella has also been crushed by Stanley's act. Blanche has told her sister what Stanley did to her, but Stella has chosen to turn a blind eye. Stella tells Eunice that she can't believe Blanche and go on living with her husband. Eunice backs her up, agreeing that life has to go on. These are the conditions of their survival, as women. But it's clear that Stella is already doubting her decision. So we can see that Stanley and Stella's marriage is far from 'saved' and may well have been irrevocably damaged.

When the doctor and nurse arrive to collect their ward, Stella is forced to watch as the nurse manhandles Blanche and threatens to put her in a straitjacket. Stella weeps inconsolably as Blanche is escorted out of the apartment, dressed in her finery, believing she is going on vacation with a rich lover. When Stanley tries to comfort Stella, she doesn't respond. Then, as she holds her newborn baby, crying, Stanley's fingers wander into her blouse. It's a gripping final image – the dominant male, now with an heir to prove his virility, narcissistically fondling his grief-stricken wife. (Remember, Stanley is the ultimate 'id' character.) Has Stanley really 'won?' Stella is the person he values most in the world, and it's looking likely that he has lost her emotionally as a direct consequence of his actions. So there is dramatic ambiguity within this resolution of the main plotline, which is driven all along by clear character goals.

The other ambiguous element of the ending, as I've already mentioned, is whether or not Blanche is actually better off at the end. When she entered the play she was grieving, vulnerable, and walking a tightrope between the harsh reality of her life and her fantasies of the life she *should* have had – full of romance, love and financial security. By the play's end, she is living firmly in her fantasy world – it has become her refuge from the unbearable experiences she has been forced to endure. Despite the fact that Blanche is now living a false reality, mistaking the ripe stink of Elysian Fields and psychiatric doctors for sea breezes and rich gentleman callers, I can't help feeling a terrible sense of relief. I can see her living out her days in a hospital ward, dressed in her ruffles and brooches, enacting an imaginary life of tea parties, balls and cruises. And part of me would rather her stay there, blissfully ignorant, then constantly have to relive the brutality of her treatment by Stanley and separation from her beloved Stella. In effect, Blanche hasn't got what she *wanted*, but somehow she has what she *needs* within the tragic circumstances of her downfall. However painful that is to witness, it is also deeply satisfying in narrative terms.

CREATING CHARACTER DETAIL

So. You've thought about what goals motivate your characters. About what they consciously want, and unconsciously need, and how that tension might create story. About which different psychological drives might affect them at different moments of the play, or if in fact they are led by one particular drive which sets them in conflict with others with conflicting drives. About the difference between short- and long-term goals, and how these might shape the narrative; and how and when in the story their initial goals might change or no longer serve them. And what it will take to stimulate those changes.

Writers can get very bogged down in all this sort of complex analysis and start overthinking (I speak from painful experience). So I want to round up the chapter by getting you to pull back a little from all this very detailed intellectual work and try to connect with character in more theatrical terms. In effect, to move from a miniaturist portrait of your character to a broader and more simplistic thumbnail sketch, retaining a few key characteristics that will help them stay alive in your imagination.

I recently heard a radio presenter characterising an American celebrity entertainer with this pithy description: *She's a strong woman who's constantly having a nervous breakdown.* I thought this was both a wonderful micro character sketch and a great illustration of the inherent conflict at the heart of most intriguing characters. The woman being discussed was Cher; it's perhaps no accident that many of our most iconic celebrities are flawed and complex. We adore them for their superhuman talents, but we are equally intrigued by their human weaknesses – they are fallible gods. It got me thinking about using this sort of micro thumbnail sketch to capture well-known theatrical characters. And in the great plays, with the enduring protagonists, it's surprisingly easy. The trick is to highlight the inherent conflict.

How about:

→ *A good little girl who's secretly a rebellious woman.* (Nora in *A Doll's House*)
→ *A displaced Southern belle thrown into a workingman's lair.* (Blanche DuBois in *A Streetcar Named Desire*)
→ *A successful salesman who has sold himself a lie of his own making.* (Willy Loman in *Death of a Salesman*)

Note how each description contains a central conflict – with others or with themselves, or both. Nora hides her true nature for the sake of social convention. Blanche, with all her old-world values, is fighting a modern and, in her eyes, brutal system. (An extra-personal conflict as well as the inner conflict of her own self-delusion.) Willy Loman's one great skill has been corrupted due to his duplicity.

Some more modern examples might be:

→ *The last free Briton in the modern age.* (Rooster Byron in *Jerusalem*)

→ *A woman who is brutally honest to complete strangers but who cannot tell the truth to herself.* (Fleabag in *Fleabag* by Phoebe Waller-Bridge)

→ *A bigoted nationalist who doesn't know his own heritage.* (Michael in *Death of England* by Roy Williams and Clint Dyer)

Memorable characters will often have activities, habits, tics, tropes – details which physically externalise those flaws or conflicts. Nora eats macaroons in secret, away from the judgement of her strict husband. Blanche spends hours indulgently bathing and dressing up (and avoiding harsh light) to protect her feminine mystique. Willy Loman wishes to plant seeds and grow plants in his garden but keeps getting distracted. In contrast, Mama in *A Raisin in the Sun* doggedly tends to her one sickly houseplant, which is the closest thing she's ever had to a garden. Rooster Byron tells tall stories, Hamlet procrastinates, and so on.

Can you identify a habit or trope in your character that might help express their true nature? And can you identify a central flaw, contradiction or conflict that helps summarise the essence of their personality? It might be a good way of reconnecting with your character after you've put them through the analytical wringer.

To finish the chapter, here's an example of a working writer whose diligent character work allowed her to turn an unsatisfying first draft into a well-rounded and emotionally engaging play.

CASE STUDY: *I Vow to Thee* by Anne Doherty

Anne's play is set in Birmingham in 1953, just before Queen Elizabeth's coronation. The protagonists are a young, impoverished Scottish couple, Lawrie and Agnes, who've recently moved from Glasgow to Birmingham to find work. The story takes place over one week, and is set in and around their small flat as the neighbourhood prepares for the Coronation Day street celebrations. During this time, Agnes discovers she is pregnant, Lawrie has problems paying the rent, and, with money a constant anxiety, the marriage spirals into crisis. These were the basic ingredients Anne began with.

The genesis of Anne's play began with a desire to write about her two main characters. She knew these people well – they were loosely based on her own family members, and the characters talked to her in very clear voices. She knew they were poor, and outsiders, and finding this new, transplanted world very difficult. She spent time thinking about their relationship and their new social context as Scots living in hostile Birmingham – there was plenty of conflict there. But it wasn't enough. As Anne puts it succinctly, 'There was a critical stage of writing the first draft when the play just seemed to be people talking in rooms.'

Anne was also convinced when she wrote her first draft that she wanted the ending of the play to be ambiguous, in that the couple will probably stay together but we aren't sure if that's a good thing or a bad thing. She wanted to show how these decent, hard-working people are trapped by their social backgrounds and put under pressure by the conflicting demands of their personal and social expectations around love, marriage and moral duty. She felt it was important that the outcome of the play should plant a seed of doubt in the audience's mind about a) whether Lawrie will stick at his marriage or leave Agnes and go off to pursue another dream life that will also probably fail, and b) whether Agnes can accept that the man she married is not who she thought he was, and recognise that she is in fact the stronger one. The beauty of the play came from this push and pull between longing for home (and each other), and a need to escape both (and each other) – but it wasn't yet quite delivering.

Anne knew she needed to give her characters goals and choices to create a more substantial story. Because they were merely *reacting* to their environment, rather than *actively* pursuing concrete desires, the play was treading water. The characters didn't have enough to do. Anne couldn't find the story motor until she'd thought more strategically about the wants and needs of both characters. What were their dreams, hopes, desires, ambitions? Over the next draft, she came up with the following answers:

Lawrie is a dreamer who is constantly chasing a better life but can't accept his lot. He has moved away from his home town because he wants more opportunities for himself and his wife (*long-term goal*) and also to be far away from his domineering father Jack (*long-term goal*). But Lawrie's sacrifices are many. He works for a factory where he is picked on by the English, and made to feel like an outsider in his community. Understandably he doesn't want to socialise with his English neighbours (*short-term goal*) – apart from with Violet, a young barmaid who lives in the flat downstairs and is something of a good-time girl. He is also happy for Agnes *not* to fall pregnant (*short-term goal*), as a baby would mean they will be stuck here in Birmingham and become even poorer. Despite his desperate need for money, he won't allow Agnes to work and be independent, because it goes against his belief that women should primarily be wives and mothers (the common view of the era). He's conflicted between old traditions and modernity; his home town and his new home; his wife and his neighbour Violet.

Note how many of Lawrie's concrete goals are negative – i.e. he *doesn't* want certain things to happen: a child, to assimilate with the English, to return to Scotland which would mean that he has failed. There's nothing wrong with starting this way – it can be illuminating to consider what a character's worst fears are, as a way of investigating wants and needs.

In contrast, Agnes is making the best of their new home and trying to carve out a place for herself and Lawrie in their community. Unlike Lawrie, she sees an opportunity to assimilate in the pending coronation celebrations (*short-term goal*). She wants to have a child (*mid-term goal*) and accepts Lawrie's role as breadwinner, although she knows if she's pregnant it'll stay that way forever.

If we do a quick summary of the material using the devices outlined in this chapter we get something like this:

→ Thumbnail of Lawrie: a big dreamer living in a small world (*more id-driven*).

→ Thumbnail of Agnes: a realist who accepts her lot but still hopes for a better life (*more ego and, at times, superego-driven*).

Also note that Lawrie has more inherent dramatic potential as a character because of an inner conflict. Agnes has less, perhaps (at least at the beginning of the play) because she accepts things as they are. But Agnes discovers she is in conflict with her husband over several significant things as the story progresses, such as having a baby, and his attitude to their English neighbours. And, usefully, she is a realist to Lawrie's dreamer. There was juice to be extracted from that key personality conflict. Anne's hope was to use that juice to give Agnes more to do in the story, so she didn't just exist as a foil for Lawrie.

We've outlined what Anne created as character *wants*, but what did they *need*? Anne came up with the following:

→ Lawrie needs to prove to himself that he is not destined to turn out like his drunken failure of a father – that he can be a successful and responsible husband and father. He needs to escape the confines of his strangled childhood. He also needs to stop dreaming and take action.

→ *What is stopping him from resolving those needs? A combination of pride, anger, his 'head-in-the-clouds' attitude and his old-fashioned values about women and the home.*

→ Agnes needs Lawrie to honour his vows to her, be more realistic about their difficulties and become more resilient – like her. She also needs to find some sense of personal agency, despite the limitations forced on her by her husband and her society.

→ *What is stopping her from resolving those needs? A combination of acceptance of social norms regarding her expected role as wife and mother; perhaps her own tendency not to rock the boat in order to avoid conflict; but, mainly, Lawrie himself.*

Anne was very conscious that Agnes was a woman of her era and didn't want to impose a more modern feminist awareness on to her character that she felt was unrealistic. Agnes was, on the one hand, happy to be a subservient wife and mother, and to accept Lawrie's authority as her husband – as most women did at the time. On the other hand, Agnes slowly realises that she is the one holding everything together. As Anne puts it: 'By the end of the play, Agnes may have to realise that "Lawrie as Master" is a fiction they will both have to inhabit in order to survive.' This was the crux of the ambiguity that Anne was leaning towards. The challenge was how to dramatise the characters' interesting and complex emotional journeys and provide a satisfying story narrative. Neither character was fully aware of their needs at the start of the play. So the events of the play should enable self-knowledge in both characters, which in turn enables choices.

Now that Anne had a clearer idea of what her characters wants and needs were, she could begin to identify what she calls the 'dramatic screws' of the story (her term, and a very useful one). Think of each screw as a sort of pressure point in the story which tightens the conflict and tension between characters. In her first draft there was a money screw. A 'Lawrie's father' screw (although the father is an offstage 'back home' character creating pressure from afar). A pregnancy screw (no pun intended). But no clear sense of how they created a narrative. By twisting the existing screws harder and thinking about how to dramatise them, Anne came up with some new plot points.

→ The father screw: Anne brought Lawrie's difficult alcoholic father Jack into the play and onto the stage by having him come and stay with the couple. This ramped up the stakes and tension greatly, *showing* the audience the pressure that Jack put on his son, rather than keeping him as an offstage '*telling*' character. Jack is a reminder of what Lawrie has tried to leave behind – and what perhaps he might become himself. Jack's interfering presence ends up being the final straw that forces the couple to choose their marriage over familial – and national – loyalty.

→ The pregnancy screw: Anne created a bigger conflict by making Agnes desperate for a baby and Lawrie the opposite. When the pregnancy does come about, it gives Agnes a huge choice: should she abort the baby to save her marriage, or keep it? (A complex and rich conflation of id/ego/superego drives. You might be interested to know that Anne tried both outcomes in different drafts.) And, in a nice reversal, the pregnancy also gives Agnes a chance to forge a friendship with her neighbour Violet, who offers help and solidarity. Agnes had previously looked down on Violet for being a barmaid, but now has her own preconceptions and judgements challenged.

→ The money screw: this was the key conflict that drove Anne's first draft, but there was plenty more to be extracted from it. Anne's couple were already very poor in Draft 1, but in her next draft she introduced an opportunity for Lawrie to make extra money selling black-market cigarettes, something Agnes really disapproves of. Anne also tightened this screw by showing us that Agnes would like to work, but that Lawrie won't allow it. It became another source of tension, secrets and conflict between the couple. And, of course, there would be money needed for a potential abortion, which could put great pressure on both characters.

We might say that the cosmic justice for this couple would be a strong and enduring marriage (the most valuable thing in the play for the audience to invest in). We care about the characters, with all their flaws, because they are struggling against poverty, discrimination and anti-Scottish sentiment. We want their marriage to succeed. The cosmic *injustice*, which Anne initially believed the play needed at the end, was that they maintained an uneasy peace but that the threat of failure hung over them. But this changed in later drafts because their relationship, by the end of the play, has also fundamentally changed. Both Agnes and Lawrie have been forced to address the reality of their marriage, along with their own strengths and weaknesses.

As we've seen with *Streetcar*, it's fine for an audience to feel ambiguous about the final story outcomes and final resting place for the characters – as long as the main dramatic conflicts have been played out and resolved. As writers we must do as much as we can to answer the questions our play sets up on the page.

I wrote, at the time of her play workshop:

> The 'vows' of your title relate to both marriage and national identity. What are you saying about both? How are they related? What ideals do both Lawrie and Agnes have, which are changed and challenged during the course of the play? What truths are uncovered about them? What weaknesses and strengths are played out?

The new draft answered many of these questions by creating a story out of the conflict between familial, social, national duty and personal desires. Now there was a clear character arc for both Agnes and Lawrie. Agnes gains agency through having to make a huge decision about her pregnancy, and also in demanding that Lawrie honour his vows to her. Lawrie is empowered to finally reject his father, overcome some of his demons, and appears to accept his lot, his stronger wife and their imminent baby, for better or worse. All of this plays out as the Coronation Day finally arrives and their neighbours gather to watch the new Queen make her vows to her country on a single television set – a lovely symbolic echo of Anne's themes.

A final note, and I hope a useful one: Anne realised during the writing process that her own parents' struggles as Scottish migrants in the hostile 1950s had influenced her a great deal. She wanted an audience to bear witness to their struggle and their stubborn resilience, which fed into her characters. She also wanted to explore how the dreams and hopes of post-war Britain (particularly for women) came into conflict with both the realities of austerity and the traditional ideas still held about marriage, motherhood and national duty. Although this meant that Anne was emotionally connected to the idea of an ending that didn't easily solve the problems of this marriage, she realised that to give her characters a dramatic journey, she needed to take them further away from real life, and fictionalise them more. They needed to take on a life of their own as dramatic characters. This is often the case when we write plays rooted in real experiences. If in doubt, and if reality is hindering you – fictionalise. That's what our job is as creative writers, after all.

Anne's play went on to be longlisted for the Bruntwood Prize for Playwriting in 2015.

EXERCISES: EXPLORING CHARACTER

You can use these questions to investigate at any point during the writing of your play. Answer whichever ones are useful to you at your current stage, and leave those that feel premature until you've reached the end of a draft or are approaching a new draft.

→ Make a list of conscious goals for each main character that exist in the play. Are they short-term goals, long-term goals? Do those goals give shape to the action of a moment, scene, act, or the entire play?

→ What are the obstacles to those goals? Who knowingly or unknowingly blocks them?

→ Make a list of conscious and/or unconscious needs for each main character. Are they aware of their needs during the play? If an unconscious need becomes conscious at any point, what does it take for that change to come about?

→ Is there a tension between your characters' wants and needs? Could that tension drive the action?

→ Think about your main characters in terms of Freudian breakdown; id, ego, superego. Do they lead with one drive more than others? Is there a clash between id, ego and superego drives for each key character that creates a key action, moment or scene?

→ Are there any literal or symbolic 'treasures' or objects of value in the play that your characters compete over, and how might this competition give rise to action?

→ What's your sense of cosmic justice or injustice for your characters? What feels inevitable or inexorable as an outcome of their character journey?

→ Make a list of activities, quirks, habits and tropes your character has which show who they are or reveal their desires or needs.

→ What questions, issues or challenges do you want your characters to solve? Where are they stuck in their lives or situation? What kinds of wants, needs and/or 'unwants' might liberate them or create change, and create 'story screws' in your play?

→ Where do we leave your characters at the end of the play? Does their journey feel complete within the play narrative, even if their fate is not entirely clear?

4
EMOTIONAL LOGIC:
THE WHAT OF PLOT
AND THE WHY OF STORY

EMOTIONAL LOGIC:
THE WHAT OF PLOT AND THE WHY OF STORY

'Where's the emotional logic?' is one of the questions I ask the most frequently in group workshops when we're discussing a writer's play. But what the hell *is* emotional logic? It sounds like an oxymoron – but it's really just another way to get at why a character is doing what they're doing. To be really clear, I'm not talking about the *characters* having a logical understanding of their emotions here, but the *writer's* (and audience's) understanding of what the character's emotions are, and how they create their behaviour. This isn't always easy. In some ways it *should* be difficult to figure out who our characters are and why they act as they do, because we want to create three-dimensional, complex, unique human beings. We are also balancing what the *characters* understand about themselves at any one point in the play, with what the *audience* understands about them – and these aren't always in sync. For all these reasons, characters can remain slippery until many drafts in.

The problem is that if you (the writer) and/or we (the audience) don't understand what's motivating the characters to feel, behave and act – if you/we can't sense a logic to their actions arising from their emotions – then the story will ultimately disappoint. So when I ask a writer, 'Where's the emotional logic?' I am really asking, 'How do the key events of your play relate to the nature/desires/needs of your protagonist?', or 'Where's the narrative cause and effect in relation to human behaviour?' And the most damning question of all: 'Why don't we care enough about your story?'

CAUSALITY

One of the key elements that all good stories share is causality – a relationship between cause and effect – and it should exist in the story events of your play as well as the characters' actions. The external events are what make up your plot. By this I mean concrete things that the audience can see happening on stage, alongside those that take place before the play starts, and/or offstage. We can usually identify the opening plot point of a play because it kickstarts the whole story (sometimes known as the 'inciting incident'): Hamlet finds out who murdered his father. (In fact there's a pre-play inciting incident in this case; the murder itself.) In Hinrich's play *Coma Girl*, a landlord hires someone to intimidate his tenant. In Rachael's play *The Lighthouse*, St Nicholas crashes his sleigh on an iceberg. Plots are escalations of one-thing-leading-to-another, following a cause-and-effect pathway, with consequences at every turn. There's a famous, anonymous proverb that sets this out beautifully.

> For want of a nail the shoe was lost;
> For want of a shoe the horse was lost;
> For want of a horse the battle was lost;
> For the failure of battle the kingdom was lost

> And all for the want of a horse-shoe nail.

What is missing from this thumbnail plot is a sense of *emotional and psychological behaviour*. We don't know how the blacksmith felt about his error, or why and how he came to make it, nor how the king dealt with his loss of power when his kingdom fell. A good play will weave together both plot logic and character behaviour into a seamless narrative.

We could sum up the plot of *Hamlet* like this: a young prince whose beloved father, the king, has recently died, receives a supernatural message that his uncle murdered the king. He swears to avenge his father and embarks on a journey to find out if this is true, and then to trap his uncle into confessing he was the murderer, using subterfuge, bullying, and finally theatrics. Along the way he betrays his sister and his mother and ultimately dies after poisoning his uncle. (We might say it's a classic convergence of id, ego and superego drives.) In this very condensed breakdown we nonetheless start to get a sense of character. It's clear that the driving action of the play is motivated by Hamlet's desire for revenge as well as his grief for his murdered father. So there is a causality to his behaviour as well as an emotional logic – both apparent in this most basic outline.

The plots of plays may be dramatic in the sense of seismic events within institutions: deaths of kings and queens, wars, betrayals, murders, decisions with far-reaching consequences. Or they may be dramatic in a very small way: men and women putting their differences aside for a few hours in a bar while they drink and share stories. But the plot – or the *what* – is only one part of a story. To create a truly dramatic story, you also need plenty of *why*.

THE 'WHY' OF STORY VERSUS THE 'WHAT' OF PLOT

I read a useful definition of 'story' in an article by the writer and story coach Lisa Cron. For Cron, a story is: *about how what happens affects someone in pursuit of a deceptively difficult goal and then how that person, the protagonist, changes internally as a result, how their world view changes.* (Interview, 'The Creative Penn'.)

Cron analyses and works with novels, not plays, but I think the principle she is articulating transcends form. If the *plot* is the events in a play that take place in a particular place or time over a particular period of time, and the *structure* of a play is how you choose to arrange, sequence and present those events, then *story* is what the experience of those events *means* to your characters. Story is really emotion. Internal change only comes about when characters experience, process, reflect and adjust. In other words, how they look for meaning in their lives – as we all do.

'I broke up with my boyfriend because I didn't trust him.' 'I decided not to have a certain medical test because I was worried about the results'. 'I was an overprotective parent because I was determined not to repeat my mother's mistakes.' We are constantly assessing our motivations, needs and desires – and, with hindsight, our mistakes, regrets and turning points. Hamlet's desire for revenge (his conscious ego-driven goal), plus his particular nature (he's an intellectual procrastinator and an id-driven narcissist) plus his political duty (his country is under threat of invasion and his superego drives him to protect it) all create an emotional logic that drives the story.

In real life, we might watch the news one night and see a clip of a bombed-out family in Syria – grief-stricken families mourning the loss of loved ones; angry soldiers crowding around the cold impartial lens of a Western photo-journalist. Why are we, watching from our safe houses, moved? Not because of the actual explosion, or the complex political machinations that led to its detonation. But because of what it means to the people whose lives it has just changed forever. As human beings, we may have no power to change the external events that life throws at us – including war, betrayal, love and death – but we will internalise and process the experience of them. So will dramatic characters. Characters act and react, act and react, act and react. What these events mean to them and how they cause them to feel, think, speak and act, are at the heart of all good plays. Dramatic characters thus effect *and* affect the plot – they create the story.

STORY IS CHARACTER

All of this is another way of saying, as Aristotle did, that story is character. Your sense of your character will be rooted in a unique particularity based on environment, genes and biology, life experience, emotional make-up, habits; what we could reduce rather crassly to three '-ology's: psychology, physiology and sociology. This doesn't mean that every single character in your play must have a driving goal, a series of obstacles, and a grand climactic battle resulting in some sort of epiphany or catharsis. But it's usually the case that one or two characters in every play *will* drive the action – and in every case it's the psychological and emotional wrangling between them that holds our attention. This is where the work starts, often before you've written a single word of dialogue. Story is created when we understand – or want to understand – why characters are acting as they are.

Have you ever lurked in a theatre bar at the end of a play and listened to audience members discussing what they've just watched? If so, you'll know that you will rarely hear anyone say, 'I really enjoyed the plot of that play.' Instead you'll probably hear them enthusing (or the opposite) about the characters, the actors, the set, the laughs they had (or didn't have), the emotion they felt (or didn't feel), the plausibility of the world, set-up or character decisions, or any variation thereof. Audience members will, however, much more often bemoan the 'lack' of plot or the 'clunky' plot or the 'implausible' plot. I think this is because when a plot works, it becomes sort of invisible. The audience is too busy being emotionally affected and entertained by the characters to think analytically about the machinations of plot or structure.

THE PERILS OF OVERPLOTTING

So how do we achieve this 'invisible plot'? As audience members we invest in a play when we are let into the characters' inner secret lives, and are able to intimately share their motivations, desires, secrets, anguish and joys. However, new writers often worry that not enough is 'happening' in their play. Our insatiable desire for plot, as we know it, often leads new playwrights to believe they must invent the important external events of the story first (War! Betrayal! Love! Death!) and build the play around them. But those things themselves don't make a story. It's common for a writer struggling with a new play to conclude that if they simply kill off a character this will immediately make their story more compelling and more dramatic. In fact, it can have the opposite effect. In trying to make sure that enough significant or downright epic things happen to their characters, the writer forgets to think about what it all actually *feels* like to those characters.

Part of the problem is that we are all plot junkies. Our most popular, mass-market monomyth films are relentless plot bombs. Much mainstream television is also driven by insatiable audience desire for cracking plot, with dramatic event heaped on dramatic event. And, of course, there's a daily 'big story' at the top of the news. Pandemics, political coups, global wars, genocides, economic crashes, wide-scale institutional corruption. There's so much *big stuff* happening that we can become both numbed by and addicted to it. I wonder sometimes if globalisation has actually changed the human narrative palette. Does it partly explain the mass popularity of the blockbuster franchise movie, which basically replays variations on the same story of impending Armageddon and a last-minute reprieve thanks to the heroism of a small group of heroic (and very attractive) individuals? Then I remember *The Odyssey*, *Beowulf*, *Macbeth*; perhaps our thirst for big stories has always been there.

But although the theatrical canon is full of epic stories, from the Greeks through Shakespeare to Brecht and onwards, the theatre is also the rightful home of the small story painted on the miniature canvas. Stories that tend to be concerned less with huge plot machinations than with intimate details of human psychology and behaviour. Theatre gives the audience (and writer) the luxury of real time in which to observe people at close range, in detailed focus. And under such a bright light, a lack of emotional character logic can scupper a play. However brilliant your dialogue is and scintillating your characters are, we won't care about them unless we are able to understand how they are affected by things.

STRIPPING BACK THE STORY

The sartorial revolutionary Coco Chanel had a famous piece of advice to fashionable women: 'Before you leave the house, look in the mirror and take one thing off.' She was referring to the baubles, bangles and beads that the women of the era commonly bedecked themselves with, and who were, in the words of journalist Janet Flanner, writing in 1931, 'Full of gussets, garters, corsets, whalebones, plackets, false hair, and brassières.'

It's a useful dictum for playwrights, too. Sometimes we overornament our stories in our desire to be 'dramatic', in the false sense of the word. I once spent several weeks trying to crowbar a particular event into a key scene of a play I was writing. It involved a jilted older man hearing a romantic exchange between his female love interest and his adult son play out on a baby monitor in another room. I'd convinced myself that it was a brilliant theatrical moment, but actually it was holding up the play completely. Firstly, I just couldn't get the couple into the next room on any reasonable pretext, so the logic of the scene didn't work; but more importantly, my refusal to drop the baby-monitor moment was stopping me from writing the actual confrontation between the father, son and lover. And that is what I needed to do in order to really understand what this difficult love triangle meant to each character. After days of wrangling I gave up and put all three characters in the same room, with a couple of others for good measure, and had them all thrash it out. Finally it became a scene with real emotional punch.

So, next time you finish a segment of your play that you feel in your bones isn't quite working yet, ask yourself if there's something plotty and external – a dramatic placket – that you might remove to create more breathing space for your characters. (Incidentally, I managed to recycle the baby-monitor moment to much better effect in my play *Genesis Inc.* years later.)

Of course, sometimes you *do* know exactly who your characters are in their bones. You've lived with them for months or years; their voices in your head are crystal clear; you have a deep sense of their emotions and thoughts and feelings. As a dramatist, your job is to then externalise all of that into action on the stage. That means, yes, giving the characters enough to do, but also giving the audience a sense of how the characters are emotionally joining the dots in the story.

Many first plays are full of interesting people doing interesting things, saying interesting sentences, and experiencing interesting predicaments.

But none of this will constitute a truly engaging story unless we, the audience, understand what is driving the people reacting to the events, making the choices, and dealing with the consequences.

The moral of the chapter is – *never underestimate an audience's desire for story.*

It's so important I'll say it again.

Never underestimate an audience's desire for story.

I mean *true* story – the meaningful internal trajectory of your character – not just a cracking plot.

THE BIG STUFF

It may be that you're writing a sprawling epic spanning continents and eras – if so, that's great – but you will still need to find ways to ensure that your big external events don't overshadow your characters' inner journeys. *Hamlet* has a pretty racy plot involving war, murder and treason, but that's not really why the play affects us. It's because we understand the emotional logic behind all Hamlet's actions. Note that to *us*, the audience, it's logical, by which I mean, *we* can see his strange behaviour stems from concrete issues and problems.

As a contemporary example, *3 Winters* by Tena Štivičić has a plot that is based on empirically big events. The Croatian Kos family have lived through three different sets of seismic national political events over three generations and seventy years: the Communist regime of 1945, the independence of Croatia in 1990, and the present day of the play, 2011, as Croatia is about to join the EU. The action is situated in all three eras, and examines the impact of these three historical moments on the family – particularly on its women: grandmother, mother and daughters.

Were these external events in Croatia's political history the starting point for the writer? Actually, no.

> I didn't set out to write a play about the war or the history of Croatia or Yugoslavia,' says Štivičić. 'I don't think the history of a country is a story: it's a context in which a story takes place. So the story of this family, and these women, how people cope, or don't cope, with systems and values collapsing – these were the things that I wanted to explore. (*Financial Times* interview)

And:

> The very first moments of inspiration for this play came from stories
> in my family. My mother's, my aunt's, my grandmother's and even
> my great-grandmother's when I was very little. These women spoke
> in very different voices, each with a different set of tools, or, in
> fact, lack of tools, to express their circumstances and articulate the
> plight of their life. (National Theatre blog)

I think this deep sense of connection to character is what enabled the
writer to write a great play, which never sacrifices characterisation for
driving plot. So how did she manage to balance the two?

The key dramatic elements of the play are a) the political events happening
offstage but impacting the onstage lives; b) a past/present time frame which
takes us back and forth between the 'present' of this particular family and
the 'past' family history which has shaped them; and c) a single theatrical
location – the family home – seen in the three different eras. This cleverly
unifies the action and themes of the play. The house was once a private
aristocratic home; then nationalised under Communism and owned by
all; then owned by a few (the family) at the time of independence, and now,
in the present (2011), it's about to be bought by daughter Lucia's rich but
dodgy fiancé, to save the family home. So the setting of the play creates a
useful dramatic metaphor.

It's also an ensemble piece, so there's no one main character driving the
narrative. We could say that the family is the communal central character
of the play. We could also say that the house itself is a character, as its fate
forms the main dramatic question of the play – will it stay in the family?
We also want to see if this family will survive the many changes thrust
on to it and retain some connection, even as their lives and experiences
diverge. The power of the story lies in the comparative struggles, choices
and relationships of the characters. We root for them, laugh with them, cry
with them. We can't ask for much more than that.

THE SMALL STUFF

It's often thought that it's far easier to create true story (in the sense I've
already mentioned) with a conventional 'big'-plot, single-protagonist
play, and far harder to do so with a one-room, one-character, one-horse
play. Or is it? I actually think that all good plays can withstand this sort of
interrogation, however small their plot is.

Take Alexander Zeldin's play *Love*, which was staged at the National Theatre in 2016. Part-devised with the company and part-authored by Zeldin, it was a naturalistic play about a group of people living in temporary social housing under very difficult circumstances, while waiting to be rehoused. The accommodation is cramped, dirty, cold and lacking any privacy. The characters have nothing in common; they are evicted families, immigrants, carers and their relatives. The very slight plot, as such, is about how the individual characters annoy, disgust, goad and frustrate each other, leading to various showdowns. It is also about how they manage to find compassion, empathy and solidarity with each other. Stuff happens. But it's not the stuff of *big story* as we know it.

Except to them. For those characters, this is the stuff of life and death. What we're watching is humans behaving under extreme emotional pressure and revealing their true natures. We are flies on the wall of the hostel, watching new arrivals emerge from their rooms, brush against each other in the hallway, share a brief conversation or a row. We don't know what happens to the two main families. Will they get rehoused? Will they survive this period in their lives? These plot questions aren't answered by the end of the play. It didn't matter to me, when I saw it. While I couldn't easily describe the plot of the play, I could tell you what the characters went through, and why they did what they did. And, magically, by spending an hour in their company, I could imagine all of their individual backstories – decades' worth of lives lived. Drama can be created on stage simply through pace, energetic shifts and surprises and dramatic payoffs for the audience, however small they might seem on the surface.

STORY IS TENSION

Finally, if you're still wrangling with your characters and don't have all the answers yet, another way to come at the questions I've posed in this chapter is to think about theatrical storytelling as a form of tension – psychological, emotional and/or performative. Humans – and therefore characters – are constantly negotiating with each other about the private and public selves they present to the world, and there is often tension to be mined in these competing personal narratives. Is Hamlet the man he thinks he is? How does he present himself to others, and who in the play accepts or rejects these presentations? It's no surprise that storytelling itself – as a human action through which we create meaning in our lives – is a frequent subject of plays.

In Annie Baker's play *The Antipodes*, a group of screenwriters sit around a table struggling to come up with a new commercial storyline for a film. As their deadline looms, and the characters' imagined storylines and their own personal stories begin to blur and overlap, the narrative sands begin to shift. What is real and what is imagined? Is a 'true' story intrinsically more valuable than one constructed by a group? Although the play on one level is a dramatisation of dramaturgy itself and lacks a conventional plot, don't for a minute think that playwrights such as Baker or Zeldin or Conor McPherson – masters and mistresses of the 'small' story – don't understand storytelling. They know exactly how to craft story out of onstage theatrical tension – and so can you.

CASE STUDY: *The Bevin Boys* by Viv Edwards

I've already mentioned (in Chapter Two) Viv's play about the Bevin Boys – the young men chosen by ballot to go and work in the mines around the UK for the war effort. Viv had done plenty of research, and as a Welshman, knew a lot about this period of time from his own family background.

The basic events of his plot were as follows:

→ In 1944 two young British men, Billy and Jim, are recruited to work in a Welsh village, mining coal to fuel the war effort. Billy is middle-class and timid; Jim is working-class, ebullient and a show-off. They are billeted with a local family: Mam, Dad, and their daughter Megan.

→ Billy and Jim don't get on initially. But on their first day down the pit, Jim panics and admits he's terrified of the dark. When he tries to escape, Billy punches Jim – acting against his pacifist beliefs – in an attempt to get him to stay calm. Jim makes Billy promise to keep this incident a secret, to save his pride. Billy agrees.

→ Billy and Jim compete over Megan's affections, and fall out again. Mam and Dad are drawn into their row, particularly when Jim tries to entreat Megan to run away with him to England to work in a munitions factory.

→ Billy, a fine singer, wants to join the chapel choir, but Dad won't let him. The local community resent the English Bevin Boys, and Dad doesn't want to jeopardise his chances of becoming a church deacon.

→ Billy dies in a mining accident. Jim decides to stay on in Wales and work down the pit in honour of his friend. Mam and Dad make an emotional speech to the local chapel congregation, entreating them to accept the Bevin Boys as their own.

At first read, the world, characters and setting were interesting and well drawn, the dialogue was well written, and the tone was warm and touching. Despite this, they didn't quite add up to a satisfying story. Viv's great desire was to show audiences how frustrating it was for these young British men, who wanted to be off heroically fighting the Germans, to be shoved down a coal mine – how their pride was hurt, how alone they felt, and how hard it was to be ostracised by the Welsh communities. Viv felt very strongly that the efforts of the Bevin boys should be acknowledged for their service. He wanted his play to reveal a forgotten aspect of the war effort, and dramatise the struggles of both Welsh and Englishmen as they rubbed up against each other.

So he had what we can call his *why* – his impetus for writing. This allowed him to come up with his *what*. A setting. A time period. A series of events happening to a group of characters. In other words, he had a plot. But those events, and those scenes he wrote around them, didn't quite create a true story, in the sense we've discussed. I was never clear what the two Englishmen Billy and Jim really wanted, and I couldn't see how their personal conflicts drove the action. It was also challenging that the conflict with the community always happened offstage. (Viv was avoiding a large-cast play for practical reasons, which meant limiting his constellation of characters to the five residents of the house and one other local Welshman.) But what most troubled me was the death of Billy.

When I asked Viv which of his invented plot events came to him first, he said, 'The ending – Billy's death.' It was completely understandable that Viv believed that the play must end with a death – after all, this is the most natural dramatisation of the risk and hardship endured by the Bevin Boys (and the Welsh miners too, of course). The problem was that the death didn't occur for any logical reason – and I mean logical within the play as a dramatic construct, rather than in the 'reality' of the play's story. This death wasn't an outcrop of Viv's theme or idea, and more importantly, it didn't come about because of character. It was just a tragic accident, occupying a sort of bubble outside the main ingredients of the play.

I wrote, rather bluntly, in notes to Viv about his play:

> Billy's death feels unearned. His death is a complete accident, and not the result of any human error, choice or judgement. So it's a *deus ex machina* * that brings your story to its end, and thus it doesn't really count as a truly dramatic climax. It is very hard to make an accident work at the end of a narrative, rather than the beginning.

> Your point seems to be, given what I know about your reasons for writing the play, that the Bevin boys were just as courageous, brave and hardy as those British troops on the German front. That they fought different battles close to home that tested them greatly, even though they went unrecognised by the British government at the time. But then you must *show* us that. Find a story that dramatises that intention. If there is to be a death, that death should be a dramatisation of human character, and of your theme. It's a surprise to me, reading the play; I didn't expect Billy to die. But it's hard to care that much, ultimately, because I don't have a sense of his death being a dramatic culmination. On stage, everything that happens must happen for a reason. Shouldn't we feel that Billy *had* to die, in order for something to be freed, salvaged, reordered, released?

Of the two English Bevin Boys, Jim was by far the more alive on the page. Viv had given him more to do and say, and he had life and energy. In discussion it occurred to us that Viv had complicated things for himself by in effect splitting Jim into two characters; resulting in Billy *and* Jim, who essentially fulfilled the same dramatic function. So, instead of being one of two Englishmen, what if Billy became a young Welshman of a similar age instead, living in the same house, who couldn't fight for health reasons? The two young men would naturally hate each other, and their interactions could

---

* Literally, 'a god from the machine' – which was a theatrical device used in Ancient Greece, where a 'god' character would be lowered onto the stage on a crane (the machine) to resolve the drama. In other words, the story's conclusion relied on divine intervention.

then help dramatise Viv's themes. For example, how might an angry English outsider and an angry Welsh insider, who consider each other enemies, find common ground and friendship – but only underground?

Viv wanted to show the hostility felt by the Welsh community to the English lads, who resented the fact that their own boys had been sent off to fight, perhaps never to return. This had given rise to a rather messy play that portrayed tragedy and deep emotion, but never followed a logical narrative that built to that sense of *inevitable action* that all good plays are striving for. After clarifying what Viv wanted to express dramatically and thematically with his story, he then had to find a way to grow the story from that place, and find the characters who could best tell it. Instead of starting with the endpoint of Billy's tragic death and working backwards, Viv started at the beginning, and rebuilt the story on the characters' desires, needs and challenges, both internal and external.

Viv went away to redraft, and the basic events of his Draft Two plot were as follows:

→ In 1944 a young Englishman, Jim, is recruited to work in a Welsh village, mining coal to fuel the war effort. Jim is working-class, ebullient and a show-off. He is billeted with a Welsh family: Mam, Dad, and their daughter Megan, along with their Welsh lodger Billy.

→ Billy is nationalistic, sensitive and physically weak. He cannot fight in the war due to a health condition and is angry about this.

→ Billy and Jim have to share a room. Billy despises Jim for being English and secretly resents him for being good-looking and physically fit. Jim finds Billy dour and haughty.

→ On their first day down the pit together, Jim panics and admits he's terrified of the dark. Jim makes Billy promise to keep this incident a secret, to save his pride. Billy agrees.

→ Jim, a fine singer, wants to join the chapel choir, but Dad won't let him. The local community resent the English Bevin Boys, and Dad doesn't want to jeopardise his chances of becoming a chapel deacon.

→ When Billy and Jim start to compete for Megan's attentions, Billy breaks his promise and tells everyone that Jim is afraid of the dark. Jim is now an object of ridicule at work and in the local community.

→ Jim, ashamed and hurt, tries to entreat Megan to run away with him to England to work in a munitions factory. Mam and Dad find out and try to stop her. Megan decides to stay.

→ Down the pit, Jim, spurred on by Mr Churchill's broadcast supporting the Bevin Boys, now accepts his lot, but is still angry about the hostility of the community. Billy suggests that he teaches Jim the Welsh words of a hymn as a means of impressing the community. As they push the tubs, Billy sings and Jim learns the words.

→ Mam and Dad make an emotional speech to the local chapel congregation, entreating them to accept the Bevin Boys as their own. Jim is allowed to sing with Billy in the chapel choir.

The play had become much more focused on the male friendship than the romantic conflict between the young men and Meg, which Viv was happy about. It felt true to his original intentions. However, I still had questions about the climactic scene down the pit when Billy teaches Jim to sing Welsh hymns. My questions were:

→ If the play has been driven by the conflict and hostility between Billy and Jim, and Jim's betrayal by Billy, why does Jim now suddenly 'accept his lot'? Is his big internal change really brought about by a radio broadcast? (*This felt too 'external' and not sufficiently character-driven.*)

→ Why/when has Jim forgiven Billy for telling everyone about his fear of the dark? Or does that happen in this scene?

→ Is there physical danger in this scene, heightening the stakes and allowing the men to realise they need each other?

One idea we discussed was that down in the pit once again, after an accident that causes Jim's fear to resurface, Billy teaches Jim the songs as a way of distracting him and helping him focus. So they pull together, finally, and become allies rather than enemies. As you can see, I was still insistently (and annoyingly) looking for a current of emotional logic in the culmination of the play's conflict. Viv, enduringly patient, supplied the following thoughts in response.

> So, why has Jim accepted his lot? A few reasons. Firstly, he is patriotic and was moved by Churchill's words, which he felt were directed at him. Secondly, both Dad and Billy have warned Jim about the reception he would get as a young man in civvies arriving alone in Cardiff – his only escape route. He'd get lynched, and he's already been in trouble with the law. He genuinely wanted to tempt Megan away to Kent to work in the munitions factory and thinks if he and Meg were travelling together to a job in munitions, there would be less risk of him been attacked. When she refuses, he feels isolated and has nowhere to turn. He threatens to escape to Kent on his own, but Billy puts it to him that working in the pit is essential, it's hard work, and he is doing his bit for the war effort. The munitions factory still doesn't meet his desire to fight in the front line, so (Billy argues) why risk getting caught and imprisoned again? Megan has admitted some affection for Jim, and whilst she has decided to stay with her family, she worries for him and implores him to stay and accept that he must work in the pit. Jim's isolation (and this is where it really helps that Billy is Welsh) forces him to admit that he needs to be accepted by the local community. Billy feels like supporting Jim, to lift the guilt of betraying him. This is where Billy suggests he teaches Jim the Welsh words of a hymn to gain acceptance.

I couldn't argue with any of that. It's the mark of a good writer that Viv was prepared to respond to my questions in such depth. However seductive it is to have a dramaturg on hand, the playwright must always follow their own nose. The dramaturg's well-intentioned desire to sniff out the (non-existent) perfect play can sometimes stifle the playwright's creative impulse, and that must be avoided at all costs. In other words, as a teacher, sometimes I need to just stop talking and listen.

Viv now had a solid outline for his new draft, which had a much stronger sense of cause and effect and clearer character arcs. After getting everything down in his first draft, he peeled back the layers and took stock. He took the inherent conflict in the setting and circumstances of his first draft *and* his emotional connection to the material, and crafted them into a much stronger story, which ended in redemption rather than destruction.

Postscript: Viv's play was produced by Pentameters Theatre company on the London fringe – but as a two-hander. His producers loved the play but as a small company could only budget for two actors, not five. So Viv went back to the drawing board yet again, and revised *The Bevin Boys* into a play for two characters. The work he had done on the drafts discussed here allowed him to tackle a new and condensed version head on. Better a small gem of a production than an unproduced playscript gathering dust in a drawer! The work paid off, as the production went on to win 'Best New Play' in the 2020 London Pub Theatre Awards.

EXERCISES: CAUSE AND EFFECT

Use these exercises to create an 'emotional logic' map for your play, interrogating the relationship between its events and its character actions.

→ Make a list of the key events that happen in your play. Some of these might happen before the play starts, and some might happen offstage. If your play has a non-linear structure it might help to write this list as the events occur in linear time. Write a line or two on each event, or plot them in a diagram, whatever is useful.

→ Note which of those events are external and circumstantial – i.e. they come about through accident, or chance, or coincidence, or are based on strong outside forces that characters have no control over – and which are based in character choice. (Using Viv's play as an example, we might say the circumstantial events of his play that take place *outside* the stage action include the outbreak of the Second World War and the conscription of the Bevin Boys in 1943. *Within* the stage action they include Jim's arrival in the village and his first day down the mine. Character choices arising from events include Billy telling everyone about Jim's panic; Jim's invitation to Meg to run away; the chapel governors' pre-existing decision not to let British boys sing in the choir, and so on.)

→ Make a note of how each event directly or indirectly affects each character differently in the play.

→ Think about where these circumstantial events take place along the continuum of your play's (linear) time frame. Are they at the beginning, the end, or somewhere in the middle? Do they slowly increase the pressure on your characters throughout, or provide a backdrop or context to the action? Or do they come in a short explosion at a particular point in the story that changes its course? Do they create dramatic stakes for your characters?

→ Now think about which of the key events count as *character actions* – i.e. things characters do as a result of internal feelings, reactions, choices and decisions, such as Billy's decision to tell everyone about Jim's irrational fear, or Jim's decision to ask Megan to run away with him.

→ Make a note of how each *action* taken by a character directly or indirectly affects each character differently in the play. What different meanings do these actions have to different characters?

→ Using your 'event map' as a guide, write a paragraph outlining how each character changes internally from the beginning of the play to the end, so you have a written arc for each one. If characters don't change, are they perhaps strong catalysts for the change of others?

5
DRAMATIC STRUCTURE: DEBUNKING THE MYTHS

DRAMATIC STRUCTURE: DEBUNKING THE MYTHS

When I ask a room of new writers what they want to take away from a writing course, or to describe what they see as their greatest writing challenge, the answer they give most often is 'structure'. For example, 'I want to understand structure'; 'I just need to figure out the structure of my play and then I'll be able to finish it'; 'I don't have a structure yet.' (All usually uttered through ground-down teeth.) Many writers conceive of dramatic structure as some sort of holy grail – a body of pre-existing wisdom that can only be mystically imparted to a chosen few (or enshrined in best-selling 'story structure' books written by screenwriting gurus). But it isn't so. Every play requires a unique structure, according to its unique needs – and the playwright discovers it by the usual trial and error.

WHAT IS DRAMATIC STRUCTURE?

In its simplest definition, structure is your play's overall layout or design – like a set of architectural plans – which present your scenes in a particular chronology and with a particular relationship between time and place. But it is also far more than this. When most people think about structure, their mind goes automatically to plot: the order of external events. They assume that as soon as they figure out this order, which events happen first, middle and last, they'll have it nailed.

Of course, knowing what happens when is crucial, but you can spend an awful lot of time ordering and reordering events like a theatrical Rubik's Cube, and still not understand what your core story is. When a writer says, 'I don't know my structure yet', they often mean, 'I don't know my story yet,' which usually means in turn, 'I don't know who my characters are.' But once you do understand whose story you're telling, and why, you'll intuitively understand more about *how* a particular structure might help you tell it. You can make it as linear, straightforward and realistic, or as fragmented, complex and symbolic as you like – either way, structure is just another storytelling tool.

It is also a very creative tool. Your structure will contribute to your play's tone, rhythm and pace, beyond its delivery of plot. In Chapter Seven we will explore how the use of scene endings, openings and transitions create meaning in a play – these are all structural elements that you can use to focus audience attention, deliver suspense and anticipation, and create theatrical energy on stage. We are all capable of creating the right structure for our play if we ask ourselves the right questions.

Let me start by debunking a few myths about dramatic structure.

MYTH 1

Dramatic structure is an empirically provable formula that a playwright must learn and employ if they want to write a good play.

Not so. Structure is, by its very definition, flexible, malleable and, above all, elective. Below is a dictionary definition of the word:

Structure (*noun*)
1. *The way in which the parts of a system or object are arranged or organised, or a system arranged in this way.*
2. *Something that has been made or built from parts, especially a large building.* (*Cambridge Dictionary*)

Both these definitions are useful in different ways. The first – arrangement – is another word for structure that is far more friendly and less mechanical. If we substitute the word 'story' for 'system' we get this:

The way in which the parts of a story are arranged or organised.

Now let's take the second definition – building – and once again substitute the word 'story' for the given noun. We get this:

Something that has been made or built from parts. Especially a large story.

Again, this is pretty simple, and pretty true (even the 'large story' part). A play is made from parts (or units of action), called, among other things: scenes, acts, plot strands, turning points, story beats, and so on. Each of those parts should contribute to the narrative trajectory of your characters.

So far then we have a notion of structure as being, at its most basic, an arrangement of those parts. That shouldn't be so frightening. We all have an instinctive understanding of narrative parts; they are taught to us in the cradle. Beginning, middle and end is the most basic triumvirate that builds a story. To further dissipate the fog of fear that surrounds the word 'structure' I'll put forward some alternative suggestions. How about:

Shape. Flow. Movement. Pattern. Organisation. Blueprint.

You can be as organic and touchy-feely in the way you conceive your story structure, or as mathematical and precise about it as you like, depending on your nature, and your writing process. You can think of your play as a classic pop song: verse, chorus, verse, chorus, bridge, chorus. Or a three-course meal. Or an act of love: foreplay, action, climax and pillow talk. Whatever helps you visualise or feel its flow of energy and its shape. Playwright Nicola Baldwin offers the following example:

> An artistic director once said their ideal play was two x forty-five-minute acts, with excitement at the end of the first half, and a decisive goal at the end of the second. This football analogy was irritating at the time, but has proved quite useful.

Let's return for a moment to the common plaints of the playwright I described at the beginning of this chapter: 'I want to understand structure.' 'I don't have a structure yet.' And let's replace it with one of these alternatives. The sentences immediately become a bit nonsensical.

I want to understand shape

If you can tell a circle from a square, you can describe the shape of your story. It might be linear. It might be episodic. It might move between past and present. It might go backwards. It might consist of three movements; quick, slow, quick, like a classical symphony. It might bookend your play with the same event, told from a different perspective. Your play might feel messy, boring or slow right now, but it will still have a shape. And if the shape's not working, then you need to change it.

I don't have a shape yet

You may not have the *best* shape for your play yet, but a completed draft will always have an arrangement of scenes; a map of action; a movement from, for example, one set of events/time period/location/character's state of mind to another. The fact that you might not be able to put your play into a conventional classical structure does not mean it doesn't have one at all.

The notion of 'building', as verb or adjective, can be helpful. Plays are written, but they are also *made*, from the building blocks of characterisation, desire, causal logic, narrative drive, plotting, and so on. And, like architects, playwrights must spend a lot of time thinking about the different potential plans of their play before they find one that works. I happen to be married to an architect, and the language he uses to discuss his buildings is often remarkably similar to the language I use in my writing.

Imagine for a moment that you are building your dream house. The building is comprised of many rooms of different shapes and sizes, which make up the whole. Each room fits together in a relational way to create an overall architectural structure with a particular logic, meaning, shape and form. When you, the architect, study your architectural blueprint, you'll see that certain groups of rooms form a substructure within the building. You could most simply divide the building into floors. Ground floor comprises kitchen, living room, dining room, utility room; where you eat, socialise, watch TV, and other communal activities. The middle floor comprises two bedrooms and a bathroom where you sleep, wash, and engage in more physically intimate and private rituals. On the top floor are an attic and a study; quiet spaces where you store memories, reflect, and work in solitude. Each floor has its own function, style and atmosphere and contributes a particular narrative of the human life lived in the house.

Broken down this way, this particular house (play) has macro and micro elements. The three floors (acts) each contribute meaning to the house, as does each room (scene). And the interrelationship *between* the rooms and the floors also contributes to the overall narrative. Of course, your house may only have one floor, or it might have five, or ten. It might be a bungalow or a skyscraper or a single room. Whatever it is, it is not a prefab. You will arrive at the right structure by feeling and thinking your way through your play and letting your story evolve organically.

MYTH 2

A play is only interesting if it has a complicated structure.

Most plays are told in a linear fashion – linear is from the Latin word *linearis*, meaning 'belonging to a line'. That is: the story follows a straight, chronological line forwards through space and time – whether that's two hours' 'real time' as in Conor McPherson's *The Weir*, or several hundred years, as in Moira Buffini's *Loveplay* or Tanya Ronder's *Table*. Shakespeare didn't spend too much time yanking his audience back and forth between past and present (with a few notable exceptions) – he just got on with telling the story in chronological order and creating plot momentum. So please be reassured – *your play is not boring if it is linear.* Linear storytelling has been going on for a few millennia now, most probably because it's the way we experience time ourselves, as an unfolding continuum.

Let's look a little deeper at some common structural forms. As we saw in the previous chapter, the basic units of action that make up a play's narrative are pretty simple. To write a scene you will need a who, a when, a where, a what and a why. Characters, a time, a place, a nugget of action and a sense of dramatic purpose and causality. A chronology and sequence of events, of course. But the way scenes are presented, ordered and arranged can and should also contribute to theme, theatricality, world and characterisation. Below are some examples of plays that use different theatrical structures to create narrative.

THE LINEAR PLAY

Most of the plays mentioned so far in this book have a linear structure, including *A Raisin in the Sun, A Streetcar Named Desire* and *Death of a Salesman.* Jez Butterworth's *Jerusalem* has a single setting and a contained time frame of a single day. The dramatic stake of the play is set up right at the beginning, in the first scene. Rooster Byron has twenty-four hours to vacate his caravan in the woods before the council will destroy it – will they succeed and will he lose his home? This question is answered at the end of the play. (The secondary dramatic question or subplot is what has happened to the missing teenage girl Phaedra – which is answered at the end of Act Two.) The tension builds as we spend the day with Rooster and his cohort of neighbours, friends and wastrels, and we learn more about why he's digging his heels in and what losing his caravan means to him. If your play has a strong plot motor and a clear suspense question at its core, then the linear structure works perfectly. It allows the audience to experience the events of the play as the characters do. So never dismiss linear storytelling as inherently dull.

THE BOOKENDED PLAY

Posh by Laura Wade was a Royal Court hit in 2010, and depicts a single night of excess in an Oxford University students' dining club named the Riot

Club, possibly inspired by the real-life Bullingdon Club. The play itself has a quick-slow-quick structure. Act One has two scenes, the first of which is a two-hander set in a private gentlemen's club, in which Conservative MP Jeremy advises his godson Guy to create havoc at Guy's impending Riot Club dinner in order to keep the old traditions alive and perhaps secure himself the club presidency. Scene Two comprises the first half of the Riot Club dinner, which turns into a bacchanalian orgy of excess as the various members, including Guy, president James, and immature Alistair compete to be the worst behaved. After the interval, Act Two begins. Scene One is a continuation of the dinner and its escalation into chaos, abuse and destruction, climaxing with the physical and verbal abuse of the young waitress and her father, the pub landlord. Scene Two (the final one of the play) is another two-hander, set in the same private gentlemen's club as Scene One, a few weeks after the dinner. This time, Jeremy has drinks with Alistair, who has been scapegoated by the other club members for the damages made at the dinner. But instead of chiding him, Jeremy seems to imply that Alistair will go far.

Although the bulk of the play, the dinner, is split into two halves and bisected by an interval, the play has more of a tripartite structure, with the bookend scenes in Jeremy's club mirroring each other's location and tone, but with a surprising twist. These two scenes therefore provide a prologue and epilogue sandwiched around the meat of the drama. It's a neat structure that has many functions. The prologue scene, or first bookend, sets up the world, the stakes for the characters, and creates a sense of anticipation for the audience about what is to come. The epilogue, and second bookend, mirrors the prologue's tone and theme, showing us that life in these rarefied circles is maintained via an unaccountable system, while also providing a surprising resolution for Alistair. The structure doesn't just serve up story, it also carries political ideas and commentary, without any heavy-handed moralising.

Lolita Chakrabarti's 2012 play *Red Velvet*, about the African-American actor Ira Aldridge, also uses a bookended structure to show the sweep of Ira's career. The play opens in 1867, as Aldridge, aged sixty and nearing the end of a successful career in Europe, arrives in the dressing room of the theatre where he will perform, and is interviewed by a female journalist. The action then moves to 1833, thirty-four years earlier, and Ira's arrival at the Theatre Royal in Drury Lane, where he has been hired to play Othello, replacing the ailing, white star Edmund Kean. The bulk of the play dramatises the hostile reception he receives from his fellow actors, the audience and theatre board members, and Ira's struggle with the theatre manager. The final scene brings us back again to 1867, as Ira prepares for his show, haunted by the ghosts of actors from the former company. In these 1867 scenes, Ira is preparing to play King Lear, and applies white face paint. This contrasts cleverly with the scenes in 1833, which focuses on the outrage that a 'real' black man is playing Othello. The bookend structure helps create meaning on many levels.

THE BACKWARDS PLAY

Harold Pinter's play *Betrayal* has a fairly simple plot: a man and a woman, Jerry and Emma, are both married to other people – Emma, in fact, to Jerry's friend Robert. The two meet, embark on a clandestine affair over a period of seven years, and finally break up. The structure of the story, and what we could call its structural device, is that the story is told backwards. We start at the end of the relationship: Scene One takes place after the break-up of Jerry and Emma. And we work backwards in time over nine scenes as we go forwards in the play, using reverse chronology. The final scene of the play takes place in a bedroom at a party, in which Jerry first tells Emma he loves her.

Stephen Sondheim's musical *Merrily We Roll Along*, with a book by George Furth, uses the same reverse chronology. So why bother with this non-linear structure? Why not tell a story with high emotional stakes and let it unfold as it plays? Doesn't it weaken the play to give away the ending right at the beginning? What do the audience have to look forward to? They are reasonable questions, but Pinter's backwards structure elevates his play from a fairly ordinary love story to something far more moving. The audience's foreknowledge of the lovers' parting infuses the play with poignant melancholy. Similarly, Sondheim's *Merrily* starts at the pinnacle of Franklin Shepard's career. Frank is a famous and wealthy but cynical and burned-out film producer. The musical moves backwards in time over twenty years, showing us moments from his life and the choices that shaped him. We end the story at the beginning of his career, with Frank as a young composer, bursting with hope and optimism. Once again there's a deep sense of loss embedded in this reverse chronology. In both cases, the backwards structure of the play helps dramatise the characters' emotional journeys to devastating effect.

THE FRAGMENTED OR KALEIDOSCOPIC PLAY

Alice Birch's *Anatomy of a Suicide* was staged at the Royal Court in 2017, and has a multi-strand tripartite structure. The play presents three women: a grandmother, her daughter, and her granddaughter, each separated by a generation, as they battle with depression. We watch all three individual stories unfold simultaneously, with the action overlapping on stage, so that sometimes we are watching three stories at once in the 1970s, 1990s and 2010s. Why did the writer structure her play this way, rather than simply presenting each character's story one after the other? By juxtaposing the action, Birch dramatises the experience of depression in a uniquely affecting way, creating an overlapping, expressionist piece of theatre. The audience witnesses each woman in her story world, alone and isolated, yet standing next to her descendant, who similarly enacts the depression she has inherited from her forebear. Through this privileged vantage point, we can feel the web of family heredity, and its pain, all the more intensely.

All these plays discussed deliberately utilise a particular organisation and shape to create meaning and tell their story. Their structure plays a role just as important as the external events of the plot, exchanges of dialogue and exposition. But we now have to deal with another behemoth lurking in the dark woods of playwriting. Classical dramatic structures, aka the Act Monster.

MYTH 3

A play must have acts to qualify as a play.

The play act is another bamboozling term. As we know, scenes are units of action that function as the building blocks of a story. Acts are just another kind of unit, comprised of groups of scenes. They are subsets, or 'containers' of scenes, and they are structural devices because they contribute to the arrangement and pattern of action.

I'm not going to bang on here about Aristotle's *Poetics* (in which he advocated a three-act structure) or Gustav Freytag's Pyramid (Freytag wrote an exhaustive – if not exhausting – analysis of five-act structure) or even the detractors of the classical dramatic-structure theorists (there are now as many books criticising what's seen as the formulaic prison of three-act structure as there are espousing it – particularly in screenwriting). Instead, the fundamental differences between three-, four- and five-act structure might be presented in three lines:

Three-act structure: beginning, middle, end.
Four-act structure: beginning, middle, late middle, end.
Five-act structure: beginning, early middle, middle, pre-ending, end.

Why not? Each form as described above has the same basic shape – or flow, or pattern, or arrangement. Any one of them might suit your own play, depending on how the action is spread out, and where the peaks and troughs fall. If you want to immerse yourself in classical structure, there is plenty of literature you can refer to. The act-based play started off as an analytical tool for the Greeks, to better understand the blossoming of their new cultural form. It was then refined and developed by writers in the Roman period, and was subsequently adopted by our most famous playwright. But Shakespeare didn't originally write his plays in this form – the structure was imposed on the texts by dramatist Nicholas Rowe when he edited the collected plays in the early eighteenth century. So our greatest dramatist may have been something of a freestyler.

Many modern writers don't bother with acts, and just use scenes to build their plays. Others use the act as the organising unit of action and dispense with scene breaks. Jez Butterworth's *The Ferryman* contains a prologue and four acts. There are no scene breaks within those acts; each presents continuous action and lasts well over thirty minutes. So, if grouping scenes or blocks of action into acts helps you understand the shape of your narrative, then go ahead – but know that there's no arcane secret knowledge hidden in these formal terms – they are just devices to help you organise your story.

TWO-ACT STRUCTURE

The two-act play is probably the most common form that you'll see on a modern stage – but it isn't necessarily following a theoretical structural model, and is often a different kind of organisational 'act' to the ones I've already talked about. Most of the time, Acts One and Two just refer to the two halves of a play, separated by an interval. If your play is anything much over ninety minutes, you'll probably need an interval, and using two acts might be the simplest way to shape your story. One of the most useful pieces of advice I ever got from a dramaturg/director early on (Purni Morell, who at that time was Director of the National Theatre Studio) was this: when the curtain comes down at the interval (if there is one) you want to make sure that the audience want to come back after their glass of wine. Especially if the seats are hard, the temperature uncomfortable, or *Bake Off* is on TV that night. So it might help to bisect your story at a point of high tension or suspense; otherwise known as a cliffhanger, or 'leave them wanting more'. This doesn't have to be a life-or-death moment – it can simply be a moment of emotional magnitude for your characters, or a crossroads, or a hotting-up of the action. It's pretty blindingly obvious now, but it was the first time I had properly thought about the *audience experience* of my play.

Some plays *do* use two-act structure in a more dramatic and/or thematic way. *The Wonderful World of Dissocia* by Anthony Neilson is a play of two very different halves. The first is set entirely in a strange and wonderful Alice-in-Wonderland type of landscape, in which Lisa, the heroine, goes on a quest to recapture a lost hour of her life. Act One ends with a moment of realisation for Lisa – and the audience – that she's not in Dissocia at all, but actually at home in her own kitchen, making a holy mess. We've just experienced an hour in her colourful, dissociative imagination. The second act opens in a stark, clinical room in a psychiatric hospital. Here, we watch Lisa recover from her episode and struggle with her condition in painful, boring, real time. Neilson really maximises his two halves here to create texture, meaning and contrast between beautiful, full-blown fantasy and painful, bland reality.

Of course, there are three- and four- and five-act plays which are also presented to their audience in two halves – with an interval in the middle. They may have two, three, four or five acts *as written*, but the staging requirement means a play in two halves *as staged*. (Cue more moaning and gnashing of teeth from mystified playwrights who want to know what's the point of having three movements presented as two halves.)

Let's look at Joe Penhall's *Blue/Orange* to illustrate this. First, a quick reminder of the basic story, which is told in three acts.

➔ In Act One, a young, white, male doctor named Bruce, expresses concerns about his patient Christopher, a young black man. Bruce believes Christopher is not ready to be released from hospital because he is experiencing delusional episodes. He explains this to his superior, senior consultant Robert, also white, who disagrees.

➔ In Act Two, Robert presents his own research to Bruce about mental illness in young black men, and his belief that the white scientific medical establishment is too quick to impose its ideology on its patients. Bruce questions Robert's motives in releasing Christopher from hospital, believing Robert is using Christopher to advance and legitimise his research and reputation.

→ In Act Three, these two conflicting beliefs go head to head, causing a major crisis. Christopher starts to display increasingly irrational behaviour and the two doctors try to take each other down. Robert encourages Christopher to file a complaint against Bruce, which he does. Bruce in turn announces he will file one against Robert.

The key dramatic questions of the play, as relating to plot outcome, are: will Christopher be released from the hospital, and is it the *right* decision? The thematic questions are a little more complex (as they should be). Whose version of medicine will triumph, and which doctor – junior Bruce or senior Robert – stands to gain the most? Penhall uses a three-act structure to present the two competing sets of beliefs about Christopher.

We could say that the play uses a dialectical structure.* Act One of *Blue/ Orange* presents a thesis by Bruce; Act Two an antithesis by Robert; and Act Three is a synthesis of both theses, from which, in this case, there is no clear victor, but from which a bigger professional and personal battle will arise.

Each time I've seen the play, the interval has come between Acts Two and Three. The curtain comes down – or the blackout happens – at the highest point of tension so far – and the audience goes away to chat at the bar and wonder whose diagnosis will play out, and whether or not Christopher will be released. The practical reason for the cut is that, at over two hours long, the audience will need a break somewhere in the middle. So the action, which takes place in three parts, is dissected in the middle by an interval. The play is presented in two halves, but its storytelling is arranged in three. The point of all this is to show you that structure has a function in both the writing of the play, and its performance. But your job is to worry about the first one. Of course, it can be helpful to think about where you want an interval to fall, if that helps you conceive of the play's energy flow, but it may well be that a director will decide to break the action elsewhere.

STRUCTURE THROUGH INSTINCT

So is our notion of beginning, middle and end merely the result of a few wise men's genius that nobody has managed to better yet? I think it's more

---

* In classical philosophy a dialectic (from the Greek: 'related to dialogue') is a debate between two people who present their principal arguments and counter-arguments until a solution combining both sets of assertions is reached, or one is refuted entirely. The concept was developed further by nineteenth-century German philosophers Georg Hegel and Heinrich Moritz Chalybäus, who identified the three key stages of dialectical development as thesis, anti-thesis and synthesis.

complex than that. Human life is inherently shaped into parts. Childhood, youth, middle-age, old-age. Birth, growth, death. The four seasons. The duality of night and day. The earliest known artworks by prehistoric man, the cave paintings, recorded key events: a harvest, a good hunt, a natural disaster. We seem programmed to look for patterns, shapes and rhythms in our experience of being alive. This isn't to downplay the amount of craft that is required to find the right structure for your play, but rather, as always, to remind you that writers must also follow their instincts.

When I asked Sebastian Born, who was Associate Director (Literary) at the National Theatre between 2007 and 2017, to talk about his understanding of dramatic structure, he drew some fascinating parallels between drama and mathematics, having studied the latter before he began working in the theatre.

> Mathematics, on one level, is about looking for shapes and patterns that occur in and between numbers. There's a certain elegance to the famous mathematical equations – a harmony that's aesthetically pleasing. And it's the same with plays. When you read a lot of plays, as I have, it becomes one of the first things you identify – a sense of the play's underlying structure (or lack of). Something in us seems to recognise and appreciate elegant, well-made structural patterns and forms, whether or not they are classical structures, or subversions of traditional ones. This sense of recognition often happens below the level of conscious appreciation, but it happens nonetheless. Structure is really about interrelationships – between narrative, plot, characters – all the different elements that make up a play. The great plays are great because on some level they appeal to us beyond their content or theme or context – they leave us feeling complete. But that's a very elusive quality, and it's hard to separate a play's magnetic 'structural energy' out from its composite elements of form and content.

It might be abstract, but the idea of dramatic structure being about the organic web of connections between the different elements of a play is rather liberating, because it takes us out of the arena of rules and formula.

This web, in as much as it contains the playwright's ideas and values, also contains moral and philosophical meaning. In *A Raisin in the Sun*, Beneatha Younger discusses the thorny issue of 'progress' within the black community with her friend Asagai:

Don't you see there isn't any real progress... there is only one large circle that we march in, around and around, each of us with our own little picture in front of us, our own little mirage that we think is the future.

I've always thought that's a pretty good description of *Waiting for Godot*, Beckett's absurdist enquiry into the essential futility of trying to understand the human condition (discuss). But Asagai disagrees with her:

It isn't a circle – it is simply a long line... And because we cannot see the end – we also cannot see how it changes. And it is very odd but those who see the changes – who dream, who will not give up – are called idealists... and those who see only the circle, we call *them* the 'realists'!

Here, two very different world views are encapsulated in two different shapes. Whatever your natural inclinations as a dramatist – whether to comedy or tragedy, realism or expressionism, gallows humour or passionate social commentary – never underestimate the potential for your story's structure to contain and create meaning.

MYTH 4

Structure is necessarily dull, difficult and painful donkey work that can impart no possible joy to the writer.

Finding the right way to tell your story can be challenging. But the more you write, and the more confident you become about playing around with structure, the more creative you will find it. Eventually it will become fun (yes, really). The key is to stay flexible while you experiment. Many students become completely unhinged when we take their story apart in workshop and play around with different shapes or arrangements. Writers, cast adrift on the sea of endless story possibilities, need anchors. This might be the last scene or moment of the play, the inciting incident that kicks off the story, or a key character action that encapsulates the entire meaning of the play to you. Once you've dropped that anchor, it can seem painfully impossible to move. But sometimes, move it must. Many times, in workshop, the thing that the playwright is convinced is the final moment of the play, actually becomes the midpoint. Or the ending becomes the beginning. Or the second half of the play becomes the first half. Any significant moment or element of your play can be a pivot from which you can start creating your structure.

I also believe that it's always worth studying beautiful structures to get a sense of their magnetic structural energy, to use Sebastian Born's term. But these don't just have to be dramatic constructions. If you get stuck with a play, go and look, listen or touch something that feels harmonious and perfect. It might be a sculpture. A Mozart symphony. A beautiful building. And, at the other end of the spectrum, if perfect structures, classical or otherwise, instil you with a strong desire to smash them up, use that too. Interrogate those feelings and try to understand what your desire for a radical structure or shape or form means. Do you want to create anarchy or chaos or fragmentation with your play? Anything is possible. But *use* your instincts. Feel them. Think them. Then shape them.

CASE STUDY: *The Gentlemen's Tales* by Sean McEnaney

Sean, who was a member of my NT group, had a very clear thematic starting point for his play. As a gay man, he was intrigued by what he perceived as a disintegration of the gay and lesbian community, in an age when gay rights have been (largely) hard won and the AIDS crisis of the 1980s is a distant memory. He felt that many gay men and women believe the big social and political battles are over – and this troubled him. Wanting to understand just how long those battles had been raging, he began to research the history of the (British) criminalisation of homosexuality. He discovered that records only really begin after the Great Fire of London in 1666, which destroyed so many previous legal papers. This was the first thing that sparked his imagination. Here is Sean on the genesis of his play.

Up till that point (1666), the crime of sodomy was defined much more broadly to include several forms of sexual deviation by men and women, and social attitudes to it were more relaxed than in the eighteenth century, when the legal records show that there was a huge surge in prosecutions for sodomy and buggery. The punishments became barbarous – pillories, tortures and executions, based on biased trials and testimony. I looked at many different court cases from over the last three hundred years, and, unquestionably, homosexuality was the ultimate crime: 'the abominable vice that must not be named' was how one law book put it. At his trial in the nineteenth century, Oscar Wilde challenged all that when he was asked to

describe 'the love that dares not speak its name'.[5] Subsequently
the crime actually *had* a name, and homosexuals suddenly had
a specific identity and a commonality. After the First World War
there was another turning point, because people's values had
changed during the war, and liberalism took root in certain
parts of society, along with what would become the twentieth-
century ideal of masculinity. So I was marking all these sea
changes across history and thinking how important it was
to remind people that life was pretty tough as a gay man or a
lesbian woman until very recently.

I started by writing scenes set in some of these different eras
with various characters; just general incidents of conflict
between different gay men and their persecutors. But there
was no cohension to any of it; I realised I was writing a sort of
'homosexuality's greatest hits'. These random scenes felt more
like a lecture put on stage. But there was one character who
stood out from all this – a savage murderer with a price on his
head who takes refuge from the law in this tavern in London, as
the embers of the Great Fire burn around him. Knowing that if
he leaves the bar he'll be arrested and hanged, he masquerades
as a barkeep in this secret seventeenth-century gay pub. The
pub becomes both his refuge and his prison. So here, clearly,
was my protagonist.

I realised he needed an antagonist, who could only be a figure of
the Authority – the man capable of prosecuting him. It was this
blatant power struggle that I was interested in building a play
around. But I didn't have a structure yet, because I still didn't
really know what – or whose – story I was telling. I was trying
to figure out how to merge all of these ideas into a theatrical,
unified plot when I was asked in class what made up the 'spine'
of my story – and that shone a light on the whole thing. I realised
I didn't need a epic plot that was unified in both place *and* time
– the spine could be a single character and a single location. I
decided that it would be the same bartender in the same pub
across all these different eras I'd been researching. The play has
no scene changes and is told straight through from 1666 to the
present day, so he would be on stage the entire time, played by

the same actor, and in the same room. The Authority would also be a single character played by one actor to provide a continuity and a relationship; only his uniform would change, depending upon the period – from King's Man to warden to twentieth-century police officer.

Building the structure was about understanding the two parallel elements of the story, and how they could coexist and intertwine. There was the microcosm of each individual scene with its period characters, and the macrocosm of my three-century timespan and the overarching social battle of gay rights. I knew I wanted to dramatise the moral idea that nothing gives you worth except the quality of your choices. That's the great test of human civility, and it was the question I wanted to put to the audience – how much moral courage does it takes to confront hostile authority and stand up for people's rights? And this hardened criminal slowly realises that his own inaction is as great a crime as any, and comes to defend the men he previously despised and teaches them how to fight back.

So that was the skeleton, the framework on which everything hung, but the whole journey didn't have a destination; structurally it still had no resolution. As I wrote the first draft, I realised that the authority figure was also making a personal journey, parallel to the barkeep's, and it's in their final incarnations that they have their showdown. Again, thinking about the story 'spine', made me see that although throughout the play we know why the barkeep *can't* leave the bar/city, in the final moments of the play we learn that there's also a secret reason why he *doesn't* (something I'm loath to give away here before the play gets a production!). It took me by surprise but it gave the story a clear finishing point. The Authority (and the audience) becomes the barkeep's confidant, and we leave him standing alone in his pub, confronting the demolition of the building that's about to take place.

The early scenes I read of Sean's had real wit and verve. As you might imagine, given the social milieu of his setting, there was the opportunity for fun, banter and male posturing, but also for danger and violence. Sean had trained and worked as a theatre director, and it was no surprise that his scenes crackled with theatrical energy – but they didn't make a play yet. By recognising that any one of his composite elements (theme, character, place, time) could form the basis of his 'spine' – or become the centre of his 'web of connections' – he started to see how they could coalesce into a coherent theatrical experience. Sean really did grow his structure organically from his original unruly mass of research and personal intent, ending up with an episodic narrative based around a single location.* This allows the audience to feel the sweep of history, while remaining invested in one main character.

EXERCISES: FINDING STRUCTURE ORGANICALLY

Digging into these questions may throw up new ideas about the existing shape and form of your play and whether it best serves your story. Try to answer as many as you can – but use this list to come back to whenever you need help.

1. *Key event*

→ Is there an event or incident that has happened in the past, present or future, that directly affects the action of the play and the lives of your characters, and might determine its shape? A birth, a death, a marriage? A row, an alliance, a threat? An escape, an arrival, a reveal? A war, an earthquake, a political crisis?

→ When and where does this event take place in the linear chronology of the play? Before the play opens? Halfway through? Right at the end? Ten years ago? In the future as yet unlived by the character?

→ Does the event happen offstage or on stage?

→ In what order do you want to present the key events of your story?

Hamlet. Past (offstage) event: The King has been murdered. Opening

---

* Episodic structure refers to a series of different stories (or episodes) which happen over different time periods, usually linked by a central character, place and theme. TV soap opera is the classic episodic form. Theatrical examples include Moira Buffini's *Loveplay*, Caryl Churchill's *Love and Information*, and my own play *Second Person Narrative*.

onstage event: The King's ghost appears to his son and demands vengeance. Dramatic question: How will Hamlet get justice for his father?

hang by debbie tucker green. Past (offstage) event: A woman was brutally assaulted by an assailant. Opening onstage event: The woman arrives at the prison to tell the authorities what punishment she has chosen for him. Dramatic question: What punishment will the woman choose for him?

In the case of this particular play, debbie tucker green might have chosen a different structure, depending on what she wanted to show in the play. For example, she could have shown: Part One, the assault itself; Part Two, the trial; Part Three, the punishment. This could arguably have made a good play, but it seems to me that writer was most interested in her protagonist's choice about her assailant's punishment than the act of violence itself. So the event happens offstage and we learn about it as the action unfolds.

2. *Opposing poles or forces in you play*

→ Are there any existing oppositional forces at work in your story? Make a list of any sets of oppositions that occur in your play, in terms of character, event, theme, symbols or idea. Might these be used to create shape or form?

→ Is there change from one elemental force (emotional, behavioural, active, visual, thematic) to another in the play, creating narrative movement? On first go, this question might throw up obvious or clumsy sets of parallels, they might also help shape your material.

Hamlet. Madness versus sanity. Theatre versus real life. Thought versus action.

Jerusalem. Country versus city. Anarchy versus social convention. Paganism versus Christianity. Morality versus immorality.

The Effect. Male versus female. Science versus emotion. Sex versus love. Euphoria versus depression.

3. *Character hot spots*

Thinking about the escalation of your characters' goals and desires and the pressures put on them will help you get a sense of the peaks and troughs of your story.

→ When do your characters know what they want and need?

→ Where/when are the turning points in their quest?

→ Where/when does the tension or conflict increase?

→ Where/when do the stakes get higher?

→ Where/when do complications happen?

→ What key decisions do your characters make and when?

→ When do your characters experience internal/external change?

4. *Theatrical devices*

→ Is there a theatrical or formal device (or several) at the heart of your play which helps give shape to your story? For example, do you have a narrator? Does your play move between past and present? Is its story presented in fragments? Does it disrupt linear time?

→ How do these devices help create shape, flow of energy, narrative complexity or thematic meaning?

6

THE GREAT SWITCHEROO:
THE PLAYWRIGHT
VERSUS THE PLAY

THE GREAT SWITCHEROO:
THE PLAYWRIGHT VERSUS THE PLAY

Some of us begin chipping away at a play with a character or set of characters in mind, using him/her/them as the chisel with which we shape our story. Others write from a more abstract intellectual, moral or political enquiry. This chapter is about the interplay – and sometimes the conflict – between the playwright's ideas and the story that the *play* is yearning to tell. It's about (playfully) turning your play's house upside down – just to see what happens – using the binary forms of classical comedy and tragedy as your tools.

I had some interesting conversations with Richard Bean when he was writing his play *The Heretic*, which was staged at the Royal Court in 2011. The play is about a controversial scientist, Dr Diane Cassell, whose recent study on stable sea levels directly challenges her university's more conformist, pessimistic stance on global warming, by suggesting it is far less extreme than popularly believed. When she publishes her study against the university's interests, she is fired. Meanwhile, Diane's naive environmentalist research student Ben falls in love with her twenty-one-year-old daughter Phoebe, who suffers from anorexia. Diane also receives death threats from Green activists called the Sacred Earth Militia, who consider her scientific position to be dangerous and heretical.

Diane retreats to her country home, where Ben and Phoebe consummate their relationship. Diane is increasingly worried about Phoebe's emotional fragility, as she's already threatened to kill herself if she ever got pregnant. As Diane tells Ben: *'I would rather have her alive than everybody in Bangladesh, or Tuvalu, or Suffolk. And every glacier in the world, and every coral reef, and every single last bloody polar bear can die, drown, melt, go impossibly acidic and fall to pieces and I honestly wouldn't care, as long as I've still got her.'* But Phoebe is angry with her mother's insistent need to prove the world wrong.

Diane, with help from colleague Kevin, eventually discovers that the university has manipulated its own research results on climate change in order to stay in line with the dominant academic position, and is offered her job back. At the climax of the play, the campus security manager, Geoff, tries to kidnap Diane at her home; we learn he is from the Sacred Earth Militia. But when Phoebe has a heart attack brought on by a row with her mother over her desire to go and live with Ben, Geoff administers CPR and saves Phoebe. The play concludes eight months later, with Phoebe pregnant and about to marry Ben, and Diane practising her wedding speech, in which she acknowledges that human life, with all its irrational inconsistencies, is more important than dead matter.

However, when I read an early draft of *The Heretic*, the play's ending was almost the polar opposite. Phoebe had her heart attack, but it killed her. Diane regained her academic reputation and her scientific propositions were proved right – but her heart was broken. I was troubled by this ending. It just didn't feel right. It wasn't about the change in tone; Richard's particular gift as a playwright is his ability to deliver serious ideas and social/political propositions while providing belly laughs. It was because Phoebe's death didn't feel *earned* within the dramatic and emotional logic of the play (like Billy's death in Viv's first draft of *The Bevin Boys*).

If the core dramatic journey of the play is Diane's quest for truth, then, in the version with the tragic ending, it seems to require the ultimate punishment – the loss of her child, who is more important to her than anything. Phoebe's death occurred during a battle with her mother about Diane's obsessive desire to expose intellectual hypocrisy. If we look at this in the context of classical tragedy, Diane's flaw is what kills Phoebe. And this seemed to somehow run counter to the point of the play, which was to show how an established scientific ideology might cause a contrarian truthsayer to be outcast as a heretic – not unlike John Proctor's role in Miller's play *The Crucible*.

Richard had written the play from a strong desire to dramatise what happens when intellectual integrity (in this case Diane's) is suppressed for the sake of political correctness or ideological conformity. The *intellectual* catastrophe he was warning his audience about took the form of a young girl's death, as a sort of cosmic punishment for his protagonist's temerity to voice 'truth'. In doing so, he was making a political point about the danger of pandering to popular wisdom, but it derailed the play's dramatic momentum.

I wondered if the play would be better served by an ending that allowed it to conclude the battle of 'knowledge versus ideology', but which also allowed Diane to complete her character journey more satisfactorily. Her scientific 'truth' does win, but she also needs to be able to let go of her own fears and to stop controlling Phoebe, who is a living, breathing person, not a set of ideas. By allowing Phoebe a sense of agency at the end of the play by finding happiness with Ben, Diane is also able to grow. These ideas chimed with Richard, who incorporated some of them into further drafts, ultimately reversing his original ending.

TRAGEDY VERSUS COMEDY

I want to take a moment to reframe the ideas behind Richard's subsequent key story change by looking more closely at the classical binary dramatic forms of tragedy and comedy. Here's a brief breakdown of both forms, in terms of the classical protagonist, according to Canadian academic Ian Johnston:

> The tragic hero characteristically sets out to deal with a conflict by himself or at least entirely on his own terms, and as things start to get more complicated, generally the tragic figure will simply redouble his efforts, increasingly persuaded that he can deal with what is happening only on his own. In that sense, tragic heroes are passionately egocentric and unwilling to compromise their powerful sense of their own identity in the face of unwelcome facts. They will not let themselves answer to any communal system of value; they answer only to themselves. Lear would sooner face the storm on the heath than compromise his sense of being horribly wronged by his daughters; Macbeth wills himself to more killings as the only means to resolve the psychological torment he feels. There is something passionately uncompromising about their obsessive egoism which will only accept life on their own terms – in a sense they are radically unsociable beings (although they may occupy, and in Shakespeare almost always do occupy, important social positions).

> But in a comedy the main characters will have the ability to adjust, to learn, to come up with the resources necessary to meet the challenges they face. They may also have a great deal of luck. But one way and another, they persevere and the conflict is resolved happily with the reintegration of the characters into a shared

community. Often an important point in the comedy is the way in which the main characters have to learn some important things about life (especially about themselves) before being able to resolve the conflict. The comic confusion will often force the individual to encounter things he or she has taken for granted, and dealing with these may well test many different resources (above all faith, flexibility, perseverance, and trust in other people). But through a final acknowledgement (earned or learned) of the importance of human interrelationships, a social harmony will be restored (commonly symbolised by a new betrothal, a reconciliation between parents, a family reunion, and so on), and a group celebration (feast, dance, procession) will endorse that New Harmony.[6]

Following this definition, Richard initially conceived of his play as a tragedy, but ultimately reversed this in later drafts by giving the play an ending that was redemptive and hopeful. In other words, a 'great switcheroo' – a total reversal or change of tack – took place. I've taken this name from a short story by Roald Dahl (which is actually about the antiquated phenomenon known as 'wife swapping', but try to see past that).

Using the Great Switcheroo enabled Richard to both celebrate Diane's dogged determination to expose the hypocrisy of institutionalised scientific wisdom and force her to reconnect with what is truly important to her. With his permission I have relayed this particular element of the play's development here to show that it's not just beginners who have to wrestle with their plays in this way, but even those playwrights at the top of their game. Richard's work paid off in the end; in 2012 *The Heretic* was joint winner of the Evening Standard Award for Best New Play along with his concurrent hit *One Man, Two Guvnors*.

I've seen the Great Switcheroo take place countless times over my years of working with novice writers on their plays, too. Interestingly, the 'switch' has always been from a tragic to a comic resolution, following Johnston's definition. So why does the phenomenon happen so often? And why not the other way round?

THE WRITER'S CONSCIENCE

I think it comes down to honourable but sometimes misplaced intentions, stemming from a sense of moral injustice, coupled with a contemporary desire to shy away from reductive and simplistic storytelling. The Greek audiences of antiquity were prepared to sit on stone benches and endure three hours of despair, witnessing murder, rape, burial alive or incest, because the Greek tragedies were meant to impart specific civic lessons to those audiences. This dominant theatrical form continued well into the twentieth century with tragedies by the likes of Arthur Miller, Tennessee Williams, Eugene O'Neill, Federico García Lorca and Lorraine Hansberry, among others. While we still respond instinctively to a great love story, or an epic 'goodies versus baddies' showdown, although many contemporary plays have *tragic* endings (including some of those already mentioned such as *The Father, Jerusalem* and *The Ferryman*), the classically tragic protagonist with the requisite fatal flaw is uncommon.

This doesn't mean for one minute that we contemporary writers are more frivolous by nature, or that we don't feel every bit as passionate about the darker sides of human nature as Sophocles did about his hero Oedipus, or Shakespeare about Macbeth. Student play topics in my last playwriting class included: the failing secondary-school system, written by a teacher with twenty years' experience working in state schools; the corruption of 'big pharma' companies who manipulate medical test results to increase financial output; the maddening bureaucracy of the social-care system for foster children; and gay rights in 1970s Sydney. Each playwright had a strong desire to tell the audience a story inspired by their own strong moral, political and philosophical beliefs. Their protagonists weren't tragic in the classic sense, but they were all the *victims* of powerful forces and their figureheads – aggressive states, economies, political regimes, and so on. However, while the desire to 'tell it like it is' is laudable, the developing writer can sometimes allow their sense of injustice about a particular topic to lead them down the wrong story path.

Here's an example from a playwright who attended my National Theatre class and who faced the same challenges.

CASE STUDY: *HIPPOLYTA'S HANDMAIDEN* BY LUCY FLANNERY

Lucy's play was based on the story of a minor character in Shakespeare's comedy *A Midsummer Night's Dream*. In Shakespeare's play, Hippolyta is Queen of the Amazons, and has recently been defeated in war by Theseus, the Duke of Athens. As part of his 'win' he will take Hippolyta as his bride. As Theseus tells her, '*I wooed you with my sword and won thy love doing thee injuries.*' Hippolyta has no choice in this marriage but seems to have no problem with it – she rather passively accepts her lot, even though this goes against the grain of her former role as a powerful woman warrior. Their wedding takes place offstage and isn't a central plot point in the *Dream*. Hippolyta and Theseus have a dramatic function in the play that is more to do with mirroring the power games between Oberon and Titania. (Titania isn't exactly a major character in the play either, but functions as part of the framing device of the 'play within the play'.)

Lucy's imagination was snared by Hippolyta, and she started devising a story around her. Here is Lucy on the genesis of the play:

> I became obsessed with Hippolyta when I directed an all-female version of *A Midsummer Night's Dream*. She's not the most sympathetic character to modern audiences – she's obsessed with status and hierarchy – but it's impossible not to feel for her terrible situation: a queen regent, a warrior, forced into the role of trophy wife in a stifling patriarchal regime. Intriguingly, she's the only member of the court to believe the lovers' tale; perhaps she was in the forest herself, I wondered – and, of course, once you have those kinds of thoughts you have no option but to run with them.

> Initially I conceived of this story as a tragedy. How could it be anything else? The handmaiden was a device, the confidante Hippolyta needed so the audience could access her desperation, her plotting. I called the servant Emilia as this is a recognisably Shakespearean name and also the name of the sister of another Hippolyta in *The Two Noble Kinsmen*.

> My original story had Hippolyta going to the forest to kill herself but being persuaded by Oberon, her former lover, to use the 'purple flower' so that life with Theseus would be bearable. She decides it would undermine her honour and integrity to take this easy way out, so at the end of the play Emilia administers the love potion secretly and mourns her lost mistress when Hippolyta, the Amazon Queen, besotted with the Athenian Duke, effectively turns into a Stepford Wife.

The draft that Lucy brought to my NT workshop ended in tragedy: although Hippolyta avoids suicide, she still effectively 'dies' in order to escape the dreadful reality of her arranged marriage. Her handmaiden Emilia brings about this living death as an act of duty and love. When we read Lucy's excerpt and looked at her outline, it became apparent that her laudable desire to take this footnote of a character and flesh out her tragedy for a modern audience, just wasn't quite working. Given that the source material is a classical comedy in its truest sense, it was interesting to consider whether or not Hippolyta's story could be said to be a true tragedy, according to Ian Johnston's definition. And it couldn't.

In the classical tragic tradition, the character must have a fatal flaw, which propels the drama. True tragedy is rooted in character weakness, such as ambition or immoral desire, and which eventually brings about the downfall of the protagonist, and the personal and/or political catharsis. But Lucy's main character had none. The fatal flaw was in the *society* that oppressed her. We discussed the relationship between Lucy's intentions to create a political feminist message with her play, and the essential ingredients – male domination, self-sacrifice and female friendship. Was her deeply political intention as a writer squashing the story? What if she turned everything around, and instead of ending the play with a tragic suicide, it ended with a liberation that allowed both Hippolyta and her handmaiden to survive – and triumph?

I asked Lucy to consider a Great Switcheroo, just to see what happened. Right away, the story started to sing. Lucy concluded:

It's hard to believe now that I thought tragedy was the right way to tell the story; I was so focused on the awful things happening to Hippolyta and what I saw as the modern parallels that I completely lost sight of how inappropriate this was as a companion piece to one of the best-loved comedies of all time. At the NT session, the scales fell from my eyes; of course *Hippolyta's Handmaiden* should be a comedy!

A chance remark led to a second epiphany: a fellow course member commented that, given the title, he expected the handmaiden to be more proactive. I realised that I'd failed to exploit a rich comic seam – the cunning, resourceful servant is such a well-known and recognisable trope. In the final version of the play, Emilia is the driving force that creates the comic havoc, mirroring in part the function of Puck in *A Midsummer Night's Dream*.

The finished play mimics the structure of the *Dream*; after a dark beginning (Egeus calling for his daughter's blood and Hippolyta contemplating suicide) it escalates into farce, with the magic flower being used for everything but the intended purpose and all the wrong people falling in love, before a final, joyful resolution in which Hippolyta can contemplate a future with a partner she genuinely respects and admires. Ironically, all the points that I wanted to make in the original treatment are still present in the final version but presented with a lightness of touch that makes the subject matter far more compelling. The new form also provided an interesting subtheme on tyranny and democracy which certainly enriched the drama.

What was wonderful about Lucy's Great Switcheroo is that she ended up with a far more powerful piece of writing. Her play, which started out as a dark study of the tragedy of female oppression, became a joyous, funny celebration of female strength in adversity. This conveyed her message just the same, but in a way that honoured the characters.

A NOTE ON GENDERED STORY FORMS

Certain feminist theorists have written about the fact that tragedy has historically been considered the province of male stories, and comedy of women's. In my experience with writers, it's actually the opposite – and as a result, the Great Switcheroo tends to happen in women's writing more frequently than men's. I think this is because for many of the female writers I've worked with – I include myself here – there is a strong drive to express the experience of gender inequality. This leads some writers to chisel out overtly political plays that are rooted in their own feelings of anger, frustration and disappointment.

This is further compounded by the fact that traditional narrative shapes and forms don't always easily act as vehicles for modern human experiences. Some of you may have heard of Joseph Campbell, an American literature professor who wrote a book called *The Hero with a Thousand Faces* in 1949. Campbell created the concept of the 'Hero's Journey' to describe the adventures of the archetypal hero – a 'monomyth' based on his analysis of existing dominant mythologies from around the world (including Shakespeare), and drawing on Jungian psychology. (Carl Jung was the founder of analytical psychology, which was in some ways a response to Freud's earlier theories of psychoanalysis.)

The concept of the Hero's Journey has become used as a kind of roadmap for storytelling, particularly within Hollywood genre screenwriting. *Star Wars* is often cited as the classic monomyth story, featuring an active hero who must fight both external and internal forces to achieve self- and world mastery. Campbell describes the journey thus:

> A hero ventures forth from the world of common day into a region of supernatural wonder: fabulous forces are there encountered and a decisive victory is won: the hero comes back from this mysterious adventure with the power to bestow boons on his fellow man.[7]

In 1981, writer and therapist Maureen Murdock interviewed Campbell, wanting to know more about the role of women in his model, which she felt was somewhat unexplored.

> I was surprised when he responded that women don't need to make the journey. 'In the whole mythological tradition, the woman is there. *All she has to do is to realise that she's the place that people are trying to get to.* When a woman realises what her wonderful character is, she's not going to get messed up with the notion of being pseudo-male. [8] (*My italics.*)

Clearly Joseph Campbell never spent much time hanging out with female playwrights, which is just as well, or he might have suffered substantial injuries.

Murdock's response was to use her own therapeutic work with female clients to devise an alternative map, the Heroine's Journey, as a new model for the female narrative quest. For her, this was less about integrating female nature into the patriarchal model found in Campbell's studied myths, and more about integrating masculine *and* feminine aspects to create psychological wholeness. As you might expect, this meant a greater focus on the more inner journey, and less emphasis on a linear narrative trajectory. The female journey, Murdock argued, *meanders*. It is messy and non-linear, reflecting, for her, the chaos of the female body and the female nature fractured by patriarchy. This might, of course, extend to other key aspects of human identity that have traditionally been excluded from the dominant colonial male narrative, including racial/ethnic and sexual identity.

BEYOND THE BINARY

As a structure geek, I find this fascinating. It demonstrates not only how much our storytelling forms reflect our deep human experiences – but also how limiting some of the traditional forms might be. In our brave new world, where we endure a daily tsunami of narratives on social media, and where fake news has become the new normal, our personal and collective identities are shifting in seismic ways. This is giving rise to some difficult but important political and cultural conversations – about 'trans' identities, personal fluidity, intersectionality. It's no surprise that we are seeing these shifts reflected and deconstructed on our stages.

Interestingly, it's actually in television, traditionally the most conventional dramatic medium, where some of the greatest innovation in narrative form and style is being used to reflect this chaos and fragmentation of self. Series like Donald Glover's *Atlanta*, Lucy Prebble's *I Hate Suzie* and Michaela Coel's *I May Destroy You* all have used inherently theatrical tropes such as direct 'to camera' address, non-linear storytelling and musical sequences to dramatise their characters' psychological and emotional disassociation as a result of trauma, along with a refusal to offer neat narrative resolutions. Coel, who started out in the theatre as a writer and actress, has talked about her own desire to challenge the dominant narrative tropes in drama, which are predominantly naturalistic, linear and Aristotelian in form – and which audiences have long been conditioned to expect.

So, although the classical binary dramatic forms may feel limiting and old-fashioned to contemporary writers, they are worth studying – firstly to help us better understand our own narrative conditioning, and then to find new ways of telling stories that satisfy us both in their form *and* content. Ultimately it takes trial and error to find the best form for your story. Just always try to be aware of your intention to create meaning *in your own world as a cultural creator*; and balance that with your understanding of the meaning created by the play *in its own world as a piece of art,* governed by its own dramatic laws and philosophical cosmology.

EXERCISES: THE GREAT SWITCHEROO

If you're clear and happy about your intentions with your play and its overall meaning, you can skip this exercise – although it might be interesting just to see what happens. It might work best for those of you who are really stuck with some central aspect of your play – a character who won't do what you want (or do anything); a sense that your ending doesn't serve your story; a burning desire to write about a particular subject that still won't coagulate into a narrative; or just a general feeling that your play is a square peg that won't fit into a round hole.

→ In a sentence or two, try to articulate what you want to communicate with your play as a cultural creator. This doesn't have to be an overtly political idea – it might be to portray a certain kind of human experience, or to express a theme. What are your own feelings about what the play is about? What does your subject matter rouse in you – passion, anger, hope, optimism, sadness?

→ Take a key character (you can repeat this for any character in the play) and think about how they currently dramatise and externalise your feelings or ideas. Is your desire to 'say something', or to make the audience feel a certain way, burdening the character? Might they actually want to behave in a different way in the story, but are constrained by your authorial desires?

→ Reimagine your character as the protagonist of a classic tragedy. This may mean changing them formulaically into an archetype and probably erasing much of their complexity for now, as well as altering the ingredients of your play – but it's just an exercise!

→ Think particularly about the character in terms of Ian Johnston's definition of someone with an 'unwillingness to compromise their sense of their own identity in the face of unwelcome facts'. Who or what are they railing against in your play? What communal system of value are they fighting against? What overarching goal is driving them to act? What flaws or weaknesses do they have that eventually prove to be their downfall? And what is lost (or gained) for their community as a direct result of their actions? Write a paragraph outlining the basic action of your tragic version.

→ How does this tragic reimagining sit with you in your gut? Does it throw up any questions about the nature of your play as it stands? Does it allow you to distinguish between the *internal* forces and the *external* forces that cause your character to act?

→ Put this to one side, and now go through the same steps, but this time, reimagine your key character as a comic protagonist. Again using Johnston's definition, think about how they learn to adjust in the face of challenges, and what they ultimately learn about themselves over the course of the play. Is 'the conflict resolved happily with the reintegration of the characters into a shared community'? How is social harmony restored at the end, and what form does that take? ('A new betrothal, a reconciliation between parents, a family reunion, a group celebration.') Write a paragraph outlining the basic action of your comic version.

→ Remember to be playful. This is all intended to remove the current 'givens' in your story and to temporarily push it off balance. Does your story naturally lean more towards one form than the other? Does this exercise allow you to separate what you want the *audience* to feel from what your *characters* currently feel or do? Try to be mindful of the emotional logic at the heart of the play... and allow it to follow its natural course.

7
HOW TO
WRITE A SCENE

HOW TO WRITE A SCENE

I'll open with an optimistic provocation: if you can learn how to write a good scene, you can learn how to write a good play. Plays are, after all, made up of scenes – those units of action that form the story spine, vertebra by vertebra. As regular television and film watchers, we are all familiar with scenic storytelling, and play scenes share many of the same basic elements. But films primarily reveal their meaning through visual storytelling, rather than through spoken dialogue. A film scene's information is also conveyed by camera angles, lighting, shot set-ups, musical underscore, and so on. (Remember the scene from *Psycho* as described in Chapter One.) In contrast, as a theatre audience we watch a mostly fixed space through which characters enter and exit, in which words are spoken and behaviour unfolds. Alongside a play's language and visuals, the shape and structure of its scenes are also key carriers of information both literal and symbolic.

WHAT IS A SCENE AND WHY DO WE NEED THEM?

For clarity I'm going to propose that we define a scene overall as *a unit of dramatic action*. The *unit* part of that term is easy to grasp. That is, a section, or chunk, or nugget of your play, which contributes to your overall narrative. In most cases, a good scene has a clear beginning, middle and end, and will stand alone as a complete part of the story. So far, so simple.

A dramatic unit usually involves a single and specific place and time. This might be a smoky kitchen at dawn in rural Northern Ireland; the hallway of a cramped flat in London's Zone 4; an economy aeroplane cabin en route from New York to China; a crater on the moon – whatever your story demands. Commonly, a dramatic scene usually employs what's known as *unity of time and place*; that is, events unfold in the specific place in linear time moving forwards (but not always) until the action of the scene is played out and the scene ends, necessitating a change of setting, an acceleration of time, and/or a new set of circumstances for the characters. Scene by scene, location by location, hour by day by year, the story evolves.

WHAT IS DRAMATIC ACTION?

New playwrights often start to sweat whenever they hear this phrase. *Dramatic action* is an unfortunate term, really, as the words themselves conjure up exactly the sort of overblown and melodramatic action that we usually want to avoid on stage. If you stopped an average somebody in the street and asked them to give you an example of a dramatic action, you might hear; 'Throwing a dog out of a window'; 'Blowing up a car'; 'Murdering my ex-wife's new husband'. Dramatic, yes; unexpected, surely; but unhelpful for our purposes. In fact the basic human action of many plays is far more subtle, complex and ambiguous than this. To complicate things further, there seem to be various definitions of the term used by theatre practitioners, academics, acting coaches, and so on. I've heard dramatic action defined as 'Anything that happens on stage that creates conflict and tension', and 'Character intention', as well as 'Something a character does to another character that has a clear outcome'.

Those definitions are all true, but for me, the simplest way to think about a dramatic action is something that has *direct consequences* in the story. When any action taken by a character has a clear cause and a clear effect, however small it is, it has the potential, like the proverbial rolling snowball, to create an avalanche. A story gains velocity and momentum when characters are forced to act and react, act and react, act and react. In this way, a good scene will contribute to the story's unfolding plot logic as well as the emotional logic of the characters' behaviour as witnessed by the audience. Only through containing some sort of catalyst for further action will a scene truly earn its place in the play.

One way to get your head around this is to think of a series of scenes like a series of links in a chain. Each link is connected to the next – together they form a strong and unbreakable length of narrative. The best question you can ask of a scene once written, is: if you took it out of your play, would the play narrative fall apart? If the answer is yes, you know that your scene contains some crucial aspect of dramatic action that is necessary to move your story on. If the answer is no, then it probably needs more work – or perhaps even to be cut altogether.

Beginning writers, gripped with fervour for their characters, themes and ideas, will tend to write scenes that, despite plenty of energy, wit and imagination, fall flat because they are dramatically empty. If you've ever written and rewritten a scene twenty times over and still not been satisfied, it's probably because there's nothing in the scene *that the story depends on.* You may have textbook conflict or clash of wills between two characters with strong feelings. But this still isn't enough. Something may seem to be inherently dramatic – let's say, a jilted husband's murderous rage. You may decide to build a scene around that emotion. It might be a scene full of cursing and breast-beating. But unless something happens in that scene that has the potential to dramatically affect a future scene and the future action of your characters, then it's not really earning its place. Each scene should act as a stone thrown into a pool, causing ripples that spread outwards until the edges of the story have been reached. (To clarify: I'm talking about more traditional forms of storytelling here. Other kinds of experimental, less narrative-driven stage writing won't – nor should – necessarily fit these guidelines so easily.)

HOW TO BEGIN CONSTRUCTING A SCENE

Let's start with the basics. Before you start writing a scene you will need some key ingredients and, if not a detailed recipe for those ingredients, a set of questions you want to answer. Let's call them the Who (characters), the Where (specific location), the When (specific time), the What (plot/ events), and the Why (dramatic/artistic necessity to the play as a whole). You'll need to know something about *who* the characters are that you're interested in (and why you are interested in them), *when* and *where* the scene is set. Then you'll also need to know roughly *what* happens in the scene, as the unit of action in the play as a whole, and *why* it contributes to the play overall. What do you want to unlock in this scene? What key conflict, struggle or value is at stake here? What emotional dynamic is playing out? Why does the scene need to exist?

Below I've outlined some of the key elements of a good scene. Then we'll put the list together and apply it to a couple of published plays.

CHARACTER GOAL

As discussed in Chapter Three, what your characters want or need, whether they are aware of it or not, is one of the primary drives behind all good storytelling. As in the overarching narrative of your play, a goal and an obstacle to achieving that goal are usually at the heart of a dramatic (in the true sense) scene. So, as always, spend some time thinking about what your characters want in this unit of the play. Is it a short-term goal that might be resolved within this scene or unit? Or something that will pay off in a future scene? Is there another character working against them? And how conscious is your character of their desire, intention or need?

PLACE AND TIME

Where is your scene set? How will your setting help underpin your action? How would your characters' behaviour be affected in a different setting? We all act under different constraints in our bedrooms, in our offices, at a children's tea party, at a police station in an interview room. Consider the impact of your setting on the drama and character, and also think about how it is theatrical (or not).

EXPOSITION

Exposition simply means an assembly of information that the audience needs to understand what's going on at any given moment. One of the great challenges for the playwright is how to disguise their exposition in dialogue and action (and staging), so that the audience isn't overloaded with information. Exposition that carries backstory, which might help the audience to understand the present day story, is particularly hard to impart well – and one of the reasons why opening scenes in first drafts are stuffed full of it.

Writers often bombard the audience in the first five minutes of their play with exposition that they think is essential, but actually isn't. It often results in leaden, clunky writing:

> Do you remember before Mum died she gave me that valuable ring that was so precious to her? I've gone and lost it.

> Yes, I do, the one with the ruby that I was always jealous of because you were Mum's favourite which made childhood really difficult for me.

This might be a better use of exposition using the same ingredients:

Why are you in such a bad mood today?

I can't find the ring.

What ring?

You know what ring. *The* ring.

Oh, your heirloom.

A one-carat ruby hardly qualifies as an heirloom. And I didn't ask Mum to give it to me.

Funny how many things in life you got without having to ask.

The trick with exposition is to give the audience information with one hand and withhold it with the other. Conor McPherson has said that his greatest lesson as a playwright has been that the play must be one step ahead of the audience. In other words, we (the audience) need just enough exposition to be able to bed into the story, but we also need to want to know more. There will usually be questions left unanswered in each scene for both characters *and* audience, so that we have forward momentum as we move through the play.

USING TREASURE/OBJECTS OF VALUE IN A SCENE

Individual scenes can be constructed around smaller treasures, which might relate to a short-term goal, as we saw in Chapter Three. For example, in *Streetcar*, Scene Seven is built around a conflict between Stanley and Blanche over a long bath she's taking in the only bathroom. Today is her birthday and she is expecting a visit from her beau Mitch: we can hear her splashing happily and singing to herself offstage. Throughout the scene Stanley grows increasingly impatient with Blanche's selfish monopolisation of the space. Stanley wants his bathroom back, yes, but also his apartment, and his wife Stella – all have been overtaken by Blanche.

The scene also contains a far more important dramatic action. Stanley has found out that Blanche is not the virginal Southern Belle she has previously claimed to be, but was sacked from her teaching job for having an affair with a young pupil. Stanley reveals to Stella in the scene that he has just shared all of this with Mitch, effectively ruining Blanche's chances of marriage to a decent man. We could say that Blanche's reputation is another treasure in the play overall, and in this scene. As she soaks in the tub, the idealised self that she has worked so hard to project is torn down by Stanley. Williams uses the surface, concrete 'treasure' of the bath/ bathroom to create a counterpoint to this other, more significant 'treasure' of Blanche's reputation. This gives texture, tension and metaphorical life to the scene.

ACTION VERSUS ACTIVITY

I find this another very useful distinction to help understand how to build a scene. If dramatic *action* is the real stuff of the scene, then the *activity* undertaken by characters in the scene is the ornamentation. But don't underestimate its value. Characters will always need something to do on stage – nobody wants to watch a play in which characters just sit around on chairs, talking (Beckett fans – there are always exceptions – and the talking itself is always active). Creating activities can help underpin themes, show character, and provide a context for dramatic action, just as described above in the *Streetcar* scene, in which Blanche bathes while Stella decorates the table for Blanche's birthday supper.

Jez Butterworth's *The Ferryman* opens (after a short prologue in a separate location) in a kitchen where a man and a woman are hanging out together. It's almost dawn. Quinn and Caitlin have clearly been up all night drinking whiskey, smoking, and enjoying each other's company. They play a crazy game of Connect 4. A lampshade catches fire and is extinguished. These seemingly inconsequential activities allow us to understand that this is an intimate friendship between two people who are very comfortable together. So far, the scene's function has been to establish context and relationships. And then things take a step forward when they dance blindfolded. Quinn takes his blindfold off and watches Caitlin dancing alone, completely possessed by the music and impervious to his scrutiny. In that moment we understand (without any dialogue) that he longs for her – and so the story is moved on. It will move on again when we find out that they're not man and wife; in fact Quinn is married, and Caitlin is his sister-in-law.

ARRIVE LATE

The classic wisdom, which holds pretty true in my opinion, is: 'Get into the action as late as possible and get out as early as possible.' In other words, cut to the chase, and don't hang around. For example, as a general note, I would try to avoid obvious signifiers of arrival. The doorbell ringing, the phone ringing, the knock at the door. While you might think this creates a sense of anticipation in the audience – and it may – it usually also involves the tempting opportunity for heavy-handed exposition. 'Hello John, well this is unexpected, it's past midnight, anyway, let me take your coat' is probably a less interesting opening line than a grumpy: 'Do you know what time it is?' Audiences invariably need less information than we think – they just want to get into the story, and if you postpone too long, you might lose them.

Think about the energy of your opening. What atmosphere do you want to drop us into the middle of? A strained silence in a boardroom? A dance of unrequited love? A pre-confession, declaration, argument? David Harrower's play *Presence* opens with three young men rushing into a dormitory and fighting over the beds. The men happen to be Beatles George, Paul and Ringo, who are living in squalid digs in Hamburg for their first band residency. It's a simple activity but it creates a visceral sense of the youthful energy, hijinks and competition that will form the dramatic tension in the play.

LEAVE EARLY

Finding a way to end a scene is notoriously hard, far more so than making a good beginning. First draft scenes often fizzle out, or end up trapped in meandering dialogue. Unfortunately the only real answer to the question 'How do I end my scene?' is: 'When the action has played out and the energy of the scene is spent.' Will you introduce a new piece of information or a decisive action by a particular character at the scene's climax that moves the story on? Will a character problem or desire become resolved or thwarted, necessitating a new course of action, or a retaliation in a new scene? Has the scene escalated your characters' problems and desires? Once you know how the action plays out, think about how might you put a 'button' on the scene – as you might button the top of your shirt – to help show the audience that the scene is now closed. More often than not this is achieved with a line of dialogue but it might also be a physical action. For example, Scene One of *Streetcar* ends with Blanche leaping up, about to be sick after one too many sips of Stanley's whiskey. A taste of what's to come, perhaps.

SCENE TRANSITIONS

Transitions in theatre and onscreen transitions have notable differences in their technical presentation. When we're watching a film, the scenes are cut or edited together using a variety of techniques; read a shooting film script and you'll often see screen directions such as: *jump cut to; fade in; fade out; montage*. While we are, of course, aware that we've just jumped from '*Interior. Bedroom. Morning*', to '*Exterior. Cliff top. Night*', when we watch a film, we are usually too busy joining the dots in the narrative and anticipating what will happen next to consciously think about the transition.

Now think about the relationship between two scenes on a stage. How do we know the action has moved on? We may get a quick blackout to signal the end of the scene, and then lights up again on a changed set. At the other end of the spectrum we may get a scene change that lasts three minutes and is an entertainment in its own right. *One Man, Two Guvnors* featured songs performed by different cast members in front of the curtain as the scenery was changed. Either way, you as the playwright have to create clear and strong points of entry and points of departure on the page, so that the director can interpret them in stagecraft. Try to think about your transitions in terms of their theatrical energy. Is there a need for a change of pace, a difference in tone or shade? It's often the case that intensely emotional play scenes are followed by a lighter scene which allows the audience to let off steam, reset themselves, and gather their strength before the next dramatic onslaught.

PUTTING IT ALL TOGETHER

Now for some examples of opening scenes from existing plays so you can see how the playwrights shaped them. Here's a reminder of the questions we've explored above.

→ Who is in the scene? Why are they there? What do they want and who might be blocking them from getting it? Is their goal resolved in the scene or not?

→ Where is the scene set?

→ When is the scene set?

→ What's the basic dramatic action that takes place in the scene? Can you put it into a sentence or two?

→ What are the future consequences for these actions? What are the possibilities for future action at the end of the scene?

→ What kind of exposition is contained in the scene, and is it all necessary?

→ Is there any kind of 'treasure' in the scene, literal or metaphorical? Who competes to win it, and why?

→ What are the different kinds of activity in the scene? How do they add complexity, theatricality and symbolism, and/or deepen characterisation? Are they entertaining for an audience?

→ Why is the scene in the play?

Let's answer these questions for Scene One of *A Streetcar Named Desire*.

Who is in the scene and what do they want?

Blanche DuBois, sister of Stella and her husband Stanley Kowalski. Blanche wants a place to stay (long-term goal) and a drink (short-term goal). She also wants to be reassured by her sister and to feel welcome. Stella wants to make her sister comfortable. Stanley's immediate wants are more negative – to *not* make Blanche feel welcome. To show her who is boss.

Where is the scene set?

Outside the apartment block where the Kowalskis live in Elysian Fields, New Orleans, and in the cramped apartment itself. Williams opens the story on the street so that the audience can experience this impoverished neighbourhood in all its smelly, intimate glory. He not only builds a strong sensory world, but he shows us just how hard it will be for his protagonist, the refined Southern Belle, Blanche, to fit into this (to her) alien world.

When is the scene set?

Evening. Stanley is still at work. This allows Blanche and Stella to have a private reunion before Stanley comes home, in which we learn about the basic circumstances of Blanche's arrival. Williams could have had Blanche arrive straight off the bus and meet with both Stanley *and* Stella, but we'd lose the sense of anticipation that builds around Stanley before he finally arrives.

What's the basic dramatic action of the scene?

The following three steps roughly form the beginning, middle and end of the scene: 1. Blanche arrives in Elysian Fields, penniless. Stella is expecting her, but her husband Stanley doesn't yet know that Blanche will be coming to stay; 2. Blanche reveals the family home Belle Reve has been sold to pay debts and there is no money left over; 3. Blanche meets Stella's husband Stanley for the first time, and he crudely interrogates her.

What are the future consequences of these actions, and what are the possibilities for continuing dramatic stakes?

Potentially, manifold. Will Blanche be allowed to stay? How will this affect everyone? Will Stella and Stanley's marriage withstand Blanche's presence? What happened back at Belle Reve that has made Blanche so anxious and alcohol-dependent? (Once Stanley learns about the loss of Belle Reve in Scene Two, his determination to find out if Blanche is lying about the money, and if so, to extract from it his fair share, fuels the whole play.) The scene ends with Blanche about to be sick after secretly drinking Stanley's whiskey – and our sense that Stanley has 'won' this round of the fight. How will Blanche parry Stanley's attack? Surely she will, or the play would be over and she would meekly return home.

What kind of exposition is contained in the scene?

We learn about the socio-political world of Stella and Stanley's neighbourhood. We learn about the DuBois sisters' upbringing and Blanche's recent difficulties. We learn about the status of the Kowalskis' marriage. Because the sisters haven't seen each other for some time ('a stranger comes to town'), there is an opportunity for plenty of natural exposition, or 'telling' – but it never overshadows the 'showing' contained in the emotional interactions between the characters, in which we learn about their natures, desires and emotions.

Is there a treasure in the scene, literal or metaphorical? Who competes to win it?

Concrete things of value that are competed over include Belle Reve, the DuBois family estate, and its financial value or lack thereof; Stella and Stanley's flat (and symbolically their marital territory); Stanley's bottle of whiskey; and Stella herself. It soon becomes clear that Blanche and Stanley will vie for Stella's love and attention at every opportunity.

What are the different kinds of activity in the scene? How do they add colour, provide context and/or deepen characterisation?

There are lots of small activities in the scene once Blanche has turned up. Blanche advises Stella on her hairstyle and dress, in an effort to reinstate her 'big sister' status. Blanche drinks Stanley's whiskey on the sly. And, famously, Stanley arrives home from work and throws a bloody package of meat up to the balcony for Stella to catch. As previous students of mine will know, this, to my mind, is one of the greatest moments in theatre history. Here's an alpha man with his day's killing returning home to his cave where his woman is waiting. We can only quiver with anticipation at what he'll make of the limp butterfly Blanche. It's not a plot point without which the story would fall apart, but it is a wonderful theatrical activity which shows us exactly who Stanley is.

Why is the scene in the play?

Blanche's arrival kicks off the action of the entire play. The key *reveal* – the fact that the family home has been sold – will become a driving force in the story. The scene also perfectly sets up what we might call the geo-political world of the play, with enough backstory to answer some of our key questions, but leaving plenty of room for further revelation.

Now let's look at a more recent text – *Love and Understanding* by Joe Penhall – to analyse some of the choices made by the playwright to effect scene transitions, openings and endings.

The play is built around a simple conflict between two old friends. Neal shares a cramped one-bedroom flat with his girlfriend Rachel. Neal and Rachel are junior doctors, and both are permanently overworked, knackered and ill, which has put their relationship under strain. Into this small, domestic, intimate space, arrives Richie, Neal's oldest friend. Richie is (at first glance) a charming, manipulative, hard-drinking, truth-bending, argumentative loose cannon. By contrast, his old pal and now host Neal is (at first glance) a people-pleasing, conventional, conciliatory, rule-obeying man who lacks the conviction or energy to put up much of a fight. You can see from this basic character breakdown that the seeds of conflict are inherent, and much of the play centres around this dual clash of nature and will, which, once Rachel has entered the story, becomes a triangular one.

SCENE OPENING

SCENE ONE

NEAL *and* RACHEL's *flat. Early morning.* NEAL *and* RICHIE *standing in the kitchen.* RICHIE *drinking a pint of milk, a suitcase at his feet. A plane is heard overhead.*

NEAL.   We're under the flightpath. One every two minutes.

RICHIE.   Very nice. All yours?

NEAL.   Will be one day.

RICHIE.   I'm impressed.

NEAL.   It actually works out a lot cheaper than renting.

RICHIE.   Well, that's the clincher, isn't it?

NEAL.   It's got a good bathroom.

RICHIE.   A bathroom and everything. Wow. Have you got a
           shower?

NEAL.   Got a very nice shower.

RICHIE.   A very nice shower? Well, that's very nice, isn't it?

He looks around, takes a few steps.

           Very clean.

Pause.

NEAL.   How's Nicky?

RICHIE.   Who?

NEAL.   Nicky, your girlfriend.

Pause.

RICHIE.   Oh, we split up.

NEAL.   Again?

RICHIE.   It's for real this time.

NEAL.   That's what you said last time.

RICHIE.   It's for real this time.

This opening simply but effectively introduces us to the characters and kicks off their conflict. Notice how Penhall opens his play with Richie clearly having very recently arrived, but not with the arrival itself. He could have shown us the doorbell ringing, Neal opening the door, the initial greeting. ('Hello Richie, well this is unexpected, I thought you were in South America, anyway, let me take your coat.') But that's a lot of unnecessary business. By dropping us into the scene a few seconds, or minutes after that arrival, there is already tension in the scene. There's a lot of very skilful exposition in this first page which never detracts from the humour and pace of the scene.

SCENE ENDING

In Scene One, Richie and Neal catch up, size each other up, and reassume what we believe to be their traditional friendship roles. We learn that Richie is homeless, newly single, and drifting. And that Neal is overworked, exhausted, and no real match for Richie's manipulative energy. Neal must now leave for work at the hospital, having offered Richie his sofa to sleep on for a few days. As he prepares to leave, the following happens:

NEAL *picks up his case and jacket and goes to the door.* RICHIE *suddenly winces.*

RICHIE.   Fuck.

NEAL.   Are you all right?

RICHIE.   Just a bit of a headache. Just... severe stabbing pains in my head. I've had them for months. Probably all the flying...

NEAL.   You should get out in the fresh air, clear your lungs, take your mind off things.

RICHIE.   Are you trying to get me out of the house?

NEAL.   No of course not...

   Pause.

   Of course not... I just don't want any...

RICHIE.   Any what, Neal? Wild parties? I came here because I thought you'd understand.

NEAL.   I do.

RICHIE.   Maybe you could fix me up with something. Painkillers. I am really in quite a lot of pain.

NEAL.   Well... if it's serious you should come to the hospital. Have a scan.

RICHIE.   Come to the hospital? Now?

NEAL.   When you've rested.

RICHIE.   I've love to come to the hospital. I've been waiting for you to invite me.

NEAL.   When you've rested.

RICHIE.   I'm rested now.

NEAL.   Actually, Richie, I've got a very busy morning.

RICHIE.   I don't mind.

NEAL.   No. I'm really snowed under at the moment.

RICHIE.   I don't mind.

   End of scene.

If we think of this opening scene, similarly to the opening of *Streetcar*, as a battle of wills between two very different characters, then towards the end of the scene it looks as though Neal has actually managed to 'win'. Having got over the surprise of his friend turning up uninvited, he has agreed to let Richie stay in the flat, but only under certain conditions. He has warned Richie not to disturb his girlfriend who is sleeping next door, and he has poured a little cold water on some of Richie's egotistical career claims.

But then Richie retaliates. How better to trump Neal, a doctor, than to suddenly become ill? Is Richie telling the truth about his migraines? We might suspect he's hamming it up, at the very least. As Richie attempts to manipulate Neal into taking him to the hospital, the conflict intensifies over the final six lines of the scene, giving the last line (repeated) to Richie. The ending a) leaves us on a cliffhanger (will Richie get his way or not?); b) gives us a sense of potential future action; c) has an active consequence; and d) provides an entertaining scene transition, as we'll see when we get to Scene Two, below.

SCENE TRANSITION

SCENE TWO

Hospital. Morning.

NEAL *sitting at a desk looking at scans.* RICHIE, *shirtless, sitting in a chair.*

This opening, purely as a visual tableau, offers both exposition and resolution to the questions set up in Scene Two – as well as comedy. So the scene transition between Scenes One and Two becomes in itself a moment of theatre. It provides a laugh, but more crucially, it lands a keen dart of insight into Richie's character. This is a man who knows how to get his way. How much more will Neal give in to him? As it turns out, quite a lot.

A NOTE ON PRACTICALITIES

Remember that theatre is live and involves a lot of backstage activity to make what happens on stage work seamlessly. So, if one of your characters has just ended a scene naked and covered in blood, and then has to open the following scene fully clothed, twenty years later, in wig and make-up, you may want to rethink. Similarly, if your play requires five actors to play multiple roles, consider how much time they will need to transform into a different character. Happily, these sorts of thorny practical challenges will often throw up ingenious theatrical solutions that can enhance your play, especially once you get into the rehearsal room. But it's important to do your due diligence on the page.

CONTINUOUS ACTION PLAYS

A brief note for those of you writing continuous action plays – i.e. plays without scene breaks, which operate in 'real time' (a notoriously difficult form to pull off). Even though your play may not use traditional scene breaks or changes of time and place, there will still be units of action within your form – you could think of them as invisible sequences. In rehearsal, the director and actors will always look for these dramatic units, even if your play contains no evident scene breaks, in order to understand how the play's narrative energy is created and decide how to physically 'block' the action. So it's still worth mentally breaking your play down into units as this will help you understand how your story evolves dramatically. To help you do this, look for turning points in your story, key choices taken by significant characters, major battles over valuable practical or symbolic treasures, and moments where new information comes into the play which will have direct consequences in the action. *The Weir* and *hang* are examples of continuous action plays that I've already mentioned.

AND FINALLY...

Although this chapter contains a lot of necessary technical information about scenecraft, every now and again it's good to throw everything up in the air and reconnect with your instincts. It's important to try to get a *feel* for the balance of a scene, its flow of energy, its geometry and shape – especially when your form doesn't follow the sort of theatrical conventions of the scenes analysed above. Try to sense when a scene feels unfinished, or front-loaded, or top heavy, as you would if you were trimming a hedge or building a wall.

If that seems easier said than done, remember that it is always hard for writers to objectively assess their work, especially in the beginning. We can get very attached to particular exchanges or moments that we just *know* glow with brilliance. Invariably, these are the lines that get cut in rehearsal. On the page they may be interesting and amusing, but they can often kill a scene stone dead, usually because we are either overindulging our lyrical dexterity, or because we're not allowing enough space for subtext. Developing a sixth sense about when scenes drag and when to end them is a key skill of the playwright. Be prepared, as William Faulkner reportedly said, to 'kill your darlings' for the good of the whole.

And let me reiterate that I'm not suggesting you wrestle over these sorts of questions before you've written a single line of your play – they're not intended as a rigid schematic checklist. You may need to write a rough first draft on gut alone, before you can pull back and use this sort of workout on a redraft. As always, follow your instincts and then apply your technique.

EXERCISES: WRITING SCENES

→ Take a tricky scene from your play and see if you can answer the questions outlined on page 132, in the section 'Putting It All Together'. You may well not be able to answer them all easily – it doesn't matter. Any one of them, particularly those concerning action, consequences and activity, might help you clarify the point of the scene and its dramatic function in the play. Be brutally honest with yourself. Does the scene do more than just showcase your ability with dialogue, for example?

→ Think about the balance of the scene in terms of the relationship between its beginning and ending, and transitions before and/ or after it into other scenes or units of action. How do these relationships create a sense of structure and enable the energy of the scene to flow? What is the scene's energetic relationship to the play as a whole?

→ What's your assessment of the scene's overall dramatic balance? Is it top-heavy with exposition? Thin in the middle? Are there lulls or peaks of energy, exposition, action? Are there any revelations, conflicts, turning points, questions or answers posed by the scene that might help you understand its current shape, and think about whether it needs reshaping?

→ If it helps, draw a diagram or graph, or make a sketch to get a sense of the overall shape of the scene and how your story flows through it.

8
HOW TO WRITE
STAGE DIALOGUE

HOW TO WRITE STAGE DIALOGUE

> Writing is different from other arts because our medium isn't
> paint or clay or marble or pitched sound, but words, something
> we use every day, and use unthinkingly. Words feel transparent
> to us; speaking is as natural to me as breathing. But to make
> art with words means first of all to break that transparency,
> to become aware that words are objects, as material and
> concrete as bricks – that they're something to build with.
> *Garth Greenwell, 'Stories That Sing'* (written and recorded for *The Essay*,
> BBC Radio 3)

Greenwell, a novelist, was talking about prose here, but his words apply
equally well to dialogue. Human beings may use words (or speech, in
the playwright's lexicon) *unthinkingly*, but we playwrights have to think
incredibly hard about every word that we put in our characters' mouths.
Once again, we must be architects – constructing our dialogue brick by
brick; word by word; pause by pause.

Many playwrights start writing for the theatre because they believe
they have a good ear for dialogue – an instinctive talent for creating a
linguistic personality or unique character voice via language. A 'good ear'
is something that talented actors also have naturally – and, if so, one of
the reasons that many actors in turn make good writers. Writers of good
dialogue are invariably good listeners – although possibly not to their
children/spouses/colleagues – but to strangers on buses/in restaurants/at
the dentist. (Or, in other words, good thieves.) But a talent for mimicry is
not enough by itself. Truly theatrical dialogue is always *active*.

WHAT IS ACTIVE DIALOGUE?

In drama, language *is* action. And action, remember, is about consequences
and causality. Good theatrical dialogue must always evolve your story in

some way. This doesn't mean that every line you write must be laden with *plot*. Yes, what characters say to each other should always be germane to the story, but if we isolated the spoken lines in a play which related purely to major plot points, we'd be left with slim pickings. The first act of *Hamlet* (minus subplots) might go something like this:

> HORATIO. Hamlet, my man – you're back! How was Wittenberg?
>
> HAMLET. Depressing, but not as bad as here. Can you believe my mum only waited a month after my dad died before she married his brother?
>
> HORATIO. I know, it's well out of order. Listen, Hamlet, I don't want to freak you out but your father's ghost is wandering around the castle ramparts.
>
> HAMLET. Really? (GHOST *appears*) Jesus! Dad, is that you?
>
> GHOST. Yes, son. Your uncle Claudius killed me to get to your mother. Avenge me and take the bastard down, please.
>
> HAMLET. All right. I'll pretend to be mad to snare him.
>
> GHOST.   Good idea. Just try not to drag your mum into it.

And so we'd have to forgo all the intricate character study, the gorgeous soliloquies, the fun of watching Claudius and Gertrude go about their royal business while Hamlet tries to catch them out, the machinations of Rosencrantz and Guildenstern, and so on and so on. Yes, there are digressions, diversions and waffle – the protagonist of the play is a loquacious, existentialist depressive. Nevertheless, the 'balls' of the story never get dropped. The words spoken by the characters in the play deepen our understanding of Hamlet, his desires, his challenges, as well as our emotional investment in his dilemma. The dialogue is always active, because every conversation, every soliloquy, takes us sailing further down the river of story.

When we talk to each other, however unthinkingly we do it, we are always on some level performing an action. We offer information and request it, we exchange ideas, we debate, we protest, we communicate to comfort, to accuse, to beg, to seduce, to amuse, to offend. Our speech involves an infinite variety of actions with an infinite number of outcomes. Of course, we also speak many words simply for the pleasure of them; to make each other laugh, to share banter, to reaffirm our sense of self and our relationships. But there is always intention. Theatrical dialogue must distil and condense this intention and use it to craft story. That's how dialogue becomes active, alive and dramatic.

DIALOGUE AS STAGECRAFT

It's often easier to understand active dialogue by looking at its opposite. You'll know *inactive* dialogue when you're watching a play because you'll start to drift off and think about what you're going to eat or watch on TV when you get home. You'll notice it when characters are talking but the energy of the play has stalled and when the dialogue becomes just noise. To dig into this a bit more, it's useful once again to compare the use of dialogue in film and theatre.

As we've already seen, cinematic storytelling is created primarily with images. Yes, people talk in films, and, yes, their dialogue reveals plot and character. But the central storytelling tool of cinema is the camera. If we need to show that a character is terrified in a film, all we have to do is focus the camera in close on their face, and direct the actor to emote fear. Throw in some dramatic music on top and the audience will immediately understand the character's emotional state. If, however, the character then turns to another character and says, in a terrified whisper, 'I'm terrified,' we might throw a shoe at the screen. Dialogue is not needed here because the camera's point of view (POV) does all the necessary work.

The audience POV is fixed by the camera when we watch a film – our attention goes where *it* goes. But in theatre, our POV is created in the main by the dialogue. Not only can our eyes wander where they like without being bullied by a camera, but we are watching live action, without the ability to zoom, freeze-frame or track. Of course, the director and team will skilfully manipulate our attention with lighting and blocking. But the primary thing that focuses the audience is *language*. When characters speak, we listen – and watch. Think of theatrical dialogue as the filmmaker's lens, guiding us through the story, painting its pictures, and focusing our collective POV.

First, a basic breakdown of the different functions that dialogue performs; then I'll lay out some tools of the trade which will help to make your dialogue sing.

DIALOGUE AS EXPOSITION

The most basic function of speech is to convey key information that is needed by your audience to understand the story. Creating good exposition is more difficult than it looks – not least because most developing writers invariably deliver far more information than is actually needed. Let's return for a moment (if we must) to my condensed *Hamlet* dialogue.

> HORATIO. Hamlet, my man – you're back! How was Wittenberg?

Believe it or not, even this dreadful line of mine contains some decent exposition. It tells us that Hamlet has been away, and where, and it seems like the believable utterance of a good friend (though perhaps not of the Elizabethan period). It is a better line than if Hamlet entered the stage and said:

> HAMLET. Hi, Horatio. I'm back from my trip to Wittenberg.

That's some very bad exposition right there.

My second line in the original exchange – Hamlet's response to Horatio – is likewise full of it.

> HAMLET. Depressing, but not as bad as here. Can you believe my mum only waited a month after my dad died before she married his brother?

We need that crucial information about Gertrude's marriage to his uncle Claudius in Hamlet's absence – it's the foundation of the play's revenge plot. Luckily Shakespeare delivers it rather better. Although he had at his disposal the dramatic conventions of his day, such as the aside and the soliloquy with which to deliver information directly to the audience, he gives the crucial exposition room to breathe by allowing the audience to witness Hamlet navigating a family meeting *before* we get his explosion of grief and rage at his mother's marriage.

When we first meet Hamlet, he is in grudging attendance to Gertrude and the new King Claudius, and sulkily endures his uncle's phoney sympathies at his father's death. We get to watch the psychological and emotional interplay between Hamlet, Gertrude and Claudius without being in full possession of the facts, and we learn a lot about Hamlet's personality, state of mind, and the conflicting demands of the court. Only when they leave him alone on stage do we get Hamlet's first soliloquy and see the full extent of his grief and wretchedness – *'O, that this too too solid flesh would melt / Thaw and resolve itself into a dew!'* And it's only here that we learn the hard facts; that his father has been dead two months, that his mother married Claudius a month later, and that Hamlet hates his uncle with a vengeance.

Few of us these days use soliloquies or asides in our plays – although monologue and direct address to audience can be useful tools in contemporary drama. This means we must work even harder to avoid spoonfeeding information to our audiences in a scene, beat or exchange.

Theresa Ikoko's play *Girls* opens with Tisana, Ruhab and Haleema idly discussing the usual things teenage girls do, like boys and social media. It's only ten minutes into the play that we realise they have been kidnapped and are being held in a camp somewhere in Nigeria. It's a wonderful opening that cleverly blindsides us with the informal, bantering dialogue and sets up their friendships before dropping the plot bombshell.

Good exposition, as you'll see, is invisible to an audience. It provides necessary context but never distracts them from the action that's unfolding. The trick is to never shovel information into a line, but smuggle it in, like a parent smuggling vegetables into a fussy child's dinner. And remember that less is nearly always more.

DIALOGUE AS SUBTEXT

Subtext is, simply, what is *not* said in direct speech, but the meaning that lurks below the surface of the spoken line. Of course, sometimes characters need to say exactly what they mean or want, but what they *don't* say – for whatever reason – is just as significant. We constantly monitor our behaviour according to social and personal contexts. Imagine a small child who wants something very badly: a toy, a biscuit, a reward. She might ask directly for it: *'Mummy, I want a biscuit.'* But, if she knows the answer will probably be no, she will ask for it in a very different way: *'Mummy, I love you, you're my favourite mummy in the whole world.'* The subtext of that second request will probably be crystal clear to the child's mother, especially if the child is standing near the biscuit tin. And her child's subterfuge might infuriate her, meaning no biscuit. Or it might disarm and charm her – biscuit.

Subtext allows you to practise the well-known rule: *show don't tell*. Just as the camera's close-up *shows* the character's fear instead of having her *tell* us that she's feeling it, theatrical dialogue should show the audience character emotion and thought. We are all of us crafty, desire-driven creatures who are simultaneously constrained by our personal codes, and we enjoy watching characters misunderstand each other, talk at cross purposes, and generally make a hash of things. Often, in good writing, some kind of behavioural or emotional subtext will lurk beneath a whole scene – and at the climax of the scene, the subtext leaps out from its hiding place like a spawning salmon. Then the real meaning behind a character's lines will become clear to another character, and cause a reaction – and a great deal of satisfaction for an audience.

To show you what I mean, here are some condensed lines from my play *Second Person Narrative*. The play shows the entire lifespan of one woman from birth to death and its structure is episodic, with twenty-three very short scenes bookended by a prologue and epilogue. The protagonist is present in each scene at a different age, along with different supporting characters. In this scene, the protagonist, You, is fifty-six years old, and hosting a book-club session at her house with friends. But she keeps being interrupted by her teenage daughter. I've pulled the daughter and mother dialogue from the scene, omitting the interspersed book-club discussion, so you can see how the subtext builds through the surface conflict over a piece of laundry, and climaxes with the real conflict at the heart of the maternal/daughter relationship. The scene is called 'Nobody Cares What You're Wearing'.

DAUGHTER.   Mum, where's my top?

YOU.   Which top?

DAUGHTER.   The black one, you said you washed it.

YOU.   I don't know, look in the airing cupboard.

DAUGHTER.   I did, it's not there.

YOU.   Well, if it went in the basket it got washed and if it got washed it's in the cupboard.

DAUGHTER.   It's not in either of those places.

YOU.   Then you've put it somewhere else, I can't help you.

DAUGHTER.   Why is everything always my fault!

DAUGHTER *leaves. Book-group conversation begins again.* DAUGHTER *re-enters.*

DAUGHTER.   Can I borrow your black top? The one that's too small for you.

YOU.   It's not too small for me.

DAUGHTER.   Whatever, I need a black top to go with these trousers, okay?

YOU.   Actually I was going to wear it tomorrow.

DAUGHTER.   It's for my date, all right, I'm going on a date, I told you, it's important.

YOU.   How do you know I'm not going on a date?

DAUGHTER.   I'm not joking, Mum, you're fifty-six, nobody cares what you're wearing.

DAUGHTER *leaves. Book-group conversation begins again.* DAUGHTER *re-enters wearing the black top.*

DAUGHTER.   I'm going out now, I'm wearing the black top, okay?

YOU. No, it's not okay it's rude to keep interrupting us like this I don't like the way you're talking to me for goodness sake the world's not going to end if you don't wear my black top.

DAUGHTER. Well tough I'm wearing it you're just trying to spoil everything I need it more than you you're not even busy you're just sitting around talking who even reads books any more.

YOU.   Right, take it off please, right now.

DAUGHTER.   WHY ARE YOU SO SELFISH, IT DOESN'T EVEN FIT YOU, YOU'VE HAD YOUR TIME, IT'S MY TIME NOW AND YES YOU'RE RIGHT THERE IS ABSOLUTELY NO MYSTERY TO YOU, NO WONDER DAD LEFT!

And the scene ends. It's not subtle, but it's more actively dramatic than if the row had escalated in the first two lines of their exchange.

To dig into how the subtext is functioning, here's a recap on the scene's basic action.

A middle-aged woman is hosting a book-club meeting at her house with friends. But she keeps being rudely interrupted by her teenage daughter, who is about to go on a date. First she demands her mum's help finding her favourite top, then borrows one of her mum's without asking. When the mother objects, the daughter retaliates by blaming her mother's selfishness for the fact that her father has left.

How would we describe the *subtext* of the scene? How about:

A teenage girl is nervous because she's going on a date tonight with someone she really likes, and takes out her anxiety on her mum. Her mother, who is suffering from low self-esteem, wants to show her daughter that she's not just a mum at her daughter's beck and call, but a woman in her own right. Hurt by this perceived selfishness, her daughter punishes her mother by upstaging and belittling her in front of her friends. Both mother and daughter have been hurt and traumatised by the woman's recent separation from her husband, and the girl's loss of her father.

Of course, you might have read the emotional and psychological subtext of the scene a bit differently. (If you saw it performed by actors, it would probably be slightly different again.) That's fine if so – the whole point of subtext is that it is unspoken and therefore interpretive, and the meaning behind certain lines will always be debated in rehearsal by director and actors. For example, you may not have considered that the daughter was nervous about tonight's date. I can tell you that that is what was in my head when I wrote the scene, but I didn't reveal anything directly about the date, nor the boy or girl that the daughter is meeting, so it's quite a leap of the imagination, subtextually speaking. Either way, you might infer from the exposition (she's going on a date) and her behaviour (rude and demanding) that her anxiety has a root cause that she doesn't want to admit (she really likes the person). Overall, however, this subtextual detail is far less important than the root cause of the characters' conflict, which is the loss of the husband/father. Hopefully this comes through strongly in the climax of the row, when the scene's buried meaning is revealed, regardless of any more subtle variations to your reading of the scene.

Here's another and more in-depth analysis, once more using the opening lines of Scene One of Joe Penhall's play *Love and Understanding*.

> NEAL *and* RACHEL's *flat. Early morning.* NEAL *and* RICHIE *standing in the kitchen.* RICHIE *drinking a pint of milk, a suitcase as his feet. A plane is heard overhead.*

NEAL.   We're under the flightpath. One every two minutes.

RICHIE.   Very nice. All yours?

NEAL.   Will be one day.

RICHIE.   I'm impressed.

NEAL.   It actually works out a lot cheaper than renting.

RICHIE.   Well, that's the clincher, isn't it?

NEAL.   It's got a good bathroom.

RICHIE.   A bathroom and everything. Wow. Have you got a shower?

NEAL.   Got a very nice shower.

RICHIE.   A very nice shower? Well, that's very nice, isn't it?

These simple lines are charged with subtextual emotions, intentions and conflict, and the brief exchange sets up a clear struggle for power and status between the two men.

Read again, and this time I've written my suggested subtextual meanings for each line beneath them. Remember, the subtext is what the character is thinking or feeling but, for whatever reason, not articulating directly. As above, I'm not offering up these analyses as definitive interpretations of the scenes in this chapter. No one pair of actors, depending on their direction, would create exactly the same version as another, and the lines could be played in many different ways. It's just an exercise to get you thinking about how much meaning is implied in good dialogue.

NEAL.   We're under the flightpath. One every two minutes.

Subtext: *I would have liked a better flat but I don't want to admit that. I invite you to make your own judgement.*

(*Note that although the play opens with this expository statement from Neal, the stage directions tell us that a plane can be heard overhead. So Neal's line is not there to give information to the audience – we already know the flat is under a flightpath. The line might be read, therefore, as a defensive comment, or a way of stating the obvious to get it out of the way. If he doesn't, he knows Richie might complain or be sarcastic.*)

RICHIE.   Very nice. All yours?

Subtext: *My judgement is, it's pathetic.*

NEAL.   Will be one day.

Subtext: *Can't you feel a tiny bit proud of me?*

RICHIE.   I'm impressed.

Subtext: *No, you've bought a shithole.*

NEAL.   It actually works out a lot cheaper than renting.

Subtext: *Now I feel even more defensive about my flat.*

RICHIE.   Well, that's the clincher, isn't it?

Subtext: *You should. Like I said, you bought a shithole.*

NEAL.   It's got a good bathroom.

Subtext: *Can you stop bullying me please?*

RICHIE.   A bathroom and everything. Wow. Have you got a shower?

Subtext: *I'll stop bullying you when you stop lying to yourself about your flat.*

NEAL.   Got a very nice shower.

Subtext: *I'm not lying, I'm trying to look on the bright side.*

RICHIE.   A very nice shower? Well, that's very nice, isn't it?

Subtext: *The bright side is for wusses. I win.*

(*And he closes it down with a sarcastic repetition of his own words.*)

Notice also how much these lines give the actors to do. There is a very specific emotional dynamic contained in this relationship, which allows actors to deploy all their craft to create believable and nuanced behaviour, full of intention and desire. (And a great deal of humour.)

Just to complete the analysis, I'm taking the liberty of rewriting the scene, this time using my inferred subtext in the lines and putting it into direct speech by the characters, just to see how it compares with the original version. (With apologies to Joe Penhall!)

NEAL.   I would have liked a better flat but I don't want to admit that. I invite you to make your own judgement.

RICHIE.   My judgement is, it's pathetic.

NEAL.   Can't you feel a tiny bit proud of me?

RICHIE.   No, you've bought a shithole.

NEAL.   Now I feel even more defensive about my flat.

RICHIE.   You should. Like I said, you bought a shithole.

NEAL.   Can you stop bullying me please?

RICHIE.   I'll stop bullying you when you stop lying to yourself about your flat.

NEAL.   I'm not lying, I'm trying to look on the bright side.

RICHIE.   The bright side is for wusses. I win.

It sounds odd, as it should, but it just about hangs together as a rational conversation. And, yes, there is conflict which might lead to significant action, but there's none of the thrust and parry between Neal and Richie in the real version that gives us such enjoyable depth of character, nuance and wit. Crucially, the audience isn't having to do much, if any, work.

Good playwrights understand that we, the audience, want to use our own emotional intelligence to put two and two together and, in this case, to question why these two men are friends, and to guess at what Richie is actually doing here. Getting the measure of an interesting fictional stage character is just as enjoyable (more, in fact, because there are no personal risks involved) as getting the measure of an interesting stranger we might meet down the pub or in a waiting room. In the theatre we are often given what I've called the luxury of real time to get to know characters. Freed from the constraints of galloping plot, as required in much TV drama and film, we get to observe stage characters more minutely and become attuned to very nuanced details of personality and behaviour.

As discussed in Chapter Seven, the two characters spend most of this short scene having a general catch-up. Although the dialogue is full of necessary exposition, the play creates a context for it. The fact that the two men haven't seen each other for years ('a stranger comes to town') allows them to impart a lot of information to each other (and the audience) without it feeling heavy-handed.

THE LEAPING SALMON

Earlier in the chapter I mentioned the moment in a scene when a character finally moves away from subtext to directly articulate his or her desire, intention, need or problem. We could say that the basic action of the scene is: Richie asks Neal if he can stay in his flat and Neal agrees. The *subtext* of the scene as a whole shows us that Neal isn't sure this is a good idea but he can't say no directly. Not only is Richie his oldest friend, but he's clearly somewhat unstable. So they pussyfoot around the subject until we get this:

NEAL.   You should get out in the fresh air, clear your lungs,
         take your mind off things.

RICHIE. Are you trying to get me out of the house?

NEAL.   No of course not...

Pause.

         Of course not... I just don't want any...

RICHIE. Any what, Neal? Wild parties? I came here because I
         thought you'd understand.

NEAL.   I do.

The 'leaping salmon' moment, when the subtext finally leaps out on to the surface of the scene, occurs when Richie says the unsayable (so far): 'Are you trying to get me out of the house?' and 'I thought you'd understand.' There, it's out in the open – his need, his fear and his desire are laid bare, and it's very uncomfortable for both of them. Neal is forced to backtrack – and to agree. 'I do.' The scene concludes with Richie back on top of the situation, forcing Neal to take him to work at the hospital and sort him out with painkillers. We can see his feet are firmly under Neal's coffee table, metaphorically speaking.

TACTICAL DIALOGUE

Many years ago I attended a very useful workshop given by playwright Simon Stephens on tactical dialogue. This refers to the emotional and behavioural tactics that characters use in their speech to achieve their desires at any given moment. It's really another way of coming at subtext, but it offers a clear methodology for creating it. As we've seen above, characters who baldly state their desires and achieve them quickly and easily do not always make for very good drama. We want to watch people struggle, prevaricate and, hopefully, learn things about themselves and others. The pleasure we get as an audience comes from being able to see complex human psychology at work, whether we identify with that behaviour or find it repellent.

There are other names for the methodology – some of you may know it as *actioning* – a rehearsal process of allocating an active transitive verb (i.e. something that is done to another person) to each line of dialogue in a play, so that the actor speaking the line understands the intention behind it. So, for example, Richie *cajoles* Neal; Neal *entertains* Richie; Richie *undermines* Neal. Actioning is rooted in the Russian director Stanislavsky's 'method' of giving concrete physical actions to actors to create psychological depth, and was popularised as a common rehearsal-room technique by Max Stafford-Clark at his theatre company Joint Stock. Although devised as a tool for actors, it's useful for writers too. Analysing a scene or unit of action and discovering a lack of action behind the dialogue can help alert the writer to flabby and discursive speech.

The American writer Paul C. Castagno has devised his own system for creating tactical dialogue that he calls *speech acts*, a term originally coined by English philosopher J. L. Austin. It refers to the same thing – the action behind the speech. Castagno lists speech acts such the threat, the promise, the command, the vow and the strategy. This helpfully reminds us that when characters use tactics to try and affect an outcome, their success or failure is not just achieved by *what* is said, but *how* it is said. '*A speech act demands a performative response. It is neither ideation, nor idle chat, but must involve behavior.*'[9] Language then becomes a weapon used by characters to achieve their ends.

We can put these two analyses together to dig into the same scene excerpt. Here I've chosen an active verb to suggest what tactic might be being used by the character on each line, and also indicated any speech acts that might be relevant.

NEAL. We're under the flightpath. One every two minutes.

Action: *Neal **denigrates** (his flat) to Richie.*

Speech act: **Strategy**. *Neal denigrates the flat before Richie can.*

RICHIE. Very nice. All yours?

Action: *Richie **denigrates** (Neal's flat) to Neal.*

NEAL. Will be one day.

Action: *Neal **appeals** to Richie.*
Speech act: **Strategy**. *Neal wants Richie's approval.*

RICHIE.   I'm impressed.

Action: *Richie **withholds** (approval from) Neal.*

NEAL.   It actually works out a lot cheaper than renting.

Action: *Neal **defends** (his flat) to Richie.*
Speech act: ***Strategy.*** *Neal appeals to Richie's rationality.*

RICHIE.   Well, that's the clincher, isn't it?

Action: *Richie **mocks** Neal.*

NEAL.   It's got a good bathroom.

Action: *Neal (attempts to) **impress** Richie.*

RICHIE.   A bathroom and everything. Wow. Have you got a shower?

Action: *Richie **provokes** Neal.*
Speech act: ***Threat.*** *Richie's mocking question is intended to threaten Neal's status.*

NEAL.   Got a very nice shower.

Action: *Neal **retaliates** to Richie.*

RICHIE.   A very nice shower? Well, that's very nice, isn't it?

Action: *Richie **humiliates** Neal.*
Speech act: ***Command.*** *Richie shows Neal the conversation is over – and that he has won this round.*

Here we might get a slightly different reading of the scene as compared to my prior subtext suggestions. But both exercises should illustrate a simple rule: that when people converse in a play, what they're saying to one another is also what they're *doing* to one another. By practising these techniques you are also training yourself for the sort of interrogation your play will get in a rehearsal room, whether or not the actors and director use a method like actioning.

If you really want to interrogate a scene or unit of action that's proving tricky to put into decent dialogue, it can be useful to write out the subtext first, using all the previous techniques. First, get down on paper the bald clunky version where the characters say exactly what they mean and want in direct exposition. Allow your characters to just blurt out everything in their (and your) minds without worrying about the dialogue's subtlety.

Then, once you really understand what you need your characters to say at this moment in the play, and why, you can start to transpose the bald 'direct' version into more active and theatrical dialogue using subtext and tactics.

DIALOGUE FOR SOCIAL/CULTURAL/EMOTIONAL CONTEXT

A character's vocabulary, diction, and accent will be rooted in many different factors – age, class, gender, nationality, education and upbringing – as well as their personality. But these things will also fluctuate according to specific social contexts and behavioural expectations. How I speak to a family member in the privacy of my own bedroom will be very different to how I address a classroom of students. Different again with my bank manager. Different again with a stranger on a park bench. *Where* – setting, world, scene, context – you situate your characters will always have an effect on *how* they talk.

Here's an excerpt from *hang* by debbie tucker green. It's near the opening of the play. Three characters, known only as One, Two and Three, gather in a nondescript institutional room. One (female) and Two (male or female) clearly work at this institution, whatever it is, and Three (also female) is visiting for reasons yet unknown. That's about all the audience knows at this point.

ONE.   …How have you been?

THREE.

ONE.   It's been a while.

   THREE *watches her.*

        (A) couple of years isn't it, how have you been…
        keeping?

   THREE *says nothing.*

        Stupid question I know, but…

THREE.   Yeah.

THREE.
ONE.

ONE.   I know, I – .
        No / I –

THREE.   No. You don't know.

ONE.   I can only imagine.

THREE.   No. You can't.

ONE.   ... I'm just (saying)... You do look surprisingly well considering all – .

THREE.   (*dry*) Thank you.

ONE.   I'm not trying to be – and it, I know it sounds (wrong) but you do look well, considering, with all you've...

THREE *exhales slowly.*
TWO *hustles in with two hot drinks.*

TWO.   Tea. Builder's, no sugar and... coffee for me – (*To* THREE) if you do change your mind or want me to pick you up anything just let / me –

ONE.   She doesn't want anything.

TWO.   Just saying that if she –

ONE.   she's fine. Thanks.

Note how One is trying her best to reassure Three with neutral small talk, but her attempts are falling flat. And note how powerful Three's silences are – along with her terse one- or two-word answers. She really doesn't want to be here and there's a lot of suppressed emotion in the words. Just as things are getting unbearable, Two comes in with tea he's been sent to fetch, and disrupts the dynamic by babbling in an attempt to be helpful. He is quickly shut down by One.

It's only about a minute of stage time, but it's packed with contextual and subtextual meaning. A lot of the meaning is created by the contrast in the characters' modes of speech – Three's monosyllabic terse responses/ silences sandwiched between One's nervous 'staying on safe ground' chit-chat. It immediately engages our curiosity, because we want to know why everyone is so tense, what they're all doing there, and why Three is so angry and resentful.

USING SPEECH FORMATS

Let's take a moment to look at how certain playwrights also use specific speech forms in theatrical writing to create meaning. In her stage directions, debbie tucker green specifies the following:

Words in brackets are not to be spoken.
Names without dialogue indicate an active silence between those characters.
A forward slash (/) marks an overlapping point in dialogue.

These sorts of formatting styles are increasingly popular in contemporary writing, and new writers can find them perplexing and intimidating. But they are simply conventions that some writers find useful to help clarify their intentions for the actor and director.

Overlapping dialogue is a particularly common trope of contemporary realism, and so the forward slash (/) can be a practical way of showing an actor exactly where to interrupt another character's line. But there are plenty of other ways to indicate interruption or overlap. You can use a dash (–) or three dots (…) at the end of a line to indicate a character hasn't completed their sentence before somebody else cuts in, or insert a simple speech direction – (*interrupting*) – at the beginning of a character's line. In rehearsal, actors will always unlock the right pace and structure of the dialogue. These formatting devices are simply practical writing tools, and don't hold the secrets of the universe.

THE BEAT VERSUS THE PAUSE

Meaning in dialogue, both literal and subtextual, is created not just in *what* your characters say, but *how* they say it. One of the tools the playwright has to direct the 'how' is via the use of beats and pauses. New writers often get very hung up on the difference between the two, and when and how to use them, and what they're for. Trawl the internet and you'll find entire forums devoted to the subject. If you want a more protracted discussion of it than the one I'm prepared to give here, you should check them out. For now, though, I'd summarise the difference (after various discussions with actors and directors) thus: a beat is usually shorter than a pause, and tends to sit between two different moments or thoughts, while a pause tends to sit within one moment or thought.

As I say, there is debate on the semantics, but trust me, whether you write 'beat' or 'pause' is less important than knowing what the word it precedes or follows is doing there, for the scene, the dialogue and your character. The golden rule is that with every use of a beat, pause, silence or anything in between, you are essentially giving a direction to the actor. Look again at debbie tucker green's note on her stage directions, above: *Names without dialogue indicate an **active** silence between those characters.* (My bold highlight.) Without using either term (beat or pause) in her stage directions, tucker green creates a great deal of subtext with the spaces in her dialogue. Three's silences are very active in the sense that they are full of meaning and causality. They might contain a reaction to a line that's been spoken to her, and/or an intention to provoke a response in Two. They give the actor playing Three an opportunity to show how she is feeling. I've suggested what these feelings might be in bold italics.

ONE.   ...How have you been?

THREE.   (**THREE** *doesn't answer. Is she offended by the question, is she too emotional to speak, does she want to make* **ONE** *really work for her answer? There are different ways to interpret the silence, but all have a consequence, which is that* **ONE** *tries again.*)

ONE.   It's been a while.

THREE *watches her.* (***Still, no answer. But we know* ONE *has* THREE*'s attention because of the stage direction. The silence could now be seen as a deliberate snub by* THREE... *and again it has a consequence.* ONE *tries again to draw* THREE *out.*)

(A) couple of years isn't it, how have you been... keeping?

THREE *says nothing.* (***Another snub.* ONE *keeps going gamely.*)

Stupid question I know, but...

THREE.   Yeah. (***And finally she speaks – and it's a marvellous put-down. She holds the power in the room right now.* THREE*'s one word has the power to vanquish* ONE*'s twenty-three. Yes, I counted them.*)

While you should always try to create rhythm and pace with your dialogue, make sure you leave some space for the actors and director to do their jobs, as above. Try to consider the following, as you score your script with space and silence. (I'm using 'pause' here as the unit of measurement.)

→ Is the pause active? Does it contribute specific meaning to the line, and/or the moment of interaction between characters?

→ *Why* does your character hesitate, quieten or not answer? Does the pause have a conscious intention or does it show unconscious emotion?

→ Does the pause create a change in pace, rhythm or tempo with regard to the actor's delivery?

→ Finally, if you're not clear about your intentions, it's better to leave these sorts of directions out. Actors will find their own way through your dialogue in rehearsal, and create their own pace and rhythm with the director.

A NOTE ON DIRECTIONS IN DIALOGUE

Developing playwrights are often guilty of relying too much on directions to indicate how a line should be spoken. Although the impulse stems from an understandable desire to be clear about how they want the actor to deliver the line, they can be distracting for the actor and weigh down the text. Using the same extract from debbie tucker green's *hang*, I've added in the sort of indications that I commonly see written in first drafts by less-experienced writers. My additions in bold italics.

ONE.   (*tentatively*) How have you been?

THREE *doesn't answer.*

ONE.   (*trying again after a short beat*) It's been a while.

THREE *still doesn't answer but we can tell she's upset. The silence is unnerving to* **ONE.**

(A) couple of years isn't it, how have you been... keeping? (*Goes on gamely*) Stupid question I know, but...

THREE.   (*terse*) Yeah.

THREE.
ONE.

ONE.   I know, I – (*Pause*)
           No / I –

THREE.   (*emphatic*) No. You don't know.

ONE.   I can only imagine.

THREE. (*angry*) No. You can't.

ONE. (*quickly interrupting*) I'm just saying... You do look surprisingly well considering all – (*She tails off*)

THREE. (*dry*) Thank you.

ONE has no idea what to say next. She's remembering what happened in the last disastrous meeting she had with THREE.

ONE. (*apologetic*) I'm not trying to be – and it, I know it sounds (wrong) but you do look well, considering, with all you've... (*She lapses into awkward silence*)

Can you see how all these additions I've made are superfluous? Overusing both dialogue and stage directions in this way not only makes writers lazy, but also patronises the actor, who should be able to bring their own skillset to their characterisation and delivery. Crucially, these directions add no meaning that we couldn't already deduce from tucker green's original text on the previous pages, using her exacting syntax alone. Note that the only actor's direction given in the exchange is the word 'dry'. This is practical, because that 'Thank you' could be delivered in several different ways, and the writer wants to make sure that the actor knows it's not earnest, nor angry, but ironic. This not only gives us a glimpse of Three's character, but it shows us the behavioural mechanisms that she is using to cope with the situation.

Of course, you will all have read published plays that contain liberally overwritten dialogue directions. This is partly just down to changing conventions and fashions within playwriting. Lorraine Hansberry's *Raisin in the Sun* contains, on a single page of dialogue, the following bracketed indications for different characters: *drily; senselessly; impatiently; disinterestedly; defensively; intently*, and a few others besides. It doesn't stop the play from being a masterpiece. But for those of us starting out, caution is better than overindulgence.

Also note my clanging stage direction, above: *'She's remembering what happened in the last disastrous meeting she had with* THREE.*'* This illustrates another golden rule: *Never write any action in your stage directions that cannot be acted.* An actor can physically enact a stage direction like, *'She crosses the stage'* or *'She throws the cup of water in* ONE*'s face.'* They cannot enact *'remembering what happened in the last disastrous meeting'*, because it's pure abstraction. So stick to essential and concrete directions in your play for the sake of clarity, and don't try to do the actors' and director's jobs for them.

CHARACTER'S VOICE VERSUS PLAYWRIGHT'S VOICE

A common note given to new playwrights is that their characters all sound too similar – the authorial voice (i.e. the writer's own voice) is dominating, and each character lacks differentiation. And that can be true. But I've never heard anyone complain about Tom Stoppard's or Harold Pinter's authorial voices. If you hear a few lines of Stoppard you could probably pick out the playwright from a dialogue line-up fairly easily. Ditto with Pinter. Ditto with Caryl Churchill. Ditto with debbie tucker green, as above. There are many other well-known playwrights whose language has a particular flavour and musicality – Martin Crimp, Tony Kushner, Annie Baker and Enda Walsh spring to mind. In their cases, the authorial voice is not considered a negative, but a recognisable element of their talent and skill. So take the notion of an overlying 'sameness' with a pinch of salt, but do consider the factors that might influence your characters and how this impacts their speech.

The way a single sentence is spoken by a particular individual can create an immediate thumbnail sketch of their background, nature and mood. Every writer I know has poached some sort of delicious verbal tic or habit from a real human being and given it to one of their characters. It's amazing how something so small and insignificant can throw open a door to understanding a character.

Here's Tom Kettle, from Jez Butterworth's *The Ferryman*. I've pulled out the first eight groups of sentences he speaks in the play and put them together in sequence, so although it won't all make exact sense, you can taste a sort of reduced *jus* of his character.

> TOM KETTLE. Aye she's still on actually.
>
> Did you see the rainbow?
>
> This morning actually. I came over the ridge early, out for a walk. There she was. Must have been about half a mile high.
>
> Yeah. I collect rainbows actually.
>
> Yeah. I've got a system actually.

What?

Right. Basically when I see one, I make a notch on my front door there. I've got hundreds.

Yeah, I've got different notches. In rows on the door there. Ninety-four snow, four hundred and forty-two thunder. Nineteen floods. And seven hundred and twelve rainbows. Seven hundred and thirteen. Here I brung some windfalls actually.

In eight sets of lines, Tom's unique character oozes out through his speech patterns, repetitions of words, rhythm and dialect, as well as his topic.

Try the eight-line rule for a character in your own play some time, especially one who is causing you problems. Put the character's lines together from a scene or beat and see what emerges via this isolation of voice, even if the lines don't make literal sense. It can also highlight when a character is purely reactive and not doing enough in the scene. Such lines might run something like this:

CHARACTER.   Fine, how are you?

Really? Why?

Oh dear.

You mean…

I don't understand.

And what did you say?

Right.

Oh, I see.

Wow. That's terrible.

There's nothing to say that a character speaking these sorts of lines can't be rich and active in the drama (and possibly waiting for their chance to shine) – but it's also possible that all they're doing in the scene is providing a sounding board for another more interesting character. So make sure that your all of your characters' words in any one scene are contributing enough dramatically to earn their place in it.

DIALOGUE AS MUSIC, COLOUR, METAPHOR

The final element in the dialogue toolbox concerns non-literal aspects of language. Here's an excerpt from Caryl Churchill's *Escaped Alone*. The play depicts a group of women in their seventies – Sally, Vi, Lena and Mrs Jarrett – who natter away in Sally's backyard over a series of summer afternoons. It's from the first two minutes of the play.

SALLY.	Rosie locked out in the rain
VI.	forgot her key
SALLY.	climbed over
LENA.	lucky to have neighbours who
SALLY.	such a high wall
VI.	this is Rosie her granddaughter
MRS J.	I've a son, Frank
VI.	I've a son
MRS J.	suffers from insomnia
VI.	doesn't come very often. But Thomas
LENA.	that's her nephew
SALLY.	he'd knock up the shelves in no time
VI.	a big table
SALLY.	grain of the wood
VI.	a table like that would last a lifetime
SALLY.	an heirloom
LENA.	except we all eat off our laps

Churchill effects a sense of easy camaraderie between the women, who are clearly so familiar with each other's lives that they can intuit each other's thoughts and complete each other's sentences. Churchill is the queen of interrupted dialogue, where characters constantly speak over and across each other. Although it brilliantly captures the chaos of human speech, creating an impressionistic web of thoughts and observations, the craft couldn't be more precise. Her powerfully attuned ear for the rhythm, pace and musicality of human language enables her to lull the audience into a false sense of security. We let these women's words drift over us, freed from the need to follow plot – and then, without warning, the cosy, meandering chit-chat is disrupted by a shocking monologue by Mrs Jarrett.

> MRS J.   Four hundred thousand tons of rock paid for by senior executives split off the hillside to smash through the roofs, each fragment onto the designated child's head. Villages were buried and new communities of survivors underground developed skills of feeding off the dead where possible and communicating with taps and groans. Instant celebrities rose on ropes to the flash of lights. Time passed. Rats were eaten by those who still had digestive systems, and mushrooms were traded for urine.

And on it goes – until we are suddenly dropped back into the quiet, sunny backyard, and the middle of another humdrum conversation about the merits of mini Tescos. The structure of the play repeats this pattern – chatty garden scenes intersected by Mrs Jarrett's doomsaying monologues – until slowly the fear and alienation in these separate monologues begins to seep into the garden and affect the other women. The juxtaposition of these two contrasting speech forms is powerful and unsettling. We have group dialogue versus monologue; overlapping chit-chat versus direct address to audience; incomplete impressionistic fragments of dialogue versus precise, articulate sentences with concrete images; glimpses of mundane suburbia versus glimpses of violent dystopia. Churchill pushes language far beyond its normal boundaries, finding a music in the everyday as well as the extraordinary.

All of us, including those of us who write dialogue that isn't naturally heightened or lyrical, can and should pay attention to pace, rhythm and musicality. These skills are equally present in a writer of realism, like Joe Penhall. I've highlighted his use of repetition in bold, below.

> RICHIE.   A bathroom and everything. Wow. Have you got a **shower**?

> NEAL.   Got a **very nice shower**.

> RICHIE.   A **very nice shower**? Well, that's **very nice**, isn't it?

Here he uses the 'rule of three' (on 'shower') – to create rhythm, along with a mirroring of 'very nice', just so that Richie can make sure Neal knows exactly what he thinks of his suburban, dull flat – and, by inference, his suburban, dull life.

Finally, here's an excerpt from *An Octoroon* by Branden Jacobs-Jenkins, who prefaces his play, set on a nineteenth-century slave plantation in Southern America, with the following stage directions:

> *I'm just going to say this right now so we can get it over with: I don't know what a real slave sounded like. And neither do you.*

Then, at the end of the first scene, we get the following exchange between Dido and Minnie, two slaves who work on the plantation.

MINNIE.   Girl, have you seen Solon today?

DIDO.   No, why?

MINNIE.   I just rememba'd that nigga owes me four piece of twine and some pig guts.

DIDO.   Girl, you know you ain't never gonna see that twine and them pig guts again, for real.

MINNIE.   What you mean?

DIDO.   Minnie, you know Solon a trick-ass nigga. Remember what happened to Rebecca.

MINNIE.   Wait. Lightskinned Rebecca?

DIDO.   Yeah.

MINNIE.   What Solon do to her?

DIDO.   Well, she had a baby –

MINNIE.   She did?

DIDO.   Yes, girl. And this one time, Solon was like, 'Girl, let me borrow your baby for a second?' And so Rebecca's dumb ass like gave him the baby and then that nigga turnt around and fucking sold the baby.

MINNIE.   What?

DIDO.   Yes, girl. Apparently Massa was about to sell Solon and Grace's baby, but then Solon switched Rebecca's baby out for they baby at the last minute and Massa didn't know the difference so he just sold Rebecca dumb-ass's baby.

MINNIE.   Oh my God. That is so messed up.

This madcap, hilarious and rule-breaking play uses Dion Boucicault's nineteenth-century melodrama *The Octoroon* as its foundation, and then delights in taking every clichéd historical trope it can about American slavery, wrapping them in contemporary language and idiom and throwing them back in our faces. By juxtaposing past and present in its dialogic form, the play positions the audience in a thrilling but uncomfortable place. An exchange like this one has a dizzying number of layers of wit, politics, history and provocation buried in it. In Jacobs-Jenkins's play, the dialogue doesn't just reveal story, the dialogue *is* the story.

MONOLOGUE

As seen in the excerpt from *Escaped Alone*, the monologue can be a very effective theatrical device and is an ever-popular form of theatrical storytelling in itself. Samuel Beckett is widely acknowledged as the father of the modern monologue play, which has diversified into many different forms. Brian Friel, David Hare and Conor McPherson are all well known for their monologue (and duologue) plays. More recent examples include Enda Walsh's *Misterman*, Charlene James's *Cuttin' It*, Simon McBurney's *The Encounter* and Phoebe Waller-Bridge's *Fleabag*. (If you're interested in standalone monologues, I'd also recommend reading the short works of the American playwright Will Eno, who is a master of the form.)

The monologue play can be tempting because it appears on the surface to be simpler and more achievable than a fully peopled drama. In some ways that's true. Direct address to audience means there's no obvious need for the complexities of subtext or dramatised physical action, as we are given a hotline into the character's thoughts. And its non-realistic performative element has an inherent theatricality, particularly when a single actor presents an array of different characters. But the monologue play lives or dies according to the playwright's dexterity with language.

If you want to dip your toe in, you might want to start by writing a dramatic monologue *within* your play, using some of the techniques discussed in this chapter. (There are literally thousands of published character monologues available on online archive sites that you can consult for inspiration.) Dramatic monologues are generally defined as long speeches made by a single character, either to another character on the stage or out to the audience. So why use a monologue and what effect can it have? The writer Lynn Truss, who has written dramatic monologues for radio, says:

The thing about monologue is that it's immediate. It happens now. It happens here. And it is literally 'im-mediate', in that there is ostensibly no mediation: nothing intervening between the character and the audience. That's why, in certain magical theatrical circumstances, it can seem to fill the world. Everyone can think of a moment in a great play when attention zooms in on a single character telling a story – and the audience simply stops breathing. (*Guardian*, 3 May 2005)

The contexts for using monologues are myriad, but you must always think carefully about how and where you place them, and to what end. You will need a dramatic context pertaining to the action of the play *and* a theatrical context that will support the use of heightened language to entertain, inform and intrigue the audience.

SPEECHES

Question: when does a long speech stop being a speech and start being a monologue? I'm afraid there's no standard measurement. *Who's Afraid of Virginia Woolf?* has several four- and five-minute-long speeches. There's a sixteen-page monologue in *La Bête* by David Hirson, spoken by a terrible windbag of a character called Valere (in rhyming couplets, no less).

For the uninitiated, and those of us who aren't natural poets, you might want to use a theatrical device to bed in your monologue, such as the narrator figure (or chorus thereof). A well-known example is Alfieri in Arthur Miller's *A View from the Bridge* – a character from outside the main action who introduces the protagonists and world directly to the audience and offers commentary on the events of the play. The narrator figure can work in epic storytelling, like Lucy Prebble's *ENRON*, as well as intimate two or three-handers such as Moira Buffini's *Handbagged*. In Buffini's play, the two main characters – Queen Elizabeth II and Margaret Thatcher – interact on stage in the present-day reality of the play but also talk directly to the audience with hindsight, as older versions of themselves. It's a multi-layered narrative which allows for rich characterisation. Yasmina Reza's *Art* also breaks the fourth wall by having various of her characters directly address the audience in between scenes to comment on their swiftly fragmenting friendships – as well as featuring a very famous 'in scene' monologue by the character Yvan about his fears over his forthcoming wedding.

SOLILOQUY

If a monologue is a speech given by a single person to somebody else (the audience and/or an onstage character), then a soliloquy is a speech spoken only to oneself. The classical soliloquy that we know from Shakespearean and Greek dramas, where a character employs the sort of rhetorical 'Is this a dagger I see before me?' self-address, tends not to cut much ice with a modern audience. The psychological self-questioning that is usually contained in a classical soliloquy – 'What should I do about my dilemma?' – makes up the very fabric of a modern play. It's usually the interplay *between* characters on stage that provides the bulk of the psychological insight for the audience. So you will need to think carefully about the context for your soliloquy if you're using one, and make sure it doesn't alienate your audience. Characters who talk to themselves – and not to the audience – need *very* good theatrical and dramatic reasons for doing so.

As always, there are no rules to follow when you're experimenting with one person speaking at length, but here are a few things to consider.

→ Is there a dramatic function behind the soliloquy? Does it deliver story, theme, character, theatricality – and why? Try to make sure there's some sort of logic behind the use of monologue, speech or soliloquy, not just your desire to put interesting words in your character's mouth.

→ Under what conditions is it spoken – social, emotional, circumstantial? Does it come at a moment that requires something other than simple dialogue – e.g. a speech, a declaration, a confession? Is it a moment of pressure or combustion for the characters? What warrants the focus on the character or their subject?

→ What might have come before the monologue in the scene to maximise its impact or contextualise its meaning? (Think about juxtaposition in Caryl Churchill's *Escaped Alone* between the domestic scenes and the direct address.)

→ How might it be used to change or privilege the relationship between the speaker and the audience?

→ How might your language change in a long speech? Is it more heightened, lyrical, emotive? Does it show dislocation or fragmentation of thought – confusion, digression? Or is it a torrent of words born of intense emotion? What techniques might you need to keep the audience engaged?

WRITING STYLE

All playwrights are influenced by other writers. It's natural and inescapable, and we can learn a huge amount from our predecessors and contemporaries. But be mindful that you must work to your own strengths. I admire the tautness and mystery in Harold Pinter's writing, but if I tried to pull off his style, I'd be doomed. Experiment by all means, but over time try to identify when and how you manage to create dialogue that seems the most effortless and free-flowing. When you stop trying too hard, you will invariably tap into your natural style and find your true voice. If you are a wordy, intellectual ideas-person, it might be a good idea to find wordy, intellectual characters who can express your dramatic story in a natural way. Tom Stoppard is not a master of subtext. His characters would probably spout philosophy (brilliantly, of course) whether they were Greek tutors or cleaning ladies. So don't try to be all things to all people.

Finally, remember to try and enjoy your work with words. Language is the playwright's base material, so be bold with it, be inventive – and be prepared to work very hard at and with it. If you're bored of thinking about yourself as a sculptor, consider yourself a composer, or a conductor, with words as your orchestra. Train your ear to hear when your dialogue is unbalanced or overwritten. Attune yourself to pace, rhythm, musicality – and silence.

To round off the chapter, I offer a cautionary tale/case study about one of my own plays. The central challenge I faced was how to turn a literary monologue into dramatic stage dialogue – but there are some other useful lessons in the story.

CASE STUDY: *Maggot Moon* by Sally Gardner (stage adaptation by myself)

I had teamed up with director Jesse Jones to create a stage adaptation of *Maggot Moon* – Sally Gardner's multi-award-winning novel for young people. Everybody had told us it was pretty much unadaptable. It has a first-person narrator, Standish, who is dyslexic. He can't read or write and is considered mentally deficient (the book is set in a dystopian 1950s England, which is ruled with an iron fist by the state apparatus of the cruel 'Motherland'). Not only does Standish's narration randomly jump back and forth in time, but his words are sometimes nonsensical. On the page, we experience the world through his own unique filter, and part of the novel's brilliance lies in the way Sally uses language to capture the chaotic, colourful and non-literal workings of her anti-hero's mind.

The novel is an epic David and Goliath story with a cracking plot that involves a murderous dictatorship, a breathtaking state conspiracy and a heroic battle by this schoolboy outsider to take on a powerful empire while searching for his best friend Hector, who has disappeared. Jesse and I both loved the book, and of course, being told it was impossible to stage just made us want to do it even more.

We were invited to workshop a draft at the National Theatre Studio. Naturally, as creatives with something to prove, we thought BIG. We imagined a main stage. A cast of fifteen actors or more, playing multiple roles. An epic dramatisation of Standish's first-person literary narration into a multi-character, multi-scene, multi-location play that fleshed out his 'real life' quest, while taking the audience into his rich imaginary world using Jesse's ambitious staging. Easy. Our first step was to deconstruct the novel's zigzagging, back-and-forth narrative structure and to put the story beats into linear form. A play can't recreate a single POV like a book can, unless it's a monologue play (which, of course, ours wasn't – we intended it to be full of fabulous dialogue), and we wanted to make sure the audience understood the complex plot.

Once we had the story spine laid out, I put key scenes into dialogue, using Sally's prose, and brought as many of the characters as we could on stage, using a roomful of wonderful actors. But the scenes weren't quite working. We improvised. We embellished. We struggled. The more we tried to dramatise the unique qualities of the novel, the further away we moved from them. Eventually we reached an impasse – we just couldn't turn the material into a workable play, and certainly not the sort of spectacular family show the National Theatre were interested in.

A year went by. I sent the book to Purni Morell, then Artistic Director of the Unicorn Theatre (one of the UK's leading theatres for children and young people). Her advice was, in typical Morellian style, simple, blunt and absolutely right: stop trying to reinvent a literary monologue as an all-singing, all-dancing epic, and just let Standish tell his story directly to the audience, as he tells it to the reader of the novel. Purni believed that nothing we threw at the show theatrically could or should compete with the sheer thrill of finding out what happened next in the nail-biting story, moment by moment, in Standish's own language.

Lightbulbs went off. Jesse and I realised we'd been like kids in a theatrical candy shop. In trying to externalise the linguistic brilliance of Standish's novelistic monologue by translating it into a three-dimensional *theatrical* language with a large cast of characters, we had killed off the story. We went back to the drawing board and workshopped the play again with only one actor and a small crack team of audio-visual designers. I threw out almost all the dialogue and used Sally's first-person literary narrative to sculpt an unbroken theatrical monologue, delivered 'out' by Standish, and underpinned with a soundtrack to create the world of the play. And in this way we managed to build the first half of the show in about five days straight.

During this process, we also decided that we would allow a single two-hander scene in the play to dramatise the crucial moment when Standish finally achieves his goal and finds his best friend Hector. It was a point in the story when Standish's idealism and fantasy fall away and are replaced by harsh reality and a new maturity. I wrote this scene in naturalistic dialogue, which made a stark contrast to Standish's highly stylised first-person narrative up to this point, and it really helped underpin his emotional journey in the play.

This was the version that was subsequently commissioned by Justin Audibert, Purni's successor, and produced in 2019. It was an important lesson about the power of simple theatrical storytelling – and that sometimes, less is more. Dialogue is only one way to create meaning on stage, and, seductive as it is to put exciting words into the mouths of many exciting characters – it's not always the right way. In the theatre, language is everything. When you're using it to its full capacities, formally speaking, anything is possible.

EXERCISES: WRITING DIALOGUE

1. *Finding a character's voice*

→ Pick a character – in particular one you feel you don't know very well yet. Refer back to the list of *physical* activities, quirks, habits and tropes you were asked to make in Chapter Three, to show who your characters are, or which reveal their desires or needs. (If you don't have any, invent some!)

→ Without thinking too much about the character's existing dialogue in your play, try and translate some of those quirks and habits into *verbal* tropes. You can exaggerate them for the purposes of the exercise. For example, if your character has a nervous disposition, give them a stammer. If they are pompous, find a verbal habit that might convey this.

→ This may also include repeated expressions, favourite words, idiosyncratic speech patterns, and so on, all of which might help convey your character's inner life.

→ Write a monologue in the voice of the character to try out this heightened voice, using all your new verbal tropes. Choose a specific emotional state for them (fear, anger, anxiety, joy) or a specific physical state (hunger, arousal, cold, adrenaline-pumped) and let that guide you. If it feels over the top, it doesn't matter. Let them be an exaggerated version of themselves for now. You may be able to take some residual flavour of this heightened voice back into your dialogue, to flesh out the character.

2. *Subtext*

→ Take a tricky scene where the dialogue feels clunky or melodramatic. Go through the scene line by line, noting exactly what the character is thinking and feeling, and what they want, on each line.

→ Put these thoughts, feelings and desires into direct speech, or *spoken subtext*, following the method I used in this chapter with the Penhall scene. It will look and sound odd – it's meant to.

→ Think about the context of the scene: which character has the higher status? Is it a public or private space? Can they speak freely or not? And so on. How might this affect *what* they say and *how* they speak? If it helps, change the context to create a better potential for subtext.

→ Now think about what kind of tactics the characters might use when they speak (or don't speak) in pursuit of their goals. Assign a tactic or a speech act (or both) to each line.

→ Then translate the spoken subtext back into *hidden subtext* – i.e. let the character infer their thoughts and feelings – as well as their intentions – but don't allow them to voice them directly.

→ See if you can find a 'leaping salmon' moment in the scene, where one or more characters are finally driven to speak their mind. Again, be clear about how this comes about – what forces them finally to be truthful or state something that was previously impossible?

3. *The eight-line exercise*

→ Take any one character and pull out their first eight lines, or groups of sentences, spoken in the play (or in the whole scene). Write down the groups of lines in chronological order.

→ What sense do you get from these lines? Are they just there to convey information and exposition? Is the character merely reacting to lines spoken to them by another character? Or are they driving the action of the scene and revealing character?

→ Such choices may be deliberate on your part, or they may have come about accidentally because the character doesn't have enough to do in the scene or because you don't know them well enough yet.

→ If so, rewrite their lines in isolation, fleshing out the character. Think about the function of *what* they say (carrier of information, escalation, conflict, exposition) and *how* they say it (using vocabulary, pace, rhythm, repetition and silence) to create a stronger and more consistent voice.

9
THEATRICAL SETTING
AND WORLD

THEATRICAL SETTING AND WORLD

1. *The Carney Home. 5.30 a.m. End of August 1981.*

    A farmhouse kitchen, in rural Northern Ireland, harvest time.

    Flagstone floor. Wooden beams. Washing hanging high in rows. At the back, a large coal-fired range.

    A sink and crockery board. A steep wooden staircase leads upstairs. On the walls are pinned countless children's drawings, photographs, swimming awards. A John Deere 1981 calendar. A rota for feeding the animals, on which are stuck photographs of children. An old, torn Rolling Stones poster from when the Stones played Belfast in 1965 (also covered in children's drawings, etc.). On another wall, almost completely obscured by pictures of children from communions, sports days, swimming galas, dancing competitions, is an old, very weathered Irish flag.

    A door stage-right to the larder. A boot room at the back, beyond through which entrances are made from outside – so people are seen putting on coats there, sometimes boots, before entering and leaving to the yard outside.

    Above the central fireplace at the back is an old farmhouse clock, next to which is a large dusty framed picture of Big Jack Carney. Along the shelf, under him (backed by a long knitted Celtic FC scarf), is an array of old soccer programmes, egg timers, an old squeeze box, an old hand-held fire extinguisher, an old biscuit tin, a foot-high dusty plastic model of George Harrison with his French horn from Yellow Submarine *(painted in psychedelic colours). Dozens of candles. Some birthday cards. A framed photograph of Brigitte Bardot in* Helen of Troy, *another of George Best.*

    The shutters are closed. The curtains drawn. The room is full of smoke.

    A tape playing on a big ghetto blaster. The Rolling Stones, quietly.

    On the table, candles burn. A full ashtray. A bottle of Bushmills, two inches left.

Description of play setting in Act One of *The Ferryman* by Jez Butterworth, 2017.

2. *Daylight. Christmas.*
   A small artificial Christmas tree with lights.
   The family is gathered. Mum, Dad, Granny, Grandad, Debbie, Hazel.
   Dad stares at Debbie. Silence.

Description of play setting in *In the Republic of Happiness* by Martin Crimp, 2012.

3. *Consider the idea that offstage should be as visible to the audience as possible. 'The actors' are another set of characters. Shoes – particularly high ones – should be taken off and on, lipstick removed and reapplied. If any vomiting, crying or shouting needs to happen offstage, the audience should be able to glimpse it at the very least.*

   There shouldn't be any set. The play should be performable without any props.

   Ideally the play should be performed by a cast of six.

   There should be at least one female character (that should probably be played by a female actor) in every scene.

   If a woman has to get a bit naked at any one point, then the men should get naked also to redress the balance.

   Most importantly, this play should not be well behaved.

Description of play setting in *Revolt. She Said. Revolt Again* by Alice Birch, 2014.

Three plays, three playwrights, three descriptions of different stage settings and theatrical worlds. Three different sets of instructions, provocations and intentions from the writer.

Do the words communicate too much, or not enough? Which play would you rather see? If you were a theatre director, which would you rather direct? Or act in? Now read the opening description of your own setting in your working playscript, if you have one. What world and setting does it indicate? What else does it communicate about the play? And do the exact words you've chosen really matter?

Yes, they do. A playscript is a blueprint, not a literary work, and a good blueprint is necessarily practical. But it also creates tone, energy and the potential to provoke the theatrical imagination of any directors, actors and literary managers who might read it. The fact is, when anyone looking for a produceable play reads a new playscript, they are looking far beyond the dialogue. Of course, dialogue is the main tool with which the writer creates meaning on the page – perhaps we could say that dialogue forms the river bed along which the play's meaning flows. But it isn't the only tool.

Everything on the page will communicate something about the playwright's intentions, and help give a sense of the play's theatrical potential (or lack of), including your play world and setting. One of the most exciting things that happens for the playwright in production is that you get to see your play made flesh – not just in terms of actual human beings playing your parts, but in terms of a physical, three-dimensional concrete world as created by your director in collaboration with stage, lighting, sound and costume designers. This theatrical world can go from, at one end of the spectrum, a miraculous copy of reality, complete with cooking smells, real fire and live animals, to the other: an abstract liminal space, and anything in between. Either way it forms a key part of your audience's theatrical experience, so you must think carefully about what you want your setting and world to communicate.

Many developing playwrights tend not to think too much about what their theatrical setting and world are contributing to the play's story, beyond them being a necessary 'where' to create a variety of physical contexts for the action. Unless a new writer has a very vivid theatrical imagination and a certain confidence with theatrical form, they will tend to default to a version of realism in their first forays into playwriting. This in turn tends to mean that setting and world stay firmly in the realm of the 'necessary where' and don't get explored to their full potential. New playwrights also tend to use scene settings and locations as a logical backdrop to the action, but let story dictate them, rather than using them as inspiration for action. This is natural, but can also be limiting.

The dominance of realism in new writing has a long history, but has been accelerated by the ubiquitous influence of television drama. The aim of TV stories, particularly in the dominant forms of soap opera and continuing drama series, is to mimic reality as closely as possible. (Although in this so-called 'golden age' of television, TV dramas have become less dependent on realism and more theatrical and non-naturalistic.) Cinematic storytelling uses a wider variety of techniques to create symbolic, visual and aural meaning that is not strictly speaking realistic in a diegetic sense. Diegetic basically means everything that the characters hear and see that is part of the actual scene, rather than anything imposed on top, like a soundtrack, special effects or a voice-over. For example, in the shower scene from *Psycho* described in Chapter One, the running water and the woman's screams are diegetic; the musical score is non-diegetic.

Given that today we probably watch more hours of television than any other dramatic form, it's impossible for it not to have influenced the way we unconsciously think about theatrical storytelling. But as we know, television writers employ a whole armoury of other important but rather different storytelling skills. So, as playwrights, instead of asking ourselves, 'How can I convince the audience that what is happening on stage is "real?",', we might instead ask the following questions: 'What representation of reality do I want to create for my audience and how will my setting and play world contribute to this?' 'How can I make them an essential, germane part of my storytelling craft, rather than simply a convenient backdrop to the action?' And 'How can I exploit my story setting for the stage using the forms and techniques available to me?'

SETTING VERSUS WORLD

These two terms are often used interchangeably, but for clarity I'm going to separate them. When I talk about your play's *setting* (singular or plural), I'm talking about the physical locations of your play – which will be turned into a theatrical set in production. This setting might be one room; it might be a natural setting like a forest or field; it might be a cityscape. It might involve a single location, or multiple locations spread across many scenes. It might involve a 'memory setting' taking us into the past or future, or a fantasy setting, such as a dream or hallucination. It might be set on a mound (*Happy Days* by Samuel Beckett); on a raft (*Rafts and Dreams* by Robert Holman); in a bathroom with a full bathtub (*Low Level Panic* by Clare McIntyre); a prison cell (*Someone Who'll Watch Over Me* by Frank McGuinness – among many others); a cinema (*The Flick* by Annie Baker); an urban street corner (*Pass Over* by Antoinette Nwandu) – or any combination of different locations. Think about the settings of some of the plays mentioned in the case studies in this book – a lighthouse, a coalmine, a series of interrogation rooms... and how they immediately create the potential for interesting action. Whether interior or exterior, abstract or concrete, the physical spaces of your play can also be used to create and underpin theme and metaphor on stage. We'll break these down in detail soon.

I'm using the *world* of the play to describe elements that go beyond the physical setting(s), locations, time and place, and that relate to the play's wider contexts. These may not always be visible on stage in concrete props or staging but will affect dialogue, action and behaviour. Your play world may directly refer to a specific socio-political context, historical period, class, community, cultural and geographical landscape. Or, conversely, a fantastical world, imaginary land or magical reality.

As an example, the setting of *A Raisin in the Sun* is the Younger family's shabby two-room rental apartment in Chicago's predominantly African-American South Side in the early 1950s. The world of the play outside these four walls is one of racial segregation, where the social and economic ghettoisation of urban black America contrasts starkly with aspirational and elitist white neighbourhoods such as Clybourne Park; where the legacy of slavery still casts a very long shadow, and where hope is offered by the growing Civil Rights movement along with the notion of the modern African diaspora. Various characters bring these different elements on stage, so that we have a clear sense of the world beyond the physical setting, and how it impacts the family.

HOW TO DESCRIBE YOUR SETTING AND WORLD

The question of how to convey your intentions with play setting and world on the page is a common source of anxiety for new playwrights, but there is no empirically right or wrong way to go about it. Different writers across the ages have employed a huge range of styles, from the novelistic to the minimalist and everything in between. Here are some more opening set descriptions from published texts that detail the play's setting and world (I've excluded those stage directions written specifically for actors who are meant to be on stage at the play's opening):

A very expensive hotel room in Leeds. The kind that is so expensive it could be anywhere in the world. (*Blasted* by Sarah Kane)

A Gentleman's Club in London. A wood-panelled room with two big leather armchairs and a small table between them. (*Posh* by Laura Wade)

Early spring, 1862. A slave cabin in the middle of nowhere. Far West Texas. One hour before dawn. (*Father Comes Home From the Wars (Parts 1, 2, & 3)* by Suzan-Lori Parks)

What's interesting about all these descriptions is that they communicate something beyond some pieces of furniture or an arrangement of bricks and mortar. They all contain exposition or information that contributes to a sense of physical place *and* of the potential world of the play. The private, enclosed setting for *Posh* immediately communicates a certain kind of social milieu – money, class, privilege, history – it feels concrete and specific. And, indeed, the play explores themes of money, class, privilege and history.

Blasted, in contrast, gives us something both specific and generic. A hotel room – but an expensive one: *'So expensive that it could be anywhere in the world.'* It's a curious description that suggests dislocation and blandness – along, again, with a sense of privilege. And it is a play in which that bland, comfortable, supposedly private space is invaded by war and violence, and in which the room and the play slowly fragment and explode into chaos.

In Suzan-Lori Parks's play, the setting is very concrete in terms of historical period, geographical location and social milieu, but we also have the added detail of the time of day: *'One hour before dawn.'* A detail as small as this can enrich, change or contextualise the action of a scene and create pace, rhythm and atmosphere.

Now think about your own opening set description. What might a reader of the text glean from your sentence or paragraph in terms of theme, plot or character? Are there any significant details, inherent conflicts, notable props? You don't have to list exhaustively every single visual aspect of the set as you imagine it – that is the job of the director and designers, using your text as a jumping-off point. Yours is to consider the significance of your play setting and world to the story, and then think about how to distil your intentions in your text.

Look again at the efficiency of the setting as described in *Posh*, and how, despite its brevity, it totally grounds us in the world of the play. Whether you tend towards brevity or length, think of your opening decription as the most direct way to locate your play's physical setting and world as carriers of exposition – to create meaning before any words have been spoken on stage. So be as economical or as expansive as you like – just do it with theatrical *intention*.

NATURALISTIC STAGING

For those of you who are now worrying that a) your play is a piece of realism and therefore less worthy, and b) your stage setting is therefore realistic and untheatrical, let's return to the description of the play set from Act One of *The Ferryman* by Jez Butterworth, as quoted at the beginning of this chapter. Butterworth uses his setting and world to create exposition, to root us in a socio-political world, and to carry metaphorical meaning – all within a realist setting, and without stylistic pyrotechnics.* Of course, this play has a single location (minus a brief prologue scene that takes place elsewhere the previous day). If the play had had multiple scene locations it's probably unlikely Butterworth would have spent so much time describing each one. But it's worth looking in detail at what information is contained here and why it might be useful.

The play is set in a farmhouse in County Armagh, Northern Ireland, over a period of twenty-four hours. Apart from the aforementioned prologue, the action takes place solely in and around this farmhouse – but the audience is only privy to the space of the main kitchen. The (offstage) event that kicks off the action is the discovery of the body of Seamus Carney, ten years after he disappeared in a suspected IRA murder. Once the news of the discovery of the missing man is brought into the home of his brother, Quinn Carney, a chain of events is set off over the proceeding day and night, building to a tragic climax. There are various ways in which the setting of the play contributes to its overall meaning, and I've broken them down below so we can analyse this interplay.

PHYSICAL SETTING

The farmhouse kitchen provides a strong physical, sensory world, which gives us many clues about the nature of the family that lives there before a single word is spoken on stage. As we've seen, the stage directions describe in some detail the detritus of the Carneys' collective life. It's a messy, comfortable house that's been lived in for many generations by a large extended family, currently six adults and eight children. In the large kitchen, which is the family hub, we will witness a stream of domestic activity; meals served and eaten, dancing, drunken rows, storytelling, childcare, bickering and celebration. The lack of privacy is a constant theme, and the various characters are shunted in and out of the room

---

* What the French call *mise-en-scène* – 'setting the scene' via props and staging to create story, although the term is more commonly used in film.

when confidential conversations are necessary. The physical setting captures the Carney family's warmth, humour and deep bonds – as well as the inevitable emotional cross-currents, conflicts and rivalries.

SOCIO-POLITICAL WORLD

The play is set during the autumn of 1981, during the Troubles in Northern Ireland. More specifically, it's set in August, at the same time as the culmination of the hunger strike by Irish Republican paramilitary prisoners in protest at the British government's withdrawal of their political prisoner status. Even more specifically, it's set on 20th August, the same day that real-life hunger striker Michael Devine became the tenth prisoner to die in six months. And on the same day in the Carneys' fictional lives, his death is juxtaposed with the discovery of Seamus Carney's body. In this way, Butterworth establishes a clear and concrete social, historical and political world that informs his story and grounds the audience in place and time. The death of Michael Devine is announced on stage (via a radio broadcast listened to by one of the characters offstage) bang in the middle of the Carney family's harvest dinner – a chillingly ironic moment.

Writing a play informed by actual events can be challenging, not least because the theatre writer, unlike the film or television writer who can cover much more narrative ground, may have to limit themselves to a single event, place and time, for practical staging reasons. However, dramatising a historical event (real or imagined) within a limited, condensed time frame and setting, can force the playwright to think much more theatrically. Other plays that successfully use limited single setting and condensed 'real time' to create an experience based on actual events include Katori Hall's *The Mountaintop*, Michael Frayn's *Copenhagen*, and Kemp Powers' *One Night in Miami*.

SYMBOLIC ELEMENTS OF SETTING

There is another aspect of *The Ferryman*'s 'time and place' setting that creates potent non-literal meaning. The play is set during harvest time – and more specifically, on the day that the Carneys' smallholding fields are harvested and the crops brought in by Quinn, his sons, and visiting relatives. Afterwards, the family gathers to feast and celebrate. Harvest is a time, as Butterworth has said, of both the culmination of something and the start of something new. This mirrors the play's basic plot, whereby a missing person is discovered, setting off a new chain of events, relationships and choices.

There's also a wonderful dramatic symbolism in Butterworth's placing of the family's harvest feast – representing bounty, plenty, a good winter – on a day of death for the hunger striker (as well as the death of Seamus). In a BBC Radio 4 interview, Butterworth said of the play's harvest setting: 'It's about an entrance and an exit... theatre is based entirely on entrances and exits, like our lives.' Think how often the same significant turning points occur in plays: births and deaths, weddings and funerals, birthdays and anniversaries, arrivals and exits (and the rituals that mark them, such as meals). Ritual events like this are always useful for the playwright. Not only are they usually suffused with emotion and tension, but they provide a reason for a large group of people to gather together in the same space.

USE OF INTERIOR VERSUS EXTERIOR/PRIVATE VERSUS PUBLIC SPACE

The set doesn't change during the play; all the action we witness takes place in this single room. Certain key events that have significant dramatic consequences happen *offstage* but are brought *on stage* in various ways. Characters come in from the fields and the river with mud on their boots, and on occasion animals in their arms. They come downstairs half-asleep; they enter drunk, tired from harvesting, with bad news, with blood on their hands. We constantly feel the rural isolation of the farmhouse and its sacred private spaces. Butterworth uses this confluence of interior and exterior/private and public to embed the drama, which is essentially about the invasion of a family both past and present, and the terrible sacrifices that are made to protect it.

THEATRICAL DEVICES AND PROPS

Many of you will have heard the famous Chekhovian maxim about the gun – or some version of – as written by the Russian playwright in a letter to a colleague: '*One must never place a loaded rifle on the stage if it isn't going to go off. It's wrong to make promises you don't mean to keep.*' It's a useful maxim, and in *The Ferryman* there is indeed a gun that goes off, but there is also a goose that goes off. In the first act of the play, the fattened goose that will be killed and eaten for the family's harvest dinner escapes after a young man, Oisin, mistakenly leaves an outdoor gate open. The goose is later found on the riverbank by Tom Kettle, an English odd-job man, and killed at the end of the act. In Act Two, the goose is duly roasted and eaten by the family. And at the climax of Act Three, in an act of dreadful but (theatrically) beautiful symmetry, Oisin has his neck wrung by Tom Kettle. The goose is used not only to foreshadow the tragedy that is to come, but to symbolise the very classical themes of sacrifice and payment to right wrongs (also referenced in the ferryman of the play's title, Charon, who in Greek mythology is paid to ferry the dead across the River Styx).

A less metaphorical but more practical and omnipotent prop is Aunt Pat's radio, to which the formidable matriarch is glued all day, listening to news reports about the hunger strikers. At one point Margaret Thatcher's stern voice cuts like a knife through the family's relaxed breakfast – a reminder of the war that rages outside the farmhouse. Not only is it a convenient way to bring the outside world into the room physically, but the radio becomes a source of conflict, as Aunt Pat and other family members grapple over its use.

These are just a few of the ways in which the play uses its physical setting and world to help tell the story and embed its themes. Although the play utilises a single static *set*, the drama itself is never dull nor static. Over three acts, the space is used by different characters to different ends, beginning with the intimate private dance between Quinn and his sister-in-law Caitlin, and ending in a public scene of death and violence with over ten people on stage. There is plenty of contrast in atmosphere and energy during the play's slow burn. In addition, the play uses theatrical symbolism to create deeper meaning for the audience. In this way we get a truly theatrical experience, despite the limitations of time and space – or perhaps because of them.

NON-NATURALISTIC STAGING

Of course, many other playwrights take an entirely different approach, using their plays' settings as overtly theatrical devices. Florian Zeller's *The Father* is set in a comfortably furnished bourgeois flat, inhabited by the protagonist, André. The action takes place primarily in the sitting room, with a kitchen just visible. In the first couple of scenes we learn that André is succumbing to dementia, and the play slowly and painfully charts his descent into forgetfulness and confusion.

Scene Three opens with this set description: '*Simultaneously, the same room and a different room. Some furniture has disappeared; as the scenes progress, the set sheds certain elements, until it becomes an empty, neutral space.'* And that is exactly what happens. As André's dementia progresses, the furniture disappears from the room during the scene changes, piece by piece. By the final scene, the once fully furnished room has transformed into a white hospital room, empty but for a single bed. The protagonist's world has shrunk and reduced, and he has shrunk and reduced too. Zeller cleverly uses his theatrical form to mirror the onstage action, giving the audience a devastating sensory impression of the awful confusion of dementia.

Another play in which the settings and world become almost another character is Anthony Neilson's *The Wonderful World of Dissocia*, as already mentioned in Chapter Five. The first half of the play dramatises the interior world of a woman having a psychotic episode by taking us into her imaginary kingdom, Dissocia. After an hour watching her romp through the surreal landscape of her imagination, we see her illusion reduced to a small, wrecked room. And then, in the second act, she (and we) are dumped back into harsh reality as we watch her struggle to recover in a clinical, colourless hospital room. It's not surprising that so many plays which attempt to externalise an internal psychological experience rely heavily on theatrical setting to do so.

UNIFIED PLACE, DISRUPTED TIME

Some plays successfully utilise a single theatrical setting across different time periods to juxtapose past, present and/or future. Bruce Norris's play *Clybourne Park* is set in a family house in a Chicago suburb (the same neighbourhood into which Lorraine Hansberry's Younger family are due to move in *A Raisin in the Sun*). In Act One, set in 1959, Clybourne Park is a predominately white middle-class neighbourhood. The story details the conflict between the house owners, Russ and Bev, and their neighbours, Karl and Betsy, who object to the couple's plans to sell their house to a black couple. They fear that allowing black families to live in the neighbourhood will trigger a downturn in property value. Act Two is set fifty years later in 2009. Clybourne Park is now a predominately black neighbourhood, on the cusp of gentrification. A different white couple, played by the same actors who were Karl and Betsy in the first half, wants to buy the house and rebuild it, but find their plans blocked by Lena and Kevin, a black couple, from the local housing board. Norris cements his themes of racial politics, property economics and family secrets by doubling his actors across both acts.

Tena Štivičić's *3 Winters*, described in Chapter Four, is another play that juxtaposes three generations of life within a single setting, as does Richard Bean's play *Honeymoon Suite*, which is set in the suite of a Bridlington seaside hotel on three separate wedding anniversaries of the same couple, whom we meet at eighteen, in their forties, and then their sixties. The single but multi-era setting of the play acts as a metaphor for the changing state of their marriage, through youthful optimism, middle-aged disillusion and the hard-won hindsight of old age. Bean gives us three different physical incarnations of the same couple at different stages of their lives using six actors. All six remain on stage during the play, occupying the same fixed space in three different realities. It's a lovely device that creates a funny and poignant overlapping theatrical world.

USE OF LIMINAL SPACE

Liminal derives from the Latin word 'limen', meaning threshold – it refers to a metaphorical or imagined place that might straddle or blur the boundaries of the 'real' world of the story. One of the most famous modern plays to use this device is Caryl Churchill's *Top Girls*. In Act One, her protagonist, Marlene, a woman who has just been promoted to managing director of the Top Girls recruitment company, holds a dinner in a restaurant for some female friends to celebrate her success. These guests, however, are famous real and imaginary women drawn from many historical eras from the Middle Ages onwards: Pope Joan, Lady Nijō, Patient Griselda from Chaucer's *Canterbury Tales*, Dull Gret from a Bruegel painting, and Isabella Bird, a Victorian explorer.

The women eat, drink too much, gossip and compare their difficult paths through life as spirited, independent women. It's a stunning theatrical set piece which cements the themes of the play with humour and spectacle. The play then abruptly dispenses with the 'dream space' to take us into the real world of Marlene's challenging working and personal life.

Tony Kushner's epic two-part *Angels in America* also uses liminal space throughout, particularly in the intersection between Prior and Harper. These two characters, both on strong medication – one for treatment of AIDS, one for depression – meet continually in dream spaces, where they are free of the bodily limitations placed on them in the real world.

So, no matter which of the above forms of stagecraft are to your taste, remember that your play's *where* – its physical *and* metaphorical worlds –

are as much a part of its theatrical cosmology as the plot, the characters, and the words they speak. When a literary manager or director reads your play, you want to ground them right away in a specific time, place and context that allows them to feel the play's sensory world and theatrical energy – and this can be done in a few deft lines. Remember, too, that many great plays are set in one room, one house, one village. Never fear simplicity if your play demands it.

CASE STUDY: *A True Friend of England* by Sylvia Paskin

Sylvia's play was inspired by real events that happened to a member of her own family in Berlin and England during the early days of the Second World War. The story concerns an illegal wartime love affair between a respectable middle-aged Jewish woman, Lily, and Josef, a gentile German conman twenty years her junior, who makes his living fleecing money from German Jews looking for safe harbour elsewhere in Europe.

The play begins with their initial meeting and mutual need as client and businessman. But the transaction is complicated, firstly by Lily's discovery of the web of lies Josef has spun to get her to part with her cash for a fake passport, and then again when, against the odds, they fall in love. Josef secures Lily's escape to England but is captured and sent to a concentration camp. There, he is released on the proviso that he goes to England to spy for the Reich, and duly attends a spy school in Germany, where he is seduced by a manipulative German singer, Clara. Lily settles in London safely, but Josef is captured on arriving in the UK. Lily and Josef are both interrogated by MI5 to ascertain whether or not Josef is a spy. Lily at first tries to protect Josef, but when MI5 tell her that Josef had an affair with Clara, she feels betrayed and agrees to confess that he is a spy – hoping to save herself and avoid being sent back to Germany. Josef is court-martialled and shot. Ultimately, the play is a portrayal of a doomed love affair between two people driven apart by jealousy and war.

The play had a good premise, great characters, plenty of suspense and very high stakes. But its core story in the current draft felt unsatisfying, and its dramatic purpose wasn't quite clear. What was the play asking us to bear witness to? What ideas was it articulating?

Did the narrative really deliver an emotional punch? Although true to life, and closely based on Sylvia's extensive research, the play felt hindered by its 'real' history.

The settings that Sylvia was using weren't helping. The play's action moved from Berlin to Hamburg to London, with many different locations. While those settings were interesting in themselves, including British interrogation rooms, Lily's contrasting German and English apartments, and the German spy school, they didn't feel theatrically cohesive. The story also covered two years of action. Sylvia, like me, felt the multiple settings, uneven structure and relatively long time frame were cluttering up the play and preventing her from creating a tight dramatic narrative.

On workshopping this first draft, three things emerged that had the potential to liberate the play and give Sylvia a way into her second draft. The first was a line spoken by Josef, which seemed to encapsulate a key theme of the play:

> We all have so many facets. We reflect our light or our darkness differently with each person we meet.

Reading this was an 'aha' moment for me. This wasn't just a story about a liar, Josef – it was a story about a liar who learns to tell the truth (that he loves Lily). It was also about a truth-teller (Lily), who ends up lying to save herself, in revenge. But wasn't it also about the narratives created and demanded by war, and the struggle to balance them? In pure dramatic terms, the story wasn't quite delivering because neither Lily's real-life choice to do what MI5 asked of her, nor Josef's real-life lack of choice in being recruited by the Reich gave the key characters any real agency. Both were merely reacting against superior forces of government. I suggested that Sylvia might want to move away from the 'truth' of the historical story and focus more on the theme of 'truth versus lies'.

The second thing I noticed was a prop. There was a folding screen used in two scenes: once in Lily's bedroom and once in an interrogation room, when Lily hides behind it at the request of Josef's interrogators so she can hear his confession. Sylvia and I discussed the idea of giving this screen a bigger role and allowing it to remain on stage in every scene. Not only did it have a practical use in the staging – for concealment, for undressing, for separation of space – it was a great carrier of symbolism. This simple folding screen could perhaps become more than just a physical piece of furniture, but also a symbolic prop to underpin the themes that were emerging in our discussions: appearance versus reality; truth versus falsehood; the different selves that every character in the play had to present in order to survive; as well as the obvious divide between the two 'sides' of the war, Germany and Britain. It could also provide the opportunity for interesting staging. For example, the screen might be manipulated by the actors to represent a change of location – reducing the need for elaborate scene changes with great shifting around of furniture and props.

The third thing was the realisation that one of the key *activities* in the play – interrogation – should also be its key dramatic *action*. (As discussed in Chapter Seven, a dramatic action is something a character does in service of a driving goal or intention, whereas an activity isn't necessarily outcome-related.) In every scene of Sylvia's play, one character would interrogate another in order to evaluate their trustworthiness – as a lover, an authority figure, an ally. But because they often lacked clear consequences, those various interrogations hadn't quite yet coalesced into a truly dramatic story. Thinking strategically about these forms of interrogation and the character motivations behind them helped unlock the play's potential drama.

Putting these three things together, Sylvia and I arrived at the following theatrical equation:

> *Key theme:* truth versus lies
> *Key theatrical prop:* a folding screen
> *Key dramatic action:* interrogation

From this point on, the 'real' events of the past became slightly less important than the need to create a satisfying, albeit more fictionalised, dramatic narrative. We outlined a possible map for Sylvia's next draft in the following summary:

A natural truth-seeker (Lily) and a natural liar (Josef) fall in love against the odds. In order to survive the war they must both lie to the authorities. Josef's great truth is that he loves Lily, a Jew, even though he knows it will condemn him. Lily's great truth is that she knows and loves Josef, a German spy, even though admitting this will condemn her to exile in Germany and certain death. In a world turned upside down by war, where truth and lies become relative, depending on which side you are on, both characters are given the chance to deny their love and save their own skin. But they cannot; their love is the only stable, true thing they both have left. Telling the truth condemns them both to death; but the value of the truth – and their love – survives.

By interrogating Sylvia's first draft in this way, we discovered how the settings and world and the play's structure could inform each other. We located and crystallised one of Sylvia's key themes in a piece of dialogue; we identified and amplified a central action; and we highlighted the use of a prop she had already placed in several scenes as a way of embodying theme. This allowed Sylvia to ground the world of her play more efficiently *and* more theatrically, while paring back her overly busy multiple settings into a few key public and private spaces. Her play now had the potential to become a much more satisfying piece of theatre, in which setting, world, story and theme converged organically. Of course, this analysis is only one possible way forward for Sylvia – there might be others that work even better – but doing this sort of intensive workout on a draft will usually bear fruit somewhere down the line.

EXERCISES: SETTING AND WORLD

1. *Setting as exposition*

→ Go back to your list of locations in your play, as many as you've thought of or already written around. If it's only one location, detail different parts of the room/stage space. They might be 'real' and/or liminal, public and private, natural and man-made, empty and peopled.

→ Think about how much exposition and backstory is contained in these settings – what do they tell us about world/character/mood/ time and place? What meaning do they carry?

→ Describe the outside world of the play beyond the concrete locations (including social, cultural, political, geographical, historical contexts and factors that might influence the action). How will you bring this world on stage to contextualise your action, for example in décor, props, costume, lighting, music, etc.?

→ If your settings are not specified in your play or contained in concrete stage directions, do you give any sense of a *theatrical performative world*, such as in Alice Birch's stage directions (see the start of this chapter)?

2. Maximalist versus minimalist physical settings

→ Continue with your list of the physical locations and scene settings. If your play has a single location, detail different parts of the room/stage space that contain action. If certain locations appear more than once, detail any differences in time of day or physical context that might change each time the location arises.

→ Choose one of the locations and describe it in as much detail as possible, in prose. Use the stage directions from *The Ferryman* for inspiration. If your play is a stripped-down, 'without décor' piece, just imagine the opposite – populate it with things. Write as lyrically as you like. Try to create a strong sense of the world of your play.

→ Then, just to see what happens, remove everything and think about how you'd create the feeling you want *without* décor. Instead of describing objects we can see in the space, think about how you might describe the abstract theatrical space to allow a director to understand the themes of the play.

→ Now come up with at least one new setting by going to the opposite of an existing one – e.g. if your play is set in a domestic space, go to a professional one. If it's set in a small room, go to an open public space. See if you can outline the basic action of a scene set in this new location, even if this will not remain in the draft. How does it impact on the action?

3. *Metaphorical setting*

→ Write down the key theme or idea at the heart of your play (or various, if more than one).

→ Now think about how you might bring your theme on stage using a key prop within a particular setting, along with other theatrical symbols, music and lighting, scenery, etc.

→ Is there an ongoing key dramatic action or activity in the play that also carries theme, and which may link to a prop, place or physical context?

→ Try to find one concrete piece of stagecraft for each theme or idea. Are any of these useful for your play beyond this exercise?

10

A MINIATURE CHAPTER ABOUT WRITING IN MINIATURE

A MINIATURE CHAPTER ABOUT WRITING IN MINIATURE

For the final chapter on writing craft, I'm going to leave you with a masterclass in miniature storytelling by a well-known writer. Some of you might already know the text. Either way, please just read (or even better, read aloud) the following monologue as spoken by the female character. In the original work, it takes the form of a Christmas card, but for now you can just imagine the actor speaking the lines out to the audience, rather than to another character on stage.

WOMAN. Hey Charlie, I'm pregnant, living on Ninth Street right above the dirty bookstore off Euclid Avenue. I stopped taking dope, and I quit drinking whiskey. My old man plays the trombone and works out at the track. He says that he loves me even though it's not his baby, he says that he'll raise him up like he would his own son. He gave me a ring that was worn by his mother, and he takes me out dancing every Saturday night. Hey Charlie, I think about you every time I pass the filling station, on account of all the grease you used to wear in your hair. I still have that record of Little Anthony and the Imperials, but someone stole my record player, now how do you like that! And hey Charlie, I almost went crazy after Mario got busted, so I went back to Omaha to live with my folks. But everyone I used to know was either dead or in prison, so I came back to Minneapolis... this time I think I'm gonna stay. Hey Charlie, I think I'm happy for the first time since my accident. And I wish I had all the money you used to spend on dope. I'd buy me a used-car lot and I wouldn't sell any of 'em, I'd just drive a different car every day depending on how I feel.

In a few deft lines, in a minute or so of performance time, an entire fictional universe is conjured up around this character. We are handed the following story elements:

A status quo

The character is pregnant, and sober, and with a new guy, who's good to her – but perhaps whom she doesn't really love. Her emotional state seems to be primarily nostalgic, a little sad, but also positive and looking towards the future.

A character goal/desire/need

Her objective is to communicate with Charlie, for reasons as yet unknown. Is it just to revisit the past? Does she need something from him? There are lots of juicy internal and external obstacles and goals here to be mined.

A complex backstory

She once had a relationship with Charlie, whoever he is; she's been through bad times with Mario, whoever he is; but she's survived addiction, drama and heartbreak. This is a woman who's been through the mill but she's still standing.

A setting and world

We are thrown into an immediate geographical location, Minneapolis, and a colourful blue-collar neighbourhood, a socio-political world, and a sense of era. We can easily conjure up the sights, sounds and smells of this woman's world. It's alive with sensory detail that can be transposed into staging.

A voice

The woman's personality seeps through her words. Can you visualise her? One of my favourite lines is the one where she imagines buying a used-car lot and driving different cars around every day depending on her whim. This writing flourish doesn't give us *story* per se, but it's a wonderful detail that opens a window into her psychology and character.

So what might we need to complete this monologue and turn it into a perfect and complete dramatic narrative that stands alone as a miniature play? In class I ask students to write a continuation of the character's speech and bring it to a dramatic conclusion, however small. To help them, they can use one or more of the following devices:

→ A reversal
→ A revelation
→ A new course of action
→ A choice
→ A decision
→ An answer to a dramatic question

Try the same now. To get you started, the writer of this monologue has kindly supplied you with the opening line of the final paragraph, which is as follows:

> WOMAN   Hey Charlie, for Chrissakes, if you want to know the
>   truth of it...

Taking this as the first line of your continuation, write a short paragraph or a few lines until you feel you've completed the woman's story within the monologue. Don't forget to use the listed elements above, which should help to give your story shape. Take five or ten minutes... and just *write*.

When you've finished, let's regroup.

How did you end this mini saga? Was it challenging to write? If so, where did you struggle? What did you discover about the character?

The point of the exercise is to demonstrate that it's easy enough to craft a narrative from a very few key concrete story elements if you are asking yourself the right sorts of questions. Sometimes pulling back from the overwhelming detail of a full-length play and thinking in miniature can help refresh your eye and crystallise your core story.

Here, with their permission, are some examples created by writers in class.

> Hey Charlie, for Chrissakes, if you want to know the truth of it...
> It's your kid, goddammit. I know – I should have written, told you
> sooner. I only stayed a couple of months in Omaha – didn't want
> my folks to know. But don't you worry, Charlie. I'm not asking for
> anything – I'll be fine... I guess.

> Hey Charlie, for Chrissakes, if you want to know the truth of
> it... When I say old man, I mean fucking ancient. We're talking
> dinosaurs, Charlie. The motherfucker's knocking on eighty. Sure

he can stagger round the dancefloor and he treats me good. But he's got real big moolah, stashed away in bonds and shares. Says it's all mine when he goes belly up. Me, an heiress, Charlie babe! I give him two years tops. Diabetes. Charlie, maybes you can help. Your time in the hospital... you know all about the medication. Nobody'd ever know... Then we could... you know... take off...

Hey Charlie, for Chrissakes, if you want to know the truth of it... I would swap every damn moment of this to have you back, so I'm throwing you one last line. If you're clean, then I'll give you one week to come and get me and we will just disappear. I'll wait every day at the Moonstone Café, the corner of Eighth Street. After that, I'll know not to expect anything ever again.

Hey Charlie, for Chrissakes, if you want to know the truth of it... This dress arrived in a box – strange white thing, made me look like I'd been bandaged. Couldn't look my old man in the eye. He wants to get it done before the baby makes the dress not fit. So I'm probably going to get married on Saturday. He came back this morning and said he'd booked the county hall for 12 o'clock. So, yeah. Saturday. If you can make it.

Hey Charlie, for Chrissakes, if you want to know the truth of it... I can't get you out of my head. I can't understand what you did. I'm still teasing at it, I guess. I'm not going to write to you again. What's the point of writing to a dead man? I held your head in my hands, and watched your eyes close. I can't get the hair grease off my hands, is all. Least not today I can't.

Hey Charlie, for Chrissakes, if you want to know the truth of it... It's the noise I can't stand. I told him, 'If you bring the guys back one more night!' 'What you gonna do?' he said. And he laughed. It's midnight now. Half an hour and they'll be here. Remember when we used to sneak out the house, before Dad came home? I've been thinking about the hut by the lake a lot, since I found out about the baby. So quiet. Hey Charlie... meet me there?

I like to think that this last one might be a letter written by Stella Kowalski to her first teenage sweetheart, ten years into her marriage with Stanley. But all the above successfully answer some of the mysteries of the earlier monologue in a variety of surprising ways.

THE REVEAL

The words are lyrics, of course, by the songwriter Tom Waits, and the monologue is a representation of his song 'Christmas Card from a Hooker in Minneapolis' (from the album *Blue Valentine*, 1978). Here is it in its original form, including its final devastating verse.

> Hey Charlie, I'm pregnant, living on Ninth Street
> Right above the dirty bookstore off Euclid Avenue.
> I stopped taking dope, and I quit drinking whiskey,
> My old man plays the trombone and works out at the track.
>
> He says that he loves me even though it's not his baby,
> He says that he'll raise him up like he would his own son.
> He gave me a ring that was worn by his mother,
> And he takes me out dancing every Saturday night.
>
> Hey Charlie, I think about you every time I pass the filling station,
> On account of all the grease you used to wear in your hair.
> I still have that record of Little Anthony and the Imperials,
> But someone stole my record player, now how do you like that!
>
> And hey Charlie, I almost went crazy after Mario got busted,
> So I went back to Omaha to live with my folks.
> But everyone I used to know was either dead or in prison,
> So I came back to Minneapolis, this time I think I'm gonna stay.
>
> Hey Charlie, I think I'm happy for the first time since my accident.
> And I wish I had all the money you used to spend on dope.
> I'd buy me a used-car lot and I wouldn't sell any of 'em,
> I'd just drive a different car every day depending on how I feel.
>
> Hey Charlie, for Chrissakes, if you want to know the truth of it,
> I don't have a husband, he don't play the trombone.
> I need to borrow money to pay this lawyer. Charlie, hey,
> I'll be eligible for parole come Valentine's Day.

Waits manages to get a reversal, a revelation, a new course of action, a choice, a decision and the answer to his dramatic questions into four lines – without ever sacrificing characterisation for exposition. So take inspiration from expert short-form storytellers wherever you might find them – songs, poems, short plays, librettos – whatever takes your fancy.

EXERCISES: WRITING IN MINIATURE

→ Take a character from your own play, or a new one that you're circling and want to explore. Imagine they are writing a card (Christmas or otherwise) to someone important to them (this might be another character in your play or someone with a role in their backstory) and turn it into a monologue, as above.

→ Before you start, think about the character's status quo, need, goal, desire, backstory, setting and world. Try to show these elements in the writing and use one or more of the following devices:

  → A reversal
  → A revelation
  → A new course of action
  → A choice
  → A decision
  → An answer to a dramatic question

→ Think of the card as representing a scene in your play, a turning point in your play, or even the whole play. Whatever is useful. If you prefer, you can write the card in verse, taking inspiration from Tom Waits. Who knows, by creating a miniature, you may even discover something new about your play that has eluded you so far in long form.

The writers of these responses are Annabel Adcock, Peter Jessup, Louise Richards, Rachael Claye, Caroline Lonqc and Anne Doherty.

PART 2

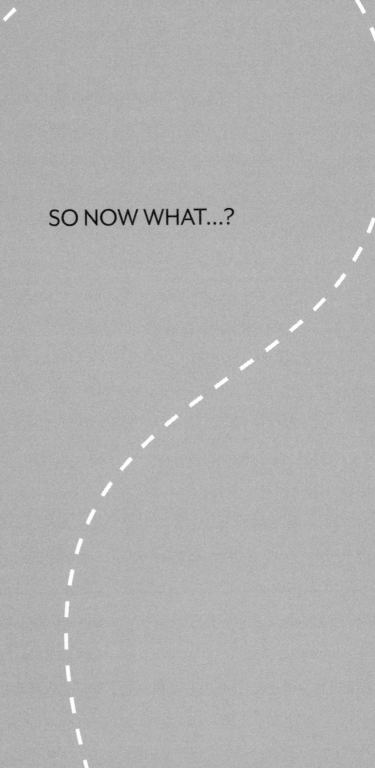

SO NOW WHAT...?

SO NOW WHAT...?

Congratulations. You have finished your play. You have written 'The End' and saved the file (and, for the love of God, backed it up). You are exhausted, elated and proud. You run your favourite lines endlessly through your head, convinced you've written a modern classic. You will have the Royal Court on the phone by Christmas begging for the rights. And then overnight, an invisible joy-leech attaches itself to the soft skin under your armpit and sucks every drop of happiness from your body. You wake the next morning knowing that the play is an embarrassment. Why have you wasted weeks, months or years of your life on this indulgent, narcissistic theatrical onanism?

This is entirely normal. It's a condition called the Post-draft Blues™ and is a rite of passage for every playwright. It will pass. But there are certain things you can do to help speed its departure. Firstly, put the play in a drawer and leave it alone. I usually experience at least two or three days of aftershocks after finishing a draft, when new ideas or problem-solving solutions suddenly magically present themselves. It's also a reason *never* to send a script to a producer, director or anyone significant the minute you've finished it.

If this happens, make a note of any useful aftershock thoughts, but don't try and stuff them into the draft straight away. As Chicago might have sung, 'Even playwrights need a holiday far away from the plays that they love.' I recommend you leave the play for at least two weeks, preferably longer. A month is good, if you're not working to deadline. Let the play settle, and then you can go back with a fresh mind.

So, now what? Now is usually when you begin the long and sometimes torturous process of redrafting, receiving feedback, redrafting again, and maybe, just maybe, having your play scheduled for production. All of which may lead you to theatrical fame and fortune. Or not.

Either way, it's better to begin with some basic knowledge about who and what you might encounter as you tread the long road from second draft to potential opening night. These next chapters are about how this process might work, and how to navigate each step.

11
THE ART OF REDRAFTING

THE ART OF REDRAFTING

Before you do anything else with your draft, if possible, arrange to hear the whole script read aloud by actors. They don't have to be professional actors. They might be fellow playwrights, or writing colleagues, or drama students – anyone who could cram into your living room. Don't worry if you can't pay them – providing some food and a bottle of wine is a good start. Taking the whole thing off the page and putting it into spoken language will help you to start thinking about the play as a map for performance, rather than a literary work. It will also give you a sense of its flow of energy, shape and balance. Try to resist the temptation to read a part yourself, even if you're an actor. Just listen. The point of the reading is to hear and see as an audience member. If you can record it for future reference, even better. At this stage, be wary of asking for feedback – just give yourself a chance to hear your play for yourself.

Whether you manage to have a table read or not, at some point you'll probably need to take the play out of the drawer and make adjustments, whether these are minor tweaks or significant rewrites, before you consider sending it out to theatres.

THE FIRST REDRAFT

If you are doing a redraft for yourself – that is, one that isn't based on professional notes, but your own reassessment after some time away from the desk – try to go in with a plan. Don't just plunge in on page 1 and start combing over the dialogue. If there are big things that need fixing, spend plenty of time thinking strategically about them. This might involve reordering and/or deleting scenes, rewriting endings and beginnings, or taking the play back to its foundations and rebuilding it brick by brick. This is when having faith in your craft becomes vital. The initial fuzzy glow of pride and love you have for your play might (and perhaps should) have faded by now, allowing for some essential objectivity. If you're seeing problems *everywhere*, don't panic. Work through them methodically (some of the exercises in this book should help). Take as long as you need to summon new strength and energy to tackle a redraft, and don't rush it.

FINDING (A) READER(S)

At some point, you will want feedback. Who should you give your play to? The obvious answer is: whoever is keen to read it. But please make sure that person is acquainted with the theatre, at the very, very least as a regular visitor. Plays are usually hard to digest on the page for those unused to reading dramatic texts, and the untrained eye may well miss some of the finer points (or the whole point) of your script. Being part of a playwriting group or acting group can be a huge support – colleagues and co-writers usually make very good initial readers, not least because they understand the processes involved in making plays, and how exposing it is to share a new piece of work.

If you're lucky, you may find someone who becomes 'your reader' over time. By this I mean a trusted someone who is interested enough to regularly read your work as you develop your career, and offer guidance and informal mentoring. For some writers this is a director they've worked with; for others it's an actor, an agent, or somebody who works in the theatre in a professional capacity (mine is an artistic director who has commissioned several plays from me over the years.) Creative relationships with non-writers such as this can be incredibly useful, not least because they are not based on a 'like for like' exchange of work, which can slightly muddy the waters.

After a while you will be ready to send your play out to theatres. What should you expect? As you'll know, many new-writing theatres in the UK, such as the Royal Court, Bush, Hampstead and Soho Theatres, Leeds Playhouse, Manchester's Royal Exchange and the National Theatre will accept unsolicited scripts and/or have a regular script window when they invite new writers to send in their work. (Just be sure to check their websites before you send in a play to ensure this is the case, otherwise the script may end up in the recycling bin.) There are also several annual and biannual playwriting competitions run by UK theatres and companies, along with new-writing festivals such as HighTide. Even if your play is rejected or doesn't get shortlisted, you might still receive some basic feedback, and occasionally receive an invitation to send in further work.

In all cases, assume your play will be read first by a script reader. These people are usually freelancers who are paid by theatres and/or competition and festival producers – whoever is in charge of decision-making on plays – to read incoming scripts and write reports on them, flagging up any interesting ones for further shortlisting and/or for passing on up the food chain. This sifting process isn't a bad thing – script readers (nearly) always have professional experience in the theatre and know how to sniff out a good play. I've been one myself many times. Just be aware that your play is unlikely to be read by the top dog in the building/organisation at this stage. This is also no bad thing: your play shouldn't be exposed to them until it's in its best possible shape.

There are plenty of websites offering useful information and guidance for developing playwrights about these sorts of opportunities, including the BBC Writersroom. You'll find advice there on every aspect of script development including basic but important stuff like how to format your script, and how to write a submission letter. So I won't spend time on these things here. Instead I'd like to delve a bit deeper into the mysterious world of dramaturgy.

WHAT IS DRAMATURGY?

Dramaturgy is a relatively new term in British theatre, and often one that seems to instil fear and confusion. It needn't be; a dramaturg is simply anyone who reads and then gives you feedback on your play. (Literary managers, the people hired by theatres to find plays and develop them with their writers, are dramaturgs by another name.) The notion of dramaturgy as a more rigorous intellectual, research-based and creative discipline has its roots in European theatre models that are less concerned with the primacy of the 'well-made play' and more with innovations in theatrical form and practice. Such innovations have slowly migrated to this country, and can be seen in the growth of, for example, devised theatre and director-led reimaginings of classic texts. The use of the term has slowly widened to encompass general development done on the single-authored play, and both term and concept have accordingly become more common within British theatre.

Still, the notion and practice of dramaturgy throws up many questions and anxieties for the new playwright. After all, dramaturgs are the people whom we playwrights hope will help our plays become their best selves. But there's actually nothing that mysterious about the process of dramaturgical development. Rob Drummer, former Associate Dramaturg at the Bush Theatre, has referred to the dramaturg's role as, at its simplest, giving the writer a 'point of resistance – something to react against'. (*The Stage*, 2015.) My analysis of the case studies earlier in this book all fall under the umbrella of dramaturgy. The work those writers and I did together took many different forms, from general discussions to detailed interrogations of particular aspects of the play, but the aims were always the same. First, to help the writer identify problems, crystallise their intentions and articulate their ideas and story aims, and second, to help them find strategic ways to rebuild their play in a way that honours the story *they want to write*, not my idea of what it should be. This is essentially what dramaturgy is.

Nina Steiger, Head of Play Development at the National Theatre Studio's New Work Department, and formerly Literary Manager of the Soho Theatre, has this to say about her work:

> When I'm working with non-text-based theatremakers my job is to help them find ways to tell a story with as many layers and as much clarity and impact as possible; to think about an overall shape and structure that serves the piece and its purpose; to find a coherence and synergy between an artistic style and the story; and explore all the opportunities to make it as consistent and powerful an experience as possible. It's about making the *how* and the *what* of the story have a dynamic relationship that can, in the most successful cases, become like a distinct character in the piece. In a sense, this form and content thinking means conceiving the piece so it isn't just about something; it *is* something. The better observed and more particular a scene, character or setting, the more chance the play has to leap off the stage and into the hearts of its audience. That's the alchemy of great playwriting but there is also the level of analysis that turns an eye on the larger context: Why now? Why here? What does this piece bring to the wider world? How does it speak to audiences and break new ground? How is this piece game-changing and why would people want to see it? Why is theatre the perfect medium for this event? (Interview, *Culture Calling*, 2015, with additions made in 2019.)

All of this sort of work falls within the same basket of 'feedback', 'note-giving' and 'script development' that you might get from a director or theatrical literary manager or script reader – although the dramaturg's

THE ART OF REDRAFTING

focus will be even more detailed and specific. You can see from the above that these are not people to fear. They earn their living trying to help playwrights and directors, and, ultimately, productions. Dramaturgy should never offer a prescription or formula. The process is also partly intuitive – like a sort of sixth sense. Good dramaturgs understand theatrical storytelling in their bones, and can relay their notes and criticisms in a way that lights up your play like an airport runway.

HOW TO TAKE NOTES

JOSEPH.   So, Mozart – a good effort. Decidedly that. A good effort.

MOZART.   Did you really like it, Sire?

JOSEPH.   I thought it was most interesting. Yes, indeed. A trifle –
           how shall one say? (*To* ORSINI-ROSENBERG) How shall
           one say, Director?

ROSENBERG. (*subserviently*) Too many notes, Your Majesty?

JOSEPH.   Very well put. Too many notes.

(From *Amadeus* by Peter Shaffer)

There are, of course, downsides to dramaturgy. Not all feedback is equally valuable, and at first it's often hard to tell the difference. New writers are generally too busy agonising over whether their work is any good to make objective judgements on the quality of the feedback they receive. But you must try to learn how. In the moment, *any* note can seem illuminating, simply because it comes from the mind of a person who has actually taken the time to read your play. But there are also notes that can inadvertently shroud it in darkness. It can happen, after you've arrived at your long-awaited meeting and shaken the hand of the Important Person, agog with expectation... that you receive a piece of advice so ambiguous, so opaque or discouraging that you may never want to write a play again.

I'll start by sharing one of my own.

'Your play is *almost* brilliant.'

That was the big note. It was followed by a sort of general explanation that the play didn't quite work and wasn't right for the theatre. There was no advice offered as to how or why it was 'almost brilliant', or, more importantly, no suggestions of what I might do to make it *completely* brilliant. It was meant well, and, of course, intended to encourage, not derail me, but the comment threw me for weeks.

MORE CLANGERS?

Here are some more gems kindly donated by some very well-known writers with years of experience between them.

> On a play set in a factory: 'We can't do your play because no one in [*the town where the play was to be staged*] has ever worked in a factory.'

> 'I think you either need to rethink it entirely or just stop.'

> 'It's a really well-written script. The problem with it is that it's *too* well-written.'

> 'Your play is a car without an engine.'

> On a play with a provocative subject matter: 'If we do this play someone in box office might get stabbed to death. Do you really want that?'

> 'Well, you could never be accused of *under*writing, could you?'

> 'Go and read 'X play by Y' because he has written something that covers this kind of subject and it's *brilliant*.'

> On a nascent first act when I was very young: 'You're not actually thinking of finishing this, are you?'

On the face of it, some of these comments might seem ridiculous, unhelpful or downright rude. And sometimes you *will* get notes that just aren't very good. But in many cases, within the context of a wider conversation about your play, notes like this might actually have something useful to contribute.

It's important always to give yourself time to digest a set of notes. If, after a few days, a particular note still makes no sense, or creates a hole in the play that stays empty, or just feels wrong in your marrow, it is your right to politely reject it. Try to remember that it's never a question of the playwright being 'wrong' and the dramaturg, in whatever form, being 'right'. Aristotle wrote the *Poetics*, yes, but he also thought the sun revolved around the earth. Thankfully, disagreements can be an essential part of a dramaturgical dialogue that ultimately helps find solutions.

It is also reasonable to go back and ask the note-giver for clarification if you aren't sure you've understood them. I know for a fact that over the years I have delivered unintentionally unhelpful notes to various students while giving feedback – probably, knowing me, buried in some florid metaphor. In my defence, and the defence of all dramaturgs, nothing said is ever intended to obfuscate or confuse the writer. It's just part of the complicated dialogue that goes on when real human beings discuss fictional human beings as though they were real human beings.

I asked the playwright Samuel Adamson for his thoughts on dramaturgical feedback, and he had the following advice on notes in general.

> It sounds obvious, but the best notes are the ones that ask a version of the question: 'What is your intention?' It's often the case that your intentions for a line, scene, character or even the whole play have gone walkabout. If you can't answer the question, you have work to do. If you *can* answer the question, but a literary manager thinks your intention isn't clear in the writing, you have work to do. It's not the literary manager's job to tell you how to write the play, or what it should be about. It is their job to make you be honest with yourself about whether you know what you want to achieve, and whether you've achieved it.

This sort of honesty can be hard won, and require huge amounts of stamina and patience (on both sides). But aim for the top.

MAGIC BELLS

On the flip side of all this agony are the ringing chimes of good notes and the sweet smell of sage advice. A good note will set off a chain reaction that leads to new insights, ideas and energy. Blessed is the playwright who receives this kind of help at any stage, whether from dramaturg, director, actor or foyer ice-cream seller. If you hear the magic bells ring, thank the note-giver fervently, and write the thing down before you forget it. It may be a general piece of advice about writing craft, or a specific note about your play.

Again, I'll start with one given to me. It came from Greg Hersov, who was at that time one of the co-Artistic Directors at the Royal Exchange Theatre in Manchester. In the play a character died just before the interval, with no other reason, I eventually realised, than to create a talking point for the characters in Act Two. Greg said (and I'm paraphrasing, because it was many years ago now), 'Never undersell your characters or exploit them in your play. Dramatic characters should be afforded the same honour as real people. Respect them, let them have a real and meaningful life in the play, and if they die, let their death be earned.' In other words, you can't expect an audience to invest in characters in whom you haven't made enough creative investment yourself. I've never forgotten it.

Here are some more examples of good notes shared by professional playwriting colleagues. (By 'good', I mean 'useful'.)

Ryan Craig

When I was starting out, the excellent playwright and screenwriter Simon Block was assigned to me as a mentor. He read an early draft of my play *Happy Savages* about young people falling in and out of love and said, 'Okay, but why am I watching these people and not their next-door neighbours?' It's a devastating critique because it's so simple and yet so all encompassing; the work has to justify its place on the stage. Every time I've started a play since, I've had that question in my mind.

Suhayla El-Bushra

Emily McLaughlin at the National Theatre Studio once said, 'If a scene isn't working it might not be that scene that's the problem, but something you've done a few pages before.' I have only recently realised how true that is. And the best note I had recently was: 'It's all in the set-up, kid', delivered in a fake New York accent.

John Donnelly

The director Joe Hill-Gibbins gave me a note about an early draft of a play of mine, *Bone* – three monologues that intertwine. He said that each character had three different types of journey: physical (moving from place to place), narrative (they were gradually revealing a story); and emotional/spiritual (confronting a place of personal pain), and that the journeys of the characters were stronger in some areas than others. The great thing about the note was he had identified something about the play that I had developed instinctively, but which was working better in some characters more than others. So the note he gave came from an engagement with the play itself rather than from an idea he was trying to impose on it from the outside.

Rebecca Lenkiewicz

Howard Davies was directing my suffragette play *Her Naked Skin*. Rob Howell had designed a fantastic set that included imposing walkways and cells for Holloway Prison. Howard said that the rhythm of the set was wrong and could I write another prison scene so that the Holloway set could pull out and be used one more time. At the time I felt a bit ruffled... the set should serve the script, surely? But I reread the play and I started to write a scene about the eldest suffragette in her cell with a doctor. It turned out to be a beating heart in the play. So it was very interesting that Howard had perceived the rhythm of the play through the set and it had dictated a new scene. He also flashed his intense eyes at me another time and said, 'There are too many endings in this play.' I got out my pen and went back to the desk.

Inua Ellams

Early in my writing career I was trying to figure out how to create suspense and conflict in a play and was struggling. The playwright Dipo Agboluaje and I met to talk about it, and Dipo kissed his teeth in an affectionate older-brotherly kind of way. I also think he actually got up to perform his explanation: imagine an empty stage with a chair on the far right. A person enters wearing white gloves, dressed perfectly, pristinely, takes out a white handkerchief and dusts down the chair. Now imagine a drunk person comes on stage, swaying from side to side. Clothes are ill-fitting and filthy, hands are dirty. All you need to do, Dipo said, for there to be drama, is to have these two characters get closer together. Not a word needs to be spoken. That is how simple it can be.

Moira Buffini

Sometimes the very best note of all is: 'You're on the right track' or 'Here are some things I loved' or 'Why are you messing with that scene? It works.' When a collaborator takes pains to praise, as well as interrogating what doesn't work, it has a great effect on a playwright. I had no idea what I'd got with my early draft of *Handbagged* (two Thatchers, two Queens, leaping about in time and space, direct audience address) until director Indhu Rubasingham said, 'This is good. This'll work.'

It's interesting how many of these cherished bits of advice came from directors. A good working relationship with a good director will always reap rewards, because they also understand theatrical storytelling in their bones. Just remember that directors are not trained to be dramaturgs. While directing will usually involve a great deal of text analysis and dissection, it is essentially a practical job that requires a 360-degree focus. You can't expect your director to fix your play by themselves, but they will hopefully contribute to a collaborative development process in which you and the company evolve the play to its best self. We'll talk more about directors in the next chapter.

So, learning to ask for, understand and take notes is a very important part of a writer's process. Writing a play is a bit like clearing a mysterious path through the woods – we follow trails that turn out to be dead ends, we trip over huge logs, we get sidetracked studying some very interesting mushrooms growing on a tree trunk... Similarly, the journey through script development may be agonisingly slow or an elated sprint, but it will always take you to places you didn't plan for. The people you meet on the way – dramaturgs, directors, literary assistants and managers, actors and producers – will be part of that journey. All playwrights need a 'point of resistance' against which to test their work, whether that happens at the redrafting stage, during workshopping, in rehearsal or on into production – usually a combination of all of these. Although we playwrights are the originators of the script, the end product is ultimately a group effort. Learn to defend your corner, if necessary (and if possible without shouting), while being open to help, guidance and input from the right people.

A (NOTE OF) WARNING

Sebastian Born (already mentioned in Chapter Five) has talked about the growing trend in what he calls 'the fetishisation of process'. He means the endless development that can suck plays into a black hole, in which they are viewed from every angle, crawled all over by various opinions, and then spat back at the writer, who has by that point often lost all sense of connection to the material and any sense of authorial ownership. Sometimes, when dramaturgy takes over and becomes an end in itself, plays and writers can be kept in a state of development limbo for months or even years before their script is finally accepted or rejected – in which time it is quite possible that their subject or theme has been covered in another play, or the topic has become dated – and they have missed their window of opportunity. Every writer I know has gone through this sort of agony. The more experience you acquire working with dramaturgs and literary departments, the better you get at sniffing out a sense of waning interest or a divergence of opinion that you know can never be made good.

If this happens to you, my advice is: seek advice. Talk to someone you trust about how to approach the theatre/manager in question, and find out what's going on. I'll also say more about cultivating relationships with theatres and managers in the next chapter.

THE SECOND (THIRD, FOURTH, FIFTH... REDRAFT)

Once you've had time to mull on your notes and understand what the theatre/dramaturg wants from your next draft(s), as I've said before, it's good to start the process with a clear plan of action. Every play and every redraft will have different requirements, but I've listed some general advice below that might help you approach your rewrite. Some are practical tips and some are more psychological. I'll start with the latter.

→ Please always make sure that you agree with all the notes before you try to execute them. *Never* start the redrafting process full of resentment or a grudging sense of having to do homework under obligation. If you're only redrafting to please somebody else, the work will not be good. So make sure that you feel ready and willing to plunge in again.

→ You probably spent a lot of time rewriting the draft that you've received notes on before you submitted it. But while it may have been 'your' Draft 8, which took you three years to complete, to your professional readers it is always Draft 1 – because it's the first draft that they read. It might help if you do a little mental reset and get in alignment with them, so you can shed the weight of your own pre-dramaturgy work on the play, and approach Draft 2 (rather than Draft 9) feeling a little lighter, energetically speaking. Sounds odd but it works, trust me.

→ Understand that no (submitted) first or second draft ever gets produced. *Ever.* This isn't to discourage you, but to give you realistic expectations about the length of the rewriting process. Try to see your redrafts not just as a means to an end, but an opportunity to learn about the play, your process and yourself.

→ Write an outline for your new draft before you start so that you have a clear map to follow. I always create a brief scene breakdown for the whole play, condensing the basic elements of each one: characters, place and time, and most importantly, the key dramatic action(s) contained in the scene. Try writing a sentence or two to describe this action, as discussed in Chapter Seven. This will help you understand how each scene earns its place in the play and creates your narrative arc.

→ Writing a brief description of each scene on blank postcards is also a useful technique that I learned from screenwriters, as it allows you to move the story units around physically, if you're playing with your structure. You can literally reshuffle and reorder your story without (for once) having to write anything down.

→ If at any point you lose sight of the core story that your play is telling, I find it helpful to step away from the script completely and spend a bit of time writing out the storyline as prose. You can do this for a scene, an act or the whole play. Try using the simplest and most familiar storytelling tropes you know to reduce the story to its absolute essence: 'Once upon a time, a Southern Belle called Blanche DuBois went to stay with her sister Stella and brother-in-law Stanley, in a cramped flat in New Orleans...'

→ If you make cuts (which you will), save them somewhere in a different file. You may want to revisit or recycle them in a future draft, or they may contain the seeds of a new scene or moment in the play. Never delete anything entirely.

→ Be prepared to go off-piste. You will always get new ideas as you write that weren't in the original draft plan. Don't be thrown by this – follow your nose and see where it takes you. If you end up writing a new scene or introducing a brand new character during your redraft that doesn't ultimately make it into the final version, so what? No writing is wasted writing.

→ Don't rush or skimp on your redrafting work. Fatigue may well set in at some point and you'll feel heartily sick of your play. If so, take a few days off and let your mind clear, then return with renewed energy. This is your chance to prove your mettle as a playwright not only to the people interested in your play, but, more importantly, to yourself.

AND FINALLY...

Taking notes and rewriting can be hard, but it can also be empowering. Try to treat it as you would any other step in your journey to becoming a playwright. And remember that while you always have the right to disagree with feedback, you also have a responsibility to make your play as good as it can possibly be. As a writer, you are *in service* of your play. Many people can stand in the way of that goal, among them, of course, dramaturgs and any others offering feedback – but sometimes *you* will be the person blocking the way. Learning to tell the difference is a truly invaluable skill. In the next chapter we will look at how this also comes in very handy when you're in the process of moving the play from the page to the stage.

12
INTO PRODUCTION

INTO PRODUCTION

All writing is a form of alchemy. We, the writers, take the base metals of our thoughts, feelings and ideas, and, by a combination of known and unknown, mathematical and formless, concrete and abstract systems and processes (aka craft and instinct), we use language to transmute them into dramatic gold. And, like the ancient alchemists, we hope that through this process we might create a universal truth that that Greeks called *gnosis* – knowledge – and share it with an audience via performance.

Among the arts, theatrical writing allows for the greatest degree of transmutation, because there are so many different layers to the process of making a play. When readers read a novel, they consume the language and create the imaginative reality of the book in their own heads. It's a deeply personal and individual experience. In theatre, however, there are three different stages of the alchemical process. Firstly, the playwright creates the script. From this, the director and company create the performance. And finally, the audience creates the theatrical experience in collaboration with the live performance. I'll talk in more detail about the relationship between playwrights and audiences in the final chapter. But first I want to guide you through the mysterious processes of production, rehearsal and working with actors, accompanied by some pieces of hard-won advice from the trenches to help you navigate this sometimes baffling world.

TAKING MEETINGS

Hooray! Someone has read your play and likes it enough to want to talk to you about it. So what might happen in that meeting? It's important not to overload yourself with expectations if you're having a general sit-down with a literary manager to talk about a play of yours that they've read. First of all, a meeting does not mean a theatre wants to produce your play. It may not mean anything other than a general vague interest in you and your work. But, whatever it is, treat it as good news – nobody arranges meetings they don't want to have.

It is also rare that finely detailed feedback will be offered in these sorts of meetings. The interested parties will want to find out more about you, hear about your writing and life experience, ask you questions about the genesis of your play, and so on. They may give you a few headline notes, but don't go in assuming that you'll be given an exhaustive analysis of your play – that is usually the stuff of the workshop or read-through.

The success or failure of this sort of introductory meeting – whether it's with an artistic director (AD), literary manager, dramaturg, director (or any combination) – will always be partly down to chemistry. It stands to reason that there are some people who will 'get' your voice and work, and others who won't. It's hard to have much control over this early in your career, when you're taking every meeting you can and considering every project that comes your way, but you'll eventually start to gravitate naturally towards people who speak your (theatrical) language. You'll also learn to nip swiftly in the bud those partnerships or collaborations that you can feel just aren't going to bear fruit.

Before you go to any meeting, make sure you do your homework. If you're having coffee with an AD who has spoken publicly about their desire to programme biting political satire, don't offer them a pantomime you wrote seven years ago. Read up about the theatre's current and past seasons, look at the directors they have hired – go in equipped with some knowledge of their tastes and interests. Also remember that while we theatre folk are always up for a vigorous debate about the merits of a particular show, you should be diplomatic. If you detested the theatre's last three plays (especially if the AD directed them), you're not obliged to pretend you adored them, but don't shoot them down in flames just to be provocative.

Always try to have another play idea up your sleeve, as you will often be asked what else you are working on. You don't then have to deliver a fully formed play pitch (and please avoid a twenty-minute monologue giving a scene-by-scene account of it), but you can mention a topic, theme or idea that you're interested in exploring, even if it's still not fully formed as a story. If in doubt, write a short paragraph that gets to the heart of the idea, why it interests you, and why it would make a good play, and practise saying it out loud before the meeting. Actors rehearse before auditions – why shouldn't you?

A cardinal rule is: never give a false impression of yourself to try and gain an 'in' with a theatre. If a literary manager mentions that they are looking for someone to adapt a historical nineteenth-century novel about the Industrial Revolution, do not tell them that your heroine is Elizabeth Gaskell when it's actually Madonna. Everyone wants opportunities to work, but make sure you are emotionally/intellectually/spiritually equipped to tackle the idea. Be true to your interests and voice – you'll be respected for it.

Finally, never be afraid to ask questions. Use the opportunity to learn from these people's experience running a working theatre.

GETTING PROGRAMMED (OR NOT)

I'm going to get this out of the way early in this chapter: roughly speaking, probably only a third of the plays commissioned by any theatre actually get produced (this estimate is born out of conversations with various theatrical agents). An unsolicited 'written on spec' play has an even smaller chance of production, simply because of the sheer volume of plays received every year by new-writing theatres that do accept unsolicited scripts. Plays rejected by their commissioning theatre may eventually get sold on to a different theatre, if the writer is lucky, but a great many sadly end up in the Great Play Graveyard for unproduced dramas.

If your play is not taken up, it will sting, of course – but just know that there will be a variety of complicated reasons for its rejection, and not all are because it's not good enough. Getting programmed by a theatre, especially on a main stage, is to be a moveable piece in a complex jigsaw puzzle. Your play has to fit with a season of work and a certain production budget; it must be matched with the right available director; it may be dependent on certain actors' availability. Artistic directors are often forced to perform heroic juggling acts to get good work on their stages, especially with dwindling public funding.

Still, it doesn't help that theatres can sometimes be incredibly opaque about their reasons for not putting on your work. A playwright recently told me of a conversation they'd had with a senior theatre employee about why their play wasn't suitable for them, who said: 'The thing is that you have to be so careful of putting new plays on that big stage (a four-hundred-seat theatre) as it's very exposing and is a huge risk.'

As a writer, it's hard not to feel instinctively patronised and insulted by this sort of comment. A risk to who and what, exactly? The theatre's income? Audience expectations? Isn't it the job of theatres – particularly new-writing theatres – to take creative risks and create opportunities for writers, rather than always playing it safe? The answer is yes, of course. But, if we look at this comment from the theatre's point of view, it might actually be more protective than simply dismissive. When plays that are not 'stage ready' get produced nonetheless, it can be devastatingly exposing for all involved – playwright, director and cast. In rare cases, entire careers can be jeopardised if an underdeveloped play is put in front of an audience and falls flat on its face. So try to remember there is as much at stake for you as there is for the theatre.

Everyone deals with rejection in different ways, but ultimately you must be prepared to write plays that don't get staged. Try to cultivate a robust attitude, and remind yourself that every play that you complete – and even the ones you abandon – will teach you something about your craft. If you end up writing a really good play, whether it's produced or not, it will nearly always become a stepping stone to something else: a relationship with a theatre, another commission, or even a different home for the play in the future. Just don't let rejection stop you from writing.

DEVELOPMENT AND PREPARATION

If you are one of the lucky ones who does receive firm interest in your play from a theatre, you might be absolutely sure that what you need now is a two-week writing workshop with a dramaturg, a renowned director, a cast of actors, costume and props, a full band and catered lunches. Know that the very most you might be offered is a table read-through using the theatre's current acting company. Theatres rarely have any extra cash available for this sort of development unless they have a funded new-writing department like the National Theatre or Royal Court. So take what is offered gratefully, but only if it's going to be useful. Don't waste anyone's resources unless you have a clear plan about how you're going to use them. There are other ways to develop your play, via theatre groups and writing schemes, and/or Research and Development and Project Grants from Arts Council England, who have funds allocated to support writers and teams of theatre artists develop work.

Development can take many forms besides workshopping the script, including more dramaturgy and research, but essentially it will mean yet more rewriting, this time probably in collaboration with your attached director. It might take ten drafts, fifty, a hundred – months, years or decades of work before the script is accepted and scheduled for production. Please note that you won't be paid for these rewrites. Unlike in film scriptwriting, where every draft and polish is contracted and has fees attached, theatres pay you flat commission and draft acceptance fees (more on this in a minute).

In terms of how to go about them, the rewriting guidelines that I outlined in the previous chapter will still apply – just bear in mind that when a script is going into production some new notes will arise out of practical necessities. For example, you may well have to rethink your character configuration if the theatre only has the budget for a smaller number of actors. (Remember how Viv bravely cut his multi-character draft of *The Bevin Boys* down to a two-hander after a theatre offered him a production for two actors.) Although creative demands like this might feel as though they threaten the integrity of your play (and sometimes they will), have courage and keep an open mind. From this point onwards, it's not just 'your' play any more, but will belong to the company of actors, directors and designers who will breathe life into your script. The theatre industry not only survives but *thrives* on compromise – sometimes amazing things can happen when practical limitations are imposed on your play. However, as with notes, if a theatre wants to take your play in a direction you think is just plain wrong – you can always leave the money on the table and walk away.

Between the initial agreement to produce your play and the beginning of rehearsals, many different decision-making processes will take place. They include the financial deal, the attaching of a director and design team, and the casting process. Playwriting students are often keen to know more about these mysterious and exciting steps towards production, so I'll say a few words about each.

THE DEAL

Forget alchemy for a moment while we focus on the hard-won gold of real earnings. I won't spend a huge amount of time on the financial side of theatre production, as you can access the standard industry terms on which writers are contracted elsewhere. (The national writers' union – the Writers' Guild of Great Britain (WGGB) – is a great resource offering free information to non-members.) But what can you expect to earn from writing a commissioned play? And who will negotiate it for you if you don't have an agent?

First of all, know that all subsidised theatres in this country are subject to minimum-rate agreements – the marketplace for plays is not a deregulated Wild West. (Talking of the West, I'm excluding West End productions from my 'top end' calculations below, as they are a) extremely rare for the developing playwright, and b) deal in theoretical sums that might turn your head. We can all but dream.)

At the top end of the scale, as negotiated by the WGGB, the TNC rate card for professional theatre writing at time of publication (an agreement between the National Theatre, Royal Shakespeare Company and Royal Court Theatre) is £8,882 for a full-length play, as an advance on royalties. This means that £4,441 is paid to the playwright on commission and another £4,441 on delivery of the script. (And relax – if the theatre decides not to programme your play, you still get to keep these two payments.) A third 'acquisition fee' payment of £4,376 is made if the play is accepted for production. That means that a playwright programmed by one of these three theatres will receive £13,258 to write their play (minus their agent's commission of ten per cent, minus any tax they pay on it) before royalties.

After the play closes, the writer will receive a percentage of net receipts of ticket sales, minus half of their prior advance payments. These royalty payments (between eight to ten per cent on a sliding scale according to box-office capacity) will, of course, vary wildly, depending on the size of the theatre and the ticket price. Forty performances in the Olivier might earn you roughly around £135,000 minus your advances. Twenty performances at the seventy-five-seat Gate Theatre in London might earn you around £1,400 on the same basis.

Other subsidised British theatres offer advances at an agreed minimum rate of between approximately £7–10,000, defined again by the WGGB as 'mid-level salary'. So what about the bottom end? Well, it varies. A studio fringe theatre might pay you something between a few hundred pounds and a couple of thousand as an advance – or offer no advance, but pay you a percentage of box office. Some writers will write for nothing at all for a fringe theatre, drama school or amateur production just for the experience of being produced. I don't know any playwright who hasn't done a bit of this early on – I certainly did – and wouldn't suggest that you rule it out, as long as you feel confident that any agreements you make are fair and reasonable.

Of course, established writers have agents to make sure any such contracts are watertight and any non-standard deals are sensible – but many new playwrights don't find agents until they've had a first production or at least a track record of commissions and professional play development. If you *are* offered a deal by a fringe theatre, festival or producer and don't have an agent, don't panic. As long as you do your research it's unlikely that you'll be unfairly exploited, but it's worth knowing what your rights are as a playwright, and how to protect yourself.

As a cautionary tale, a student of mine once wrote a play that was picked up for development by a new independent theatre-production company. The producers met with the playwright several times to give notes, who then wrote two or three new drafts. The company intended to submit the final draft to various theatres for consideration for production, and to the Arts Council for further development funding. The producers had no contract with the playwright, nor did they pay them to do any of the work – but once they were happy with the draft, they said as they'd contributed ideas to the script and had 'influenced' it, that they would need to be part of any producing contract the writer might be given down the line. What terms they were asking for were never made clear; the writer understandably parted ways with them at this point.

Although the company presumably had good intentions and wanted to support the playwright, they put the writer in a very difficult position. The lesson here is: writers can choose to write without getting paid for their work just like producers can develop work without getting paid for it – but if there *are* writing fees involved at any stage, the writer alone should get them. Producers make their money back (or don't, at their own risk) on ticket sales – they should never try to claim writers' development or writing fees. A company who has invested time and money into a new play can, of course, expect or at least hope to be involved in a future production, if that's possible, but their terms should always be explicitly spelled out at the beginning of any new relationship. If you ever find yourself in a similar position, and are in doubt about what is right or fair, seek advice from the WGGB or from theatre colleagues, and politely but firmly decline any offers that aren't kosher.

FINDING A DIRECTOR

The playwright–director relationship is the most important one you will have, before and during production. The fact is, we can't live without each other. Without our plays, directors don't have careers, and without directors, our scripts don't get staged. Like all marriages, yours and your director's will probably have a first heady flush of love, a reality check as the hard work kicks in, a few (hopefully friendly) disagreements and the odd lover's tiff. The key is to realise that, like all relationships, it needs commitment, care and trust on both sides. More on what happens in the rehearsal room in a moment.

We don't always get to choose our directors. If your work is programmed as part of a festival, for example, or you're really new to theatre and don't already have a working relationship with the industry, you may well be assigned a director without any say in the matter. This isn't a bad thing per se – you'll hopefully be matched with someone who has responded well to your script and has useful things to say about it. Otherwise, if the script is with a producing theatre, they will suggest potential candidates for consideration. Be aware that theatres often have strong directorial agendas, and are keen to court 'hot' directors on to their stages, to the point where their interest in a particular director can overshadow their interest in your play. I once had a play dropped by a theatre after a starry director who showed initial interest ended up not being available. Ouch.

Nonetheless, it's in everyone's interests – yours, the director's and the theatre's – to find the person who has the best possible fit with your play. So how can you tell when you've found 'the one'? Every play and every writer will have different requirements, but here are a few things to ask yourself when you meet a potential director for the first time:

→ Do they understand your play in its essence – story, themes and intention? If not, and they have missed its basic point on first read, and/or seem keen to turn it into an entirely different play, they are probably not the right person to make it into a show.

→ Do you like them as a person? You'll be spending many hours in their company – it's essential to have some basic camaraderie to see you through. If they make you nervous, distrustful or uncomfortable try to interrogate why (in private and to yourself, not out loud in your meeting!). Being cowed by a director's perceived brilliance is also not conducive to a good experience in the rehearsal room. You'll need the courage to disagree when needed.

→ Are you willing in your gut to trust the director with your play and take the leap of faith required to hand over your precious script?

Of course, you won't really know how things will work out until you're into rehearsal, but take time to process your sense of connection (or not) with any directors you meet. It's worth waiting for the right person, rather than jumping into bed with the first person who shows interest, even if that means delaying the production.

DESIGN TEAM

Once your director is attached, they will go about assembling a team of people (yet more theatrical alchemists) to design the set, lighting, costume, music and choreography/movement, as required by the production. You will probably have little or no say in these choices – although you should always feel free to make informed suggestions to your director. Most directors have long-standing professional relationships with favoured designers, and try to work with them whenever possible. It stands to reason that they want a team around them whose work they know and value, so don't get in the way of this process. It's another chance to practise your faith-leaping: trust that the director knows who can help turn your script into its best visual, aural and physical self.

CASTING

Casting is the next big step towards production, and one that all playwrights including myself generally adore. You should always be involved in the casting process with your director, and most theatres will expect the playwright to attend casting sessions when possible. Only the biggest theatres have an in-house casting director or department – otherwise the theatre that is producing your play will hire an independent casting agency. The casting director's job is, essentially, to read your script, put together lists of potential actors for each role, organise the auditions and then make the offers once you've all decided who you want to hire. But they are much more than this – good casting directors are also alchemists in their own right. It's their job to know about every talented actor in the industry, from recent drama-school graduates through to our most famous and in-demand artists, and their suggestions for pairing actors with roles can help make or break a show.

Casting is one of the most exciting parts of the process for writers. For many of us, it's the first time we'll see and hear our characters become three-dimensional beings, and it's easy to have our hearts stolen, and then broken, by an actor who might smash an audition and then be unavailable or not interested in doing the play. One of the most important things to bear in mind is that a company of actors is far greater, to quote Aristotle, than the sum of its parts. The individual talents of each actor are crucial, but so is the chemistry between them. You may fall in love with X actor for a particular part, but they may just not work alongside your favourite Y actor for a different one. A good casting director (in tandem with your director) will be able to spot this and help find solutions. They won't ever be the ones to make the final decisions about who is hired – that's down to you and your director – but it usually pays to listen to them carefully.

INTO REHEARSAL

We're here! It can be hard for writers to navigate the thrills, seductions and, sometimes, the betrayals of the rehearsal space, especially for those of us very new to the industry. So here are a few words of advice and reassurance for the playwright who is yet to experience a rehearsal or production.

Directors run rehearsal rooms in many different ways; each brings their own unique methodology to the process of bringing a play to life. But the basic steps are generally the same. Once a play has been cast and production scheduled, the rehearsal process usually begins on day one with a straight-through reading of the play around the table by the company. Frequently, it's not just the actors, director and playwright who are present for this, but every member of the producing company. This will include stage, costume, lighting and sound designers, musicians and musical directors, stage managers and technicians, and anyone who will be working on the show in some capacity, including theatre staff who are doing the play's marketing and PR, for example. It gives everyone a chance to hear the script in its entirety and get a feel for the play.

After that, it becomes a long and detailed process of deconstructing the script, led by the director, so that the company can, line by line, action by action, scene by scene, construct the physical show. In many ways it's a reversal of the writing process: the 'whole' of the play is stripped back into its composite parts so that each element can be discussed, questioned, and then put back together in three dimensions.

This work can take many surprising forms. Early on I was struck by just how playful the rehearsal room can be. It often resembles an extended playtime; a bunch of adults tossing balls around, playing word games, stretching, singing. These sorts of explorations may seem to the inexperienced playwright like a distraction from their sacred and important text – but nothing could be further from the truth. Actors are human beings, after all, and their bodies and vocal cords (along with their minds and hearts) are what turn your text into performance.

The point of rehearsal is not just so the actors can learn their words and where to stand, but to give everyone time to collectively and organically develop the production. Staging a play is an evolutionary process. There will (and should) always be room for growth and change in the room – but this can sometimes be hard for the writer, who might not always feel that their original intentions are being honoured. To give some insight into the director's perspective on this, I asked theatre director Blanche McIntyre, who has directed new plays on many of the UK's leading new-writing stages, for some thoughts:

> When writers ask me what my 'vision' for the play is, I say 'To do the play as written.' In other words, how can I dramatise the intrinsic qualities in the playscript? This sometimes means that I have to serve the play over the writer. I once worked on a play that was written naturalistically and could have been staged that way, but it also had many tiny, short scenes set in lots of different locations. So I also had to serve the speed of the play, which means moving away from the writer's naturalistic intentions. If I'd stopped the action to bring on a sofa during a scene change, for example, all the heat would have gone out of it and it would have ruined the intimacy on stage. Directing is partly about finding the energetic flow of the play, above and beyond the script itself.

Your director and actors will, of course, also always want to make changes to the text. It's amazing how many significant contributions to a play can be made in rehearsal, some of which might have nothing to do with altering an actual line of dialogue, but everything to do with a simple change of vocal inflection, a gesture, an arrangement of bodies in space. So we playwrights should respect the integrity of the rehearsal process, just as we would hope that actors and directors peeking into our sacred writing rooms would respect the fact that when we stare out of the window or play Sudoku or lie on the floor doing yogic breathing, we are also working on our plays. (Honest.)

Here's Blanche again with some advice for playwrights:

> The best thing a writer can bring into the rehearsal room is a really in-depth, solid knowledge of their play. The first week of rehearsal is when the actors ask the writer, 'What does this bit mean?' or 'What did you imagine happening here?' – the writer is the best resource we have. Then in weeks two and three, the actors have to find those answers themselves, although the creative choices they make should always be rooted in the text.

Of course, if you really disagree with a director's note or direction, you should speak up, but that may be something to do over a coffee or during lunch, so there's time to interrogate it properly. During scheduled rehearsal time, directors are often being pulled in twenty different directions and bombarded with questions from all sides, so find some quiet time away from the room if you really need to get into it with them.

REHEARSAL-ROOM ETIQUETTE

Rehearsal rooms are *extremely* charged places, full of imaginative and sensitive human beings working at high speed and to their fullest physical and mental capacities. A great deal rests on the positive chemistry between them and their director. At best, these are rooms full of incredible focus, energy and commitment; at worst they are plagued by discord, anxiety, competition and confusion – and the playwright always has a role to play in terms of which it will be. It's usually thrilling to watch your play evolve and improve in rehearsal, as long as you remain open to collaboration, you're not overly precious with your script, and you accept the rules of the rehearsal room. As to these rules, there is no single universal manifesto, but they are grounded in practical common sense and good manners.

➔ Let the director run the room as they see fit – you are in their territory now.

➔ Attend when you're invited, to watch, listen, and make notes.

➔ Offer your opinions and engage in debate when asked, but don't interrupt or disrupt the group process.

➔ If you are concerned about how the show is shaping up, talk privately to your director about it, but don't usurp their position and spread your doubts among the actors, individually or collectively.

→ When you're respectfully asked to leave the rehearsal process and let them get on with it, go with good grace.

→ Creative and personal catastrophes can happen during rehearsals, but nothing was ever solved by a playwright having a tantrum in front of the entire company.

→ If you feel you cannot communicate with your director, seek help elsewhere, perhaps from the producer or artistic director of the theatre, if there is one. Most problems are solvable eventually.

Finally, you'll be pleased to know that it is standard for subsidised theatres to pay writers to attend rehearsals at a daily rate of around £50–75. There's usually a maximum number of days in the production budget for this, so even though you may end up voluntarily attending an entire six-week rehearsal period, you might only get paid for two weeks. If there is no rehearsal fee in your contract you may get offered a small per diem towards expenses. Either way, you won't get financially rich in rehearsal but you will reap creative rewards. (Tip: bring your own lunches.)

LEARNING FROM ACTORS

For most theatre writers, seeing and hearing our words made flesh is a powerful and sometimes overwhelming experience. Suddenly our long-worried-over lines become spoken words. Our imaginary characters become real people. Our story skeletons acquire feathers and fur.

I have learned many valuable lessons along the way from actors, but most of them can be distilled into one very simple question, which I try to remember to ask whenever I'm creating a character, writing a line or forming a scene: *What can an actor do with this?* In other words, what of *their* craft and instinct can they bring to the play? Regardless of the various existing schools of acting, the fundamental principles that actors learn in creating a character and performing a text are essentially the same. Here are few of the things I've learned, which spill over into the rehearsal process.

Acting is far more than just speaking lines

Actors are trained to act with their bodies, not just their voices. They are acting when they are delivering dialogue, but also when they are not. Characters rarely all speak at once on stage – so it follows that they are always listening to each other. When you write, try to think beyond the single character talking at any one moment in your play. Visualise the other actors on stage around them. What are they doing? How are they feeling? What are they thinking? How are they listening? You don't have to detail constant activity for every actor on stage – where actors stand, sit and move (otherwise known as 'blocking') will be worked out in rehearsal. But do try to develop a sense of the energetic relationship between your characters in physical time and space. If a scene or moment starts to feel static, think about how you might create a better flow of energy and pace in the spoken dialogue, which may in turn stimulate the characters on stage to respond physically.

Acting is more than just 'imitation'

Actors are taught to look for 'truth' – to create a character in performance who is believable, autonomous and with an inner life. They are interested in mining real emotion, thought and behaviour in their character and presenting a truthful representation of a human being on stage. The clearer your characters' psychology, personality and behaviour are on the page, the better the actors can honour your intentions, and the more layers of detail they will be able to find. They will also try to fill in any gaps that you as the writer haven't filled, often including a detailed backstory for their character. You don't have to spell out a detailed history for each character in the play (unless it's essential to understanding the plot), but if *you* can't imagine one for them, it's unlikely an actor will find it easy either. The better you know your characters, even if not all the information you've collected about them goes into the play, the better chance the actor has of representing them.

Characters are always motivated by something at every moment

We are all of us motivated by thoughts, feelings, desires and needs – and so are our characters. One of the primary lessons all actors are taught is to think about the *intentions* of their character on any given line or action. The actor will always bring layers of nuance to their characterisation that isn't written in the script – that's a key part of their job – but character motivations should always be clear on the page. And that is your job. (This includes when they aren't speaking.)

Characters exist on a continuum through time

We meet characters in particular locations and times, and in particular contexts and states of mind. Actors will think carefully about all the detailed elements in the text that might affect their character's behaviour in a scene. They will also imagine others that you *didn't* specify, such as where their characters were and what they were doing before they entered the scene. Actors don't just look at the few lines they speak in any part of the play, but consider their character's place in the cosmology of the whole play and on a continuum of the character's lived experience in and outside the play's parameters. The more you ask yourself the same questions when writing, the more you can create nuanced behaviour and depth of character that a good actor will easily bring to life.

Dialogue is not just about what is said but how it is said

No two actors will ever read the same line in an identical way, but they will always look for clues in your characters' vocabulary, idiom, tone and rhythmic patterns in order to help them interpret character. This also includes the use of pauses, beats, silences, hesitations, and so on. *Everything* you put on the page should be there for a reason. The actor will assume it is so – try not to disappoint them!

To round off the chapter I asked six actors with whom I've worked over the years – Suzanne Ahmet, Sarah Belcher, Kobna Holdbrook-Smith, Christian Roe, Helen Schlesinger, and Peter Sullivan – what advice they would give to playwrights who are new to theatre. Here's what they said:

Suzanne Ahmet

I recently played the eldest of three sisters in an epic ensemble play (Rory Mullarkey's *Saint George and the Dragon*). My character's instinct was to keep the family dynamic under control, to dissuade any rebellious behaviour and to keep feelings in check. She had no monologues, I don't think she even had more than one sentence each time she spoke. And yet I could imagine what she *didn't* say, and this could be explored in verbal and non-verbal ways, moment to moment, throughout the piece. For example, the sisters often spoke in a trio, one after another, or slotting in between another character's dialogue. This to me became musical, so we had our own poetry, our own harmonies, our own wavelength, inside the bigger community. In our separate units and together as a village, the company built on the material in this way, linking stories, tragedies, losses and loves.

We were taught at drama school: there are no small parts, only small performances. The way I've interpreted this advice, as an actor, is to see opportunity in every line and every moment that a character is on stage, no matter how sparse their actual dialogue might be. The way the writer helps me to create a full and nuanced inner and outer life is by giving me enough to *imagine* around and to step into the thoughts of this person.

Kobna Holdbrook-Smith

An actor is understandably concerned with character. As an actor I want to know how events or situations make a character *feel* and then let that inform what a character *does*. ('Doing' includes thinking.) A play doesn't have to have an equal spread of characters scene by scene, but let everyone be a living part of the story. Creating detail for them gives more life to characters, which in turn gives life to your story. That police officer who arrests your lead woman at the end of Act Four? Make them apologetic or impatient or sleepy – let them be more than just a device to remove or imperil your protagonist. A memorable small part can be way more tantalising to play than a larger, drier one.

Sarah Belcher

My advice to playwrights when developing a script would be to allow for spaces that the actor's interpretive ability can fill. Sometimes the complexities of character that exist *between* the lines and which bring richness and colour to the show can be ironed out by too much dramaturgy. I would advise a new writer to always be unafraid of the heightened medium of theatre and if possible to allow your actors (who have been cast by the trusted director) to come with their world of experience, questions and responses. Actors are all human and are filled with the complexities of the human condition. This can bring about a kind of alchemy in rehearsal that can be lost if there's too much intellectualising of the written word. A playwright needs to trust that the rehearsal room is a place where their play can grow, perhaps far beyond what they originally imagined when they wrote it.

Christian Roe

When I look at a script I try not to make any assumptions about how to play it or what the writer means. Instead I look at the detail: the punctuation, whether the sentences are long or short, what the consonants feel like in the mouth, what the vowels feel like in my gut. That's how I start to find out how speaking like this person feels. Sometimes this can go to extremes – I once, at a read-through, reached the word *harrumph* – and so I said, 'Harrumph.' The writer shot me a look as if to say, 'Seriously?' Of course, I knew it wasn't 'harrumph' she wanted me to say, but it's not my business to second-guess anything on the page, especially on day one. I stick by this principle, because I find it saves time in the long run if I don't make assumptions based on conjecture or what's *not* there. Imagine if you were a musician – you can't just guess how the composer wants you to play, you have to follow the notes. Interpretation will come later, once those notes are second nature. So when you write, all you really need to give an actor is a score to work from. When you can, try speaking your lines out loud and find out what the words do to you; where you run out of breath, where a consonant becomes a release, where a short vowel makes you laugh or a silence feels vertiginous. If it does something to you, it will probably do something to me, and then we can begin – as long as neither of us fills gaps with guesswork,* because that's when things tend to go wrong.

* Note: guesswork is not the same as interpretation. There's more freedom to play once you know the rules.

Peter Sullivan

I've done director's theatre, and I've done work which still relies on writer and actor trying to share a vision, and they're both great in their different ways. But I have to say the best notes I've ever had as an actor have come from writers. The writer Nic Pizzolatto summed it up brilliantly when he said, 'I like working with actors because they're the only other people who care as much about the characters as I do.' So that's what I'd say to writers: we actors may be a pain in the arse and behave like children sometimes, but no one else is going to live with the people you invented like we do; to love them and care for them and take them home with us at night and get up at five in the morning worrying about them just as much as you do. When the chips are down, the actors are on your side because it's us who have to go out and live and die by what you're writing. We need to be on the same side. Ultimately, we're the only ones you can really trust. John Heilpern (as detailed in his book on Peter Brook's original company) once asked the company on a rare day off: 'What is a play?' One of the actors, quick as a whip, famously replied, 'A play is anything with me in it.' Writers need great actors, and in the end all actors really want are great parts. It seems that for the next three thousand years, we're still in this together.

Helen Schlesinger

I think it's important for playwrights to know that actors love them. The play and the part will be our major reasons for doing the job, so we want the writer to like us, and what we bring to their work. As an actor I may go on a long, slow, sometimes tedious, often unpredictable route through rehearsals, but I would encourage writers to be patient, because we often need to be very bad before we can be any good; to be fuzzy before we can be clear; to go up blind alleys before finding a way through.

Rehearsals are a thicket. Be around for all the initial questions, then go away for a bit so we can play around and get it all wrong, then come back and help again towards the end of rehearsals, or watch a run, and talk it through with the director. The writer finds their own relationship with the actors, often through the conduit of the director, who hopefully has a good sense of where we're all at.

I would encourage writers to keep listening to the music of your play – are there false notes, wrong emphases, missed beats which affect the storytelling? Tell the director, so that these can be addressed – not necessarily at the beginning of rehearsals when things are in flux, but towards the end so that your work is fully honoured, before habits harden. Be careful about giving notes directly to actors. I know I can be overly reverent to writers, which may breed a lifelessness in the work, whereas other actors may feel criticised and defensive.

But share as much as you can with the director, whose head is full of the complexities of rehearsals, and who may appreciate being reminded of the story, and of your original intentions. Finally, we love it when the writer comes to the bar. Because we love you, we love your play, and we also want to feel that you think we're doing okay!

How to summarise this strange process from page to stage? The journey from playscript to production for director, actor and every other member of the company is just as intense, playful and challenging as the writer's journey from blank page to final draft. So trust your company, allow them to practise their craft to their best abilities, and, when you go to the bar after a show, always buy the first round.

13
THE WIDE, WIDE WORLD

THE WIDE, WIDE WORLD

As writers we are, of course, in dialogue with ourselves as creators, but eventually, gods willing, we will also be in dialogue with our audience. When you're writing a play, even to commission for a particular stage, it's usually impossible to fully imagine the end result – a live performance experienced communally by a room of strangers. This unique 'liveness' has a powerful effect on us. A 2017 study by psychological and linguistic scientists (Drs Joe Devlin, Daniel C. Richardson and John Hogan of the Department of Experimental Psychology at UCL, and Dr Helen Nuttall at Lancaster University) demonstrated that watching a live theatre performance created what they call 'in-group arousal' among audience members.[10] In physical terms, while watching a play, this group of strangers' heartbeats synchronised, and their pulses increased and decreased at the same rate. Dr Devlin said, 'This clearly demonstrates that the physiological synchrony observed during the performance was strong enough to overcome social group differences and engage the audience as a whole.'

As audience members we are not only privy to, but complicit in this alchemy, suspending our disbelief so that we can immerse ourselves in the theatrical illusion. Unlike recorded screen dramas, whose magical technical processes are invisibly concealed, and whose form is essentially static and finite, theatre is a living, breathing spectacle. The meaning of a performed play will be different every single night of its run, depending on who is in the room, the mood of the actors, and the willingness or reluctance of its infinitely varied audience to engage with it. It's one of the exciting (and terrifying) things about writing for the stage. Audiences are the reward for all our hard work, but they are also judge and jury. How to cope with this?

LETTING GO...

The first thing to remember is that everyone – audience, technicians, actors, bar staff, even your mum – wants the same thing: for your play to make a great show. Every production is the culmination of many hours of work, input and commitment. Even if the production isn't the one you originally imagined, it now has a life of its own – you may as well try to enjoy it and to support its makers. You are still the show's ambassador, which comes with its own set of terrors and delights – as we'll see.

Once the initial agony of previews is over and you've seen enough performances, you might even start to be able to view it as 'the show' rather than 'my play'. It's very, very hard to do, but a little bit of letting go will give you a lot of perspective.

USING YOUR AUDIENCE

Whether joyful or painful (it's usually both), the live, public consumption of our work provides us with a huge learning curve. Witnessing a group of people united in emotion generated by your creation is a heady experience. It can be addictive, and sometimes blindsiding. It can be equally excruciating to feel an audience miss a joke or become obviously bored. Seeing an audience member fall asleep during one of your shows is a milestone. So is seeing one moved to tears. The very harshest test of your writing – also one of the most rewarding, when it works – is to put it in front of children. No amount of onstage theatrical trickery will stimulate a young audience who are baffled by your story. If the play isn't delivering, they'll start eating, chatting or fighting. (I speak from experience.)

So, once you've started to get work up in front of actual human beings, whether they are paying customers or colleagues and friends attending a reading – use them. Learn to feel when they are gripped or when they're drifting. If you get bored at the theatre watching someone else's play, watch the audience instead. It's like studying water – you will see and hear eddies of engagement, ripples of amusement, stretches of flat disinterest. And, occasionally, the deep stillness of an audience utterly engaged in every passing second. Always be alert to your own disengagement as an audience member, and always try to work out why it is happening.

CRITICS: FRIEND OR FOE?

Unfortunately, British theatre criticism can sometimes seem more like a blood sport than a cultural dialogue. Of course, the writing alone is not responsible for the success or failure of a production, even though sometimes in Britain it feels as though the writer is always the one judged most harshly. There are brilliant productions of mediocre plays, which can be elevated by a star performance or a director's flair; equally, small-scale intimate shows which have thrilled in a small studio theatre can lose much in translation when they transfer to a larger stage. But the playwright's craft – or lack of it – will usually be evident to a good critic.

Of course, if you read theatre reviews, which nowadays, given the proliferation of blogging and social media, can be a full-time and exhausting job, you'll often see entirely conflicting assessments of plays. One reviewer's four-star can be another's two-star. Who is right? Any critical response to a play is necessarily personal and subjective, and no word from any reviewer – even your mum on Twitter – is God. Good criticism is therefore not to be feared – and I mean 'good' in the sense of thoughtful, considered, illuminating – even if it doesn't garnish your play with stars.

You'll soon learn which of the critics have a genuine interest in and love for theatre – whether venerable industry stalwarts or new kids on the block. True critics, for me, are those who offer *informed subjectivity* – an opinion that stems from experience and knowledge of, and investment in the theatre. Good critiques can help crystallise or illuminate a play's meaning; provide a context for better understanding a play or its production; and/ or encourage audiences to consider their own responses. We may not agree with the critic's assessment, but their analysis will be intellectually stimulating and provoke debate. To my mind, anything that promotes the theatre as a cultural force and encourages participation is a good thing.

However, there is a breed of theatre critic that you must avoid like the plague – the most you will learn from them is about their own inflated sense of self. I call them the Statler Waldorfs, after the cantankerous Muppets who heckle the onstage players from their plush theatre box. Statler Waldorfs exist both in the mainstream press and online; they are, thankfully, few, but they can shout very loudly. You will know them by their tone, which has a pungent base note of contempt, and, occasionally, bigotry. Unfortunately they do possess one powerful weapon, which can wreck writers' lives, and that is shame. Shame is the deadliest force for any creative artist, and you must learn to turn your cheek. Never feel embarrassed by your attempts to create something meaningful and put it out into the world. To do so would be to let the Statler Waldorfs win, and this cannot be permitted.

(DON'T) LOOK BACK IN ANGER

These days a growing part of our theatre ecology is dedicated to discussions about what kinds of writers and plays get programmed, why they should be programmed, and who might have to move over a little to create room for new voices. A myriad of different decisions affects why and how a play is programmed and which plays gain value over time. Theatres are run as both businesses and charities; they are often reliant on public subsidy and therefore duty-bound to serve the public interest, while having the commercial pressure to sell tickets. The people who run the buildings are also human beings, with a variety of personal tastes and ambitions, political agendas and institutional responsibilities.

Understandably, these issues arouse a great deal of strong feeling within the theatre community, and are frequently raised in my writing classes by new playwrights, whose passion for the theatre is often marred by practical frustrations and a deep sense of historical and/or present injustice. So what is the writer's role in and among all of this? Here are some thoughts on a few of the key thorny issues.

The canon

When I first became interested in the theatre, I learned about plays by picking up published texts in second-hand bookshops. The plays I most frequently came across were, other than texts by Shakespeare, Chekhov and Ibsen, by Pinter, Stoppard, Brenton, Frayn, Hare, Williams, Miller, Albee and Mamet. So they were the ones I read. And I fell in love with many of them. They opened my mind and they taught me a lot about playwriting craft.

This particular collection of names is a small snapshot of the post-war British and American theatre canon of the late 1950s, '60s and onwards – largely a group of young, Oxford and Cambridge-educated white men, whose work was also directed largely by Oxford and Cambridge-educated white men. It wasn't until I read Caryl Churchill that I realised there was female writer with as much weight and influence in the British modern canon, as well as being one of the great innovators of post-war British theatre. It took digging and researching and being mentored to discover other writers whose work broadened my internal horizons: female playwrights, 'queer' playwrights, black and Asian playwrights. So we do have to acknowledge the other factors that affect a playwright's longevity and success, such as access, opportunity and social expectation – things that are embedded in deep-rooted social systems.

Although the theatre industry has always prided itself on finding 'new voices', it is finally starting to put its money where its mouth is in terms of actively seeking, developing and programming new writers whose backgrounds, experience and interests sit outside the limits of the mainstream canon (although at times progress can seem glacially slow).*

I'm fascinated by the potential artistic changes that might take place as a result of a drive to diversity. And when I get disheartened by the seeming sameness of frequently platformed writers, I take comfort from a quote by the late great Ursula K. Le Guin, who reminds us: 'We live in capitalism. Its power seems inescapable. So did the divine right of kings.'[11]

The right to write

There is an ongoing debate across all narrative and dramatic media about who should be 'allowed' to write about (and/or perform) certain subjects and human experiences. A 2019 London revival of the musical *Falsettos*, about a Jewish family coming to terms with the AIDS crisis in 1992, was widely condemned for having no Jewish actors nor members of the creative team. More recently the television writer Russell T Davies stated his belief that gay actors should be cast to play gay characters to ensure authenticity. Speaking to the *Radio Times*, he said:

> I feel strongly that if I cast someone in a story, I am casting them to act as a lover, or an enemy, or someone on drugs or a criminal or a saint... they are *not* there to 'act gay' because 'acting gay' is a bunch of codes for a performance.

So, do writers run the risk of creating such 'codes' in our plays when we write outside of our own experiences? Should we avoid certain subjects or giving voice to certain kind of characters? Personally I believe we all have the artistic right to write about anything that grips our imagination. 'Write what you know' is a limiting idea, which automatically dismisses a great

* At the time of writing, white male writers are still about two-thirds more likely than anyone else to have an original work programmed on a main stage.

deal of the classical canon – Shakespeare never visited Verona, fought a duel or spent time disguised as a woman (as far as we know). It's nonsense to suggest that a male playwright would, by virtue of his gender alone, be unable to create a fictional female character who is as compelling as one created by a female playwright.

I also believe it's important not to censor yourself from the outset – no good play ever got written from a place of fear or self-doubt. If you are inspired to write a particular story and feel that you have the necessary abilities to do it justice, go for it. But also be mindful that plays are not just written but *made* – and that the creative choices of those 'makers' will naturally affect the finished product. In other words, you are not just responsible for *what* you write, but *who you give your play to*, whether that's a particular theatre, director or company. Whatever you put out into the wide, wide world will have an impact on someone, somewhere, however small your audience might be. This is a both a privilege and a responsibility – try to use your platform wisely.

The theatre marketplace

Audiences like to drink and eat when they see a play. The National Theatre's audience is partial to a glass of white wine and a smoked-salmon sandwich, along with some very expensive gourmet nuts. Down the road in the Young Vic, you'll find a younger and generally more diverse audience tucking into pulled pork sandwiches and free water. A mile east, at Southwark Playhouse, students with cheap preview tickets will be drinking affordable craft beer and eating crisps. Let's float back up to the National. Let's say a couple of regular visitors are there tonight to see a new play in the Olivier. They might have paid up to £89 for a top-price ticket and they're looking forward to their glass of wine and their gourmet nuts at the interval. Taking the top-end estimation, for the tickets, perhaps a babysitter, the interval drinks and food, the travel, and possibly a programme, that couple could easily be spending upwards of £250 for their night out.

What does this have to do with playwriting? Nothing... and everything. The play gets written by a freelance writer and then made by freelance actors, directors and designers, in draughty rehearsal rooms, fuelled by Jaffa cakes and Haribo and apples (depending on how virtuous the Assistant Stage Manager feels that week) – when the gourmet nuts are still just a rumble in the audience's belly. Eventually the audience consumes the play – just as they consume their interval snacks and drinks. And so the play is in some tiny part subsidised by the price of the nuts, which boosts the theatre's income and allows it to pay its writers and theatre artists.

As I recall, a small carton of gourmet nuts at the National Theatre bars costs in the region of £4.50. I'm not bringing this up to point fingers; every theatre has to supplement its income with catering – it's part of the business. But in a cultural space where an audience member is prepared to pay almost five quid for a carton of nuts, does that create certain expectations in the audience about the kind of art they're paying to see? Does spending £125 to sit with a friend in the hush of the Olivier Theatre mean we have the right to expect 'great' writing, performance, direction and staging? And who gets to say that it *is* great or not? And when we spend a tenner on a ticket for a new show at Live Theatre in Newcastle are our expectations different? Is Shakespeare worth the nuts, but not a new play by a young Asian woman?

I'm asking these questions because it's likely that at some point you'll feel personally and/or professionally disadvantaged by the fact that the prestigious and hallowed cultural spaces of theatre are also consumer marketplaces selling particular kinds of experiences, from the art right down to the bar snacks. These experiences are not all created equal, nor are they equally accessible to a wide audience – and the majority of playwrights struggle to earn a living from most of them. Rest assured that you're not the first and you won't be the last writer to feel challenged by all of this. What's important is how you deal with these inequities – how you prevent them from stopping you writing, and how they affect what kind of writer you want to become.

So, in the dark nights of your soul, when you've left the theatre badly out of pocket after seeing a disappointing play by yet another canon-lite playwright, and none of the sixteen theatres you sent your play to have responded, or you've been heckled by a Statler Waldorf, and you can't solve the riddle of your middle half because you're too tired from working nightshifts, remember that *you don't have to write this play.* You can put the pen, or laptop, or keyboard down. Stroke your cat. Phone a friend. And then, the next morning, get up and start afresh.

AFTERWORD: FINDING THE HUMANITY

I love being a playwright, but I also find it very tough. Aside from the actual creative difficulty of writing a good play, we are operating in an overflowing workplace with thousands of playwrights competing for a handful of annual new-writing slots. It is hard to get work produced, hard finding directors and producers to commit, and hard to make any sort of real living from writing theatre. Writing is also a process of constant exposure, initially to readers – writer colleagues, teachers, actors, directors, agents – and, ultimately, to a live audience. And like every industry, the theatre industry is a mixed bag. At its best it is inclusive, accessible, open-hearted, imaginative and supportive. And at its worst it can be exclusive, privileged, savagely competitive, myopic, conservative and cliquey. It can seem at times that the hard knocks far outweigh the joys. So why do we persevere?

It's a good question. The enduring playwrights who receive multiple commissions and productions in this country and abroad, whose careers span years if not decades, are a tiny few. Longevity in this industry is rare. There is often a surfeit of unhelpful PR around these established writers, which implies that successful playwrights are born talented, and it's just a matter of time before they are discovered and given a stage. This is a myth – or half a myth. Talent is undeniably essential. But no writer is born polished, experienced and fully realised. Everyone starts off inexperienced, unknowing and unpractised.

At the climax of *Indiana Jones and the Last Crusade* (bear with me), Indiana steps into the thin air of an apparently yawning abyss. 'You must believe, boy,' his father mutters from his deathbed, in a nice echo of *Hamlet*, and so Indiana puts one foot down into apparently empty space, only to find a foothold on a hidden path invisible to the naked eye. Step by step he crosses over to the other side of the chasm, and, naturally, to redemption, heroics, the holy grail, etc., etc. (Naturally I looked for a post-colonial female anti-heroine to provide this lesson, but I know better than to ignore a good analogy when I see one. Plus, I love Harrison Ford.)

When we start a play, we are all Indiana Joneses. We can plan and discuss and strategise as much as we like, but ultimately we have to step off the cliff edge at some point with only our faith to guide us. Writers have to construct their path across the abyss with words, and keep going until they reach the other side. Success in this industry is based so much on luck, as well as talent – but I can absolutely guarantee you that the one thing that *all* successful playwrights have in common is endurance. They will succeed or die trying. And even if you don't become a star playwright, there might be another path you haven't yet discovered, like Indiana.

We live in a world that is increasingly secular, atomised and isolating. And in this world, the theatre is a rare place of community, where we learn what binds us, divides us, angers and inspires us. Where we experience the collective unconscious of different worlds that allow us to connect with people we will never meet face to face. Becoming a playwright is on one level about becoming a student of human nature. If years of writing in solitary confinement can eventually enrich an audience's heart or mind, then that is a very good way to have spent your time. It's over fifteen years since I started writing, and I'm still learning, from every feedback session, redraft, table reading, rehearsal, preview. I learn every time I go to see a play, good or bad, and when I have a useful conversation with another writer, actor or director. Most of all, of course, I learn by doing. How lucky we are, then, too, that our training as playwrights is limitless.

I'll finish the book with eight general pieces of advice that have served me well.

1. Write what moves, excites and interests you

You cannot expect an audience to invest in your story, world and characters if you're not invested yourself. Audiences are like wolves – they can sniff out your own lack of interest or conviction. Always try to stay connected to the material. If you lose the connection, step back, reassess, and then find another way in. Be rigorous in your interrogation of your material and of yourself.

2. You have the right to fail

It is better to write badly and bravely with the hope of improving than not at all. Use any criticism you get to put more fire in your belly. You'll get over a bad experience in time, and today's bad review is, as the old saying goes, tomorrow's fish-and-chip paper. Writing is a process. Not every word you write will end up in a play. Most won't. Just as athletes have to continuously exercise their muscles, so writers must continuously write to keep their own supple. If you write three plays that you eventually throw in the bin, don't mourn. Congratulate yourself on having the determination to complete three pieces of art, the making of which will have taught you many lessons. Writing is just as much about the journey as it is the end result.

3. *Don't write to be loved*

Not everybody will like your play. Divided audiences and critics are no bad thing. Better to arouse a strong response than a lukewarm *'Mmm'* of approval. Yes, it's good to consider your audience as you're writing. But don't try to make them love you by showing them how clever you are. What audiences really want is to be *moved*. So mine the emotional truth in your writing and don't smother it in theatrical tricks just for the sake of it.

4. *Be prepared to kill your darlings*

If your best lines fall flat in rehearsal or hold back a scene, be prepared to let them go. Ditto a scene. Ditto a character. Ditto a moment of what you thought on the page was theatrical brio, but which performance turns into a tumbleweed. Develop tough love. Be ruthless with your work and your audience will ultimately thank you for it. Yes, you created the play, you are its mother and father. But once it's on its feet, you have to let it fly the nest. Don't let your ego stop it from soaring.

5. *Be cautious about who you share your work with*

Every writer needs support, encouragement and help. If you are lucky enough to find a mentor or friend who you can trust to critique your work, don't ever lose their numbers. But be wary about giving your play to your mum, sister, lover, boss, if these are people who a) never go to the theatre and don't understand how a play behaves on the page, and/or b) if they have a personal agenda to support, admire and flatter (or undermine) you. Their notes will not be helpful. They may make you cry, unintentionally. Share with those who understand what it means to write – and who can be firm but fair.

6. *Be a team player*

Writing is a solitary act. But theatre is also the most wonderfully collaborative art form. Once you get to be in a rehearsal room, there are endless opportunities to learn – from directors, producers, actors, costume and lighting designers – in fact the whole company, including theatre ushers, who listen to the audience respond to your work night after night. Remember that everybody is on the same journey. Directors and actors have to find their way into a play – they never know all the answers at the beginning. You will find the way together. So respect the process, respect the craft, skill and hard work of *everybody* who contributes to the production of a play. Be thankful and appreciative. Everyone wants your play to be the best it can.

7. *Be nice*

Remember that it's extremely difficult to write even a mediocre play, let alone a great one. And nobody ever sets out to write a bad one. So on your journey as a playwright, try to respect and support the efforts of your colleagues. Every production is the culmination of many hours of work, input and commitment. This includes being nice to other writers. To waste time agonising over the hard-won success of others can drag you down and stop you writing – catastrophe! Try to use both positive and negative feelings to do one thing – write more. We are all in this together.

8. *Find the humanity*

The theatre director Howard Davies, who died in 2016, was one of the directors I had most dreamed of one day working with. He gave me some of my most enjoyable and memorable hours in the theatre, particularly with the Russian plays he directed at the National Theatre including *The White Guard* (Bulgakov) and *Philistines* (Gorky). The day he died, I was at an NT show, and its previous artistic director Nicholas Hytner came on stage and made a moving oration in Howard's memory before the show began. He said of Howard: '*He unlocked wild and contradictory passions in everything he did, and would describe a play not in terms of his concept but of its humanity.*' (His speech was later issued in a press release issued by the theatre.)

It occurred to me how right that was – how every play I'd seen directed by Howard was full of humanity. Humanity not always at its best, but often at its worst – fearful, selfish, passionate, stubborn, misjudging – but also loving, desiring, vulnerable, compassionate. The plays he directed made me want to be a better human being as well as a better playwright. They made me want to write a text of my own that might, under such expert guidance, one day unite a group of disparate strangers for two hours in their common humanity.

Nick Hytner's description of Howard's process has become a question I now ask myself whenever I'm writing. Where's the humanity? What essential quality of humanity am I trying to grapple with in this play?

I hope this book will inspire you to dig deep and ask yourself the same.

Good luck on your writer's journey, wherever it takes you.

READING LIST

There follows a list of plays I've referenced in this book. It is, of course, a very personal list according to my own tastes and experience, and is by no means intended as a definitive guide to 'what to read or see'. I hope it might lead readers to discover new work they don't already know and explore further texts by some of these playwrights.

Who's Afraid of Virginia Woolf? by Edward Albee
The Antipodes by Annie Baker
The Flick by Annie Baker
The Heretic by Richard Bean
Honeymoon Suite by Richard Bean
One Man Two Guvnors by Richard Bean
Happy Days by Samuel Beckett
Waiting for Godot by Samuel Beckett
Anatomy of a Suicide by Alice Birch
Revolt. She Said. Revolt Again. by Alice Birch
Handbagged by Moira Buffini
Loveplay by Moira Buffini
The White Guard by Mikhail Bulgakov
The Ferryman by Jez Butterworth
Jerusalem by Jez Butterworth
Skåne by Pamela Carter
Red Velvet by Lolita Chakrabarti
Escaped Alone by Caryl Churchill
Love and Information by Caryl Churchill
Top Girls by Caryl Churchill
The Lighthouse by Rachael Claye
In the Republic of Happiness by Martin Crimp
The Bevin Boys by Viv Edwards
Barber Shop Chronicles by Inua Ellams

Copenhagen by Michael Frayn
Philistines by Maxim Gorky
The Mountaintop by Katori Hall
A Raisin in the Sun by Lorraine Hansberry
Les Blancs by Lorraine Hansberry
Presence by David Harrower
La Bête by David Hirson
Rafts and Dreams by Robert Holman
A Doll's House by Henrik Ibsen
Girls by Theresa Ikoko
An Octoroon by Branden Jacobs-Jenkins
Cuttin' It by Charlene James
Blasted by Sarah Kane
Genesis Inc. by Jemma Kennedy
Maggot Moon based on the novel by Sally Gardner, adapted by Jemma
   Kennedy
Second Person Narrative by Jemma Kennedy
The Children by Lucy Kirkwood
Chimerica by Lucy Kirkwood
Angels in America by Tony Kushner
Her Naked Skin by Rebecca Lenkiewicz
People, Places and Things by Duncan Macmillan
The Encounter by Simon McBurney
Someone Who'll Watch Over Me by Frank McGuinness
Low Level Panic by Clare McIntyre
The Weir by Conor McPherson
A View from the Bridge by Arthur Miller
The Crucible by Arthur Miller
Death of a Salesman by Arthur Miller
Saint George and the Dragon by Rory Mullarkey
The Wonderful World of Dissocia by Anthony Neilson
Clybourne Park by Bruce Norris
Ruined by Lynn Nottage
Pass Over by Antoinette Nwandu
The Plough and the Stars by Seán O'Casey
Father Comes Home from the Wars (Parts 1, 2 & 3) by Suzan-Lori Parks
Blue/Orange by Joe Penhall
Love and Understanding by Joe Penhall
Betrayal by Harold Pinter
One Night in Miami by Kemp Powers
The Effect by Lucy Prebble

ENRON by Lucy Prebble
Art by Yasmina Reza
Table by Tanya Ronder
Amadeus by Peter Shaffer
A Midsummer Night's Dream by William Shakespeare
Hamlet by William Shakespeare
King Lear by William Shakespeare
Macbeth by William Shakespeare
Romeo and Juliet by William Shakespeare
The Two Noble Kinsmen by William Shakespeare
Saint Joan by George Bernard Shaw
Merrily We Roll Along by Stephen Sondheim and George Furth
Antigone by Sophocles
Oedipus Rex by Sophocles
The Curious Incident of the Dog in the Night-Time based on the novel by Mark
   Haddon, adapted by Simon Stephens
3 Winters by Tena Štivičić
generations by debbie tucker green
hang by debbie tucker green
Posh by Laura Wade
Fleabag by Phoebe Waller-Bridge
Misterman by Enda Walsh
Death of England by Roy Williams and Clint Dyer
A Streetcar Named Desire by Tennessee Williams
Love by Alexander Zeldin
The Father by Florian Zeller

Other playwrights mentioned in the book are Samuel Adamson, Alan Ayckbourn, Nicola Baldwin, Bertolt Brecht, Howard Brenton, Anton Chekhov, Ryan Craig, David Greig, John Donnelly, Suhayla El-Bushra, Will Eno, Brian Friel, David Hare, Federico García Lorca, David Mamet, Eugene O'Neill, Tom Stoppard and Lynn Truss.

The plays discussed in the case studies were written and generously shared by Rachael Claye, Anne Doherty, Lucy Flannery, Viv Edwards, Hinrich Von Haaren, Sean McEnaney and Sylvia Paskin.

CRITICAL WORKS

Poetics by Aristotle
Baldwin, Collected Essays by James Baldwin
The Seven Basic Plots: Why We Tell Stories by Christopher Booker
The Hero with a Thousand Faces by Joseph Campbell
Playwriting Strategies by Paul C. Castagno
The Origin and Development of Psychoanalysis by Sigmund Freud
The Wave in the Mind: Talks and Essays on the Writer, the Reader and the Imagination by Ursula K. Le Guin
Dramatic Structure: Comedy and Tragedy, and Shakespeare by Ian Johnston
The Collected Essays of Arthur Miller by Arthur Miller
The Heroine's Journey: Woman's Quest for Wholeness by Maureen Murdock
Various Voices: Prose, Poetry, Politics 1948–1998 by Harold Pinter

ENDNOTES

Introduction

1   James Baldwin, from 'The Devil Finds Work: An Essay' in *Baldwin, Collected Essays*, Library of America, 1998.

Chapter Two

2. Ursula K. Le Guin, *The Wave in the Mind: Talks and Essays on the Writer, the Reader, and the Imagination*, Shambhala Publications, 2004.

3. Arthur Miller, from 'Introduction to the Collected Plays' in *The Collected Essays of Arthur Miller*, ed. Matthew C. Roudané, Bloomsbury Methuen Drama, 2015.

Chapter Three

4. Freud, *The Origin and Development of Psychoanalysis*.

Chapter Five

5. A line from a poem by Lord Alfred Douglas.

Chapter Six

6. From Johnston's lecture 'Introduction to Shakespeare Studies', given at Malaspina University College, 1999, revised 2000.

7. Joseph Campbell, *The Hero with a Thousand Faces*, Princeton University Press, 1968.

8. Maureen Murdock, *The Heroine's Journey*, Shambhala Publications, 1990.

Chapter Eight

9. Paul C. Castango, *New Playwriting Strategies*, Routledge, 2001.

Chapter Thirteen

10. From 'The Psychology of Live Performance' by Daniel Richardson, John Hogan, Helen Nuttall and Joseph Devlin, ACN Applied Consumer Neuroscience Labs, 2018.

11. Excerpt from Ursula K. Le Guin's speech at the American National Book Awards, 2014.

ACKNOWLEDGEMENTS

Thanks are due to the following people for their contributions and feedback:

Samuel Adamson, Suzanne Ahmet, Nicola Baldwin, Clare Bayley, Richard Bean, Sarah Belcher, Angela Bell, Sebastian Born, Moira Buffini, Shenagh Cameron, Ryan Craig, John Donnelly, Suhayla El-Bushra, Inua Ellams, Kobna Holdbrook-Smith, Nicholas Hytner, Jesse Jones, Rebecca Lenkiewicz, Morgan Lloyd Malcolm, Blanche McIntyre, Amy Ng, Christian Roe, Victoria Sadler, Helen Schlesinger, Giles Smart, Nina Steiger, Peter Sullivan and Chris Thorpe.

Thanks to Nick Hern, Matt Applewhite, John O'Donovan and all at Nick Hern Books.

Special thanks to Joe Penhall. And to Purni Morell, the Explicator, for her editorial help.

Many thanks are also due to all my former students who generously lifted the curtain on their plays, exercises and processes: Annabel Adcock, Rachael Claye, Anne Doherty, Viv Edwards, Lucy Flannery, Hinrich Von Haaren, Peter Jessup, Joyce Lee, Caroline Loncq, Lydia Marchant, Sean McEnaney, Sylvia Paskin, Louise Richards and Catherine Willmore.

*

Heretic © 2011 Richard Bean, *Revolt. She Said. Revolt Again.* © 2014 Alice Birch, and *Posh* © 2010 Laura Wade, all published by Oberon Books, an imprint of Bloomsbury Publishing Plc, by kind permission of Bloomsbury Publishing Plc; *In the Republic of Happiness* by Martin Crimp, by kind permission of Faber & Faber Ltd; 'Stories That Sing' by Garth Greenwell, written and recorded for *The Essay*, BBC Radio 3, by kind permission of the author; 'Christmas Card from a Hooker in Minneapolis', words and music by Tom Waits, copyright © 1978 Fifth Floor Music Inc., all rights administered by BMG Rights Management (US) LLC, all rights reserved, reprinted by permission of Hal Leonard LLC; 'Introduction to Shakespeare Studies' by Ian Johnston, Professor Emeritus at Vancouver Island University, 1999 (revised 2000), by kind permission of the author; *Amadeus* © Sir Peter Shaffer Charitable Foundation, by kind permission of Macnaughton Lord Representation on behalf of the Sir Peter Shaffer Charitable Foundation; *The Ferryman* by Jez Butterworth, *Escaped Alone* by Caryl Churchill, *hang* by debbie tucker green, *An Octoroon* by Branden Jacobs-Jenkins, *Second Person Narrative* by Jemma Kennedy, *Ruined* by Lynn Nottage, and *Father Comes Home from the Wars (Parts 1, 2 & 3)* by Suzan-Lori Parks, all published by Nick Hern Books Ltd; and 'The Psychology of Live Performance' by Daniel Richardson, John Hogan, Helen Nuttall and Joseph Devlin, ACN Applied Consumer Neuroscience Labs, 2018, by kind permission of the authors.

Every effort has been made to contact copyright holders. The publisher will be glad to make good in any future editions any errors or omissions brought to their attention.

INDEX

www.nickhernbooks.co.uk

facebook.com/nickhernbooks

twitter.com/nickhernbooks